PRINCIPLES
OF
PROFESSIONAL
FUNDRAISING

Joseph R. Mixer

PRINCIPLES
OF
PROFESSIONAL
FUNDRAISING

Useful Foundations
for
Successful Practice

Jossey-Bass Publishers • San Francisco

Substantial discounts on bulk quantities of Jossey-Bass books are available to corporations, professional associations, and other organizations. For details and discount information, contact the special sales department at Jossey-Bass Inc., Publishers. (415) 433-1740; Fax (415) 433-0499.

For sales outside the United States, contact Maxwell Macmillan International Publishing Group, 866 Third Avenue, New York, New York 10022.

Manufactured in the United States of America

The paper used in this book is acid-free and meets the State of California requirements for recycled paper (50 percent recycled waste, including 10 percent postconsumer waste), which are the strictest guidelines for recycled paper currently in use in the United States.

The ink in this book is either soy- or vegetable-based and during the printing process emits fewer than half the volatile organic compounds (VOCs) emitted by petroleum-based ink.

Library of Congress Cataloging-in-Publication Data

Mixer, Joseph R., date.
    Principles of professional fundraising : Useful foundations for successful practice / Joseph R. Mixer.
        p.   cm. — (The Jossey-Bass nonprofit sector series)
    Includes bibliographical references and index.
    ISBN 1-55542-590-9
    1. Fundraising—United States.   2. Nonprofit organizations—United States.   I. Title. II. Series.
HV41.9.U5M58   1993
361.7'068'1—dc20
                                             93-14551
                                           CIP

Figure 1.1, "The Social Exchange Model for Giving," Figure 4.1, "Strategic Planning Process," and Figure 4.2, "Strategic Decision-Making Questions," are excerpts from *Fundraising Skills Training for Community Agencies* copyright 1988, Pacific Bell. Reprinted by permission from **PACIFIC ★ BELL®**

A Pacific Telesis Company

FIRST EDITION
HB Printing 10 9 8 7 6 5 4 3 2 1   *Code 9389*

*The
Jossey-Bass
Nonprofit Sector
Series*

CONTENTS

PREFACE

Nonprofit charitable fundraising activity in the United States has grown significantly over the past several decades. Giving from private sources has increased 790 percent in a span of twenty-five years, reaching an estimated $124 billion in 1992 (Kaplan, 1993). This growth exceeds the rate of inflation during the same years by almost 75 percent.

The U.S. nonprofit charitable economy, fed by more than 516,000 organizations, is estimated to be nearing half a trillion dollars in revenues (Internal Revenue Service, 1992). From 1987 to 1991, the number of new charitable organizations increased more than 7 percent annually, despite a significant decline in federal support and an economic recession. Meanwhile, the demand for services to the homeless, hungry, afflicted, and poverty-stricken outstrips available resources. Additionally, the nation's social development, cultural, and civic needs continue to increase.

In this environment of high demand, the competition among charitable nonprofits for private funds has intensified.

As a result, new fundraising skills and techniques are being developed, and nonprofits are expanding their searches for new prospects. Fundraising organizations require more staff members and volunteers who are better trained and educated than ever before.

Unfortunately, among the public, volunteers, and prospective donors alike, the practice of fundraising is often held in low esteem. For example, many citizens who are buffeted by mail and telephone solicitation view fundraising as simply a collection of slick tactics to elicit money. The pejorative labels many individuals apply to fundraising demean the practice and prevent organizations and their volunteers and staff from being optimally effective.

Negative views about fundraising arise also from a lack of understanding about the conceptual foundations on which organized fundraising rests. Certainly, the beggar on the street who roughly importunes strangers affects public attitudes about fundraising, as does the paid solicitor who uses high-pressure tactics. However, both of these overly persistent types obscure the fundamental values and principles of gift giving and getting and the true benefits to givers as well as receivers.

The numerous books on fundraising shed little light on its current image problem. They focus on specific fundraising steps, techniques, or funding sources. A few works touch briefly on the basic principles by repeating fundraising axioms. And how-to books provide little comfort in times of failure or when the prescription does not fit the situation. The existing fundraising literature lacks a strong conceptual foundation, one that would give fundraising the support, recognition, and status befitting the fundamental position it occupies in financing nonprofit organizations. This book sets out to build that foundation.

Purpose of the Book

Principles of Professional Fundraising provides a thorough exposition of the concepts underlying the behavior of individuals, groups, and organizations involved in giving and getting funds for charitable purposes. It relates existing psychological and managerial theories and applications to the practice of fundraising in three critical dimensions. The first dimension concerns the behavioral processes: influences on and motivations for individuals and organizations to become donors. The second dimension relates to the leadership, strategy, and direction organizations need if they are to obtain charitable dollars. The third dimension involves the growth and change that fundraising organizations face as a result of both fundraising success and economic and social uncertainties.

Principles of Professional Fundraising gives managers, fundraisers, academicians, and volunteers a conceptual framework to support their understanding of fundraising. The substantiated knowledge offered in the chapters that follow will enhance readers' proficiency at teaching and practicing fundraising. As an addition to the growing literature justifying the study of fundraising as a discipline, this book will help fundraising move toward the recognition it deserves in philanthropy and in society.

Need for the Book

Most theories of psychology and organizational management and behavior are not routinely made available to students or practitioners of fundraising. For example, the theory of social exchange is only occasionally cited in the fundraising literature, yet this theory provides a solid explanatory model of the interchange between donors and recipients. Here I offer greater explanations of this and other underlying concepts critical to a sound understanding of fundraising.

In practice, of course, fundraisers often apply principles without knowing that a theory exists or understanding why a particular application works. While the work done in such a state of innocence may suffice for a time, today's competitive arena demands that to achieve and maintain success, fundraisers must master certain fundamental concepts. Future fundraising managers will be judged according to their ability to draw from a repertoire of theoretically based techniques or applications to solve difficult funding challenges in ways that lead to financial success.

Recognition that fundraising endeavors are buttressed by accepted theories of human and organizational behavior will advance the status of fundraising and its practitioners. Academic communities and professional societies can use the information contained here to study and promote research. Board and staff members of nonprofit organizations will develop greater acceptance of their fundraising activities. Organizations and community groups will find it easier to recruit volunteers for fundraising. The burnout and turnover so prevalent among fundraising personnel may be reduced, once decision making and performance are more solidly based.

Audience

Principles of Professional Fundraising serves two primary audiences: professional and academic. Fundraising executives, managers, and staff will find the concepts in the book helpful in improving performance, analyzing failures, and prescribing remedies. A knowledge of which techniques work fosters rational, effective planning and organization; moreover, with improved fundraising management, more dollars are raised.

Voluntary leaders in the some 500,000 charitable nonprofit organizations, being closely allied with staff fundraisers, will profit similarly from greater understanding of fundraising. In addition, volunteers who come from backgrounds in business and public administration will welcome the book's systematic approach to the funding decisions they face.

Professional associations of fundraisers such as the Association for Healthcare Philanthropy, the Council for the Advancement and Support of Education, the Nonprofit Management Association, the National Society of Fund Raising Executives, and the United Way of America will find the content of the book helpful in their training and educational programs.

The academic audience for *Principles of Professional Fundraising* includes instructors, students, and researchers in public administration, public health, business management, education, and social welfare departments who study nonprofit organizations. INDEPENDENT SECTOR (IS), an association of nonprofit organizations, reports that more than three hundred colleges and universities offer educational opportunities to students of the nonprofit sector. IS also cites twenty-six recently formed academic centers and research institutes that focus on the study of philanthropy, voluntarism, and not-for-profit activity (Crowder and Hodgkinson, 1991). This book will serve as a reference and a research tool, and can also be used as a text in both graduate and undergraduate courses to introduce students to the basic principles and theories of fundraising and fundraising management. At the graduate level, it will also help students formulate topics for term papers, research, and theses. Instructors will be able to use the theories and concepts presented in the book as a means of integrating pertinent material from the social science disciplines into their fundraising courses.

Overview of the Contents

In recognition of the several audiences to be served, I have balanced theoretical approaches with practical applications. I focus on those aspects of organizational and management theories that apply to fundraising activities.

Part One introduces the theoretical framework of social exchange as a valid model for the interaction between donors (both organizational and individual) and seekers. I analyze the central impediments to fundraising—namely, the negative attitudes and values held by prospects, volunteers, and staff members of nonprofit organizations—and show how adoption of the social exchange model can work to counteract such attitudes. Methods of raising funds from individuals, foundations, corporations, and small businesses are examined from a psychosocial perspective.

Chapter One explores the basic transaction between prospects and fundraisers by asking what is involved in the exchange, why it works, and why people do or do not give. Motives, influences, and attitudes are classified. In Chapter Two, I apply the social exchange model to face-to-face solicitation and four other basic methods of asking. This chapter describes psychological principles for helping individuals overcome their reluctance to ask for gifts. Chapter Three investigates the process of social exchange between nonprofit agencies and corporations, small businesses, and foundations and reveals these donors' decision-making processes and rationales for giving.

Part Two relates established and emerging theories of management and organizational behavior to the conduct of fundraising. Charitable nonprofit organizations can benefit from relevant facets of those theories, such as leadership strategies.

Chapter Four establishes strategic planning as the means by which leaders and managers imbue fundraising with vision, purpose, and legitimacy. I highlight the influence of internal and external organizational environments on strategic planning and develop criteria for selecting fundraising methods. Chapter Five looks at the established patterns for organizing fundraising departments, focusing on the reporting relationships, communication patterns, reward systems, and cultural norms that reveal structures and governance patterns. Chapter Six examines concepts of strategy and leadership and applies them to the management of fundraising activities. I relate leadership styles and strategies for change to improving the effectiveness of fundraising in organizations.

Part Three explores theoretical and practical factors that affect both large and small nonprofit organizations as they grow or encounter economic and social change.

Chapter Seven identifies critical environmental changes and analyzes how shifting market resources affect internal and external relationships. Alternative revenue strategies—business ventures, increased fees, product sales, and new services—are assessed. Chapter Eight targets difficulties created by growth in small and mid-sized nonprofit agencies: for example, tensions between board and staff members, requirements for new capabilities and resources, alterations in image and direction, hazards of underadministration, and temptations to expand services. Chapter Nine analyzes the pressing problems caused by both centralization and decentralization in large fundraising organizations. I present theories of coordination and control and examine the influence of organizational culture and the roles of individuals.

The Conclusion synthesizes the concepts underlying fundraising practice, emphasizing the key factors that promote success, and looks at the growing need for knowledge about nonprofit organizations and their funding requirements. The increasing demand on managers and volunteer leaders to greater accountability and effectiveness is an inducement for them to develop a repertoire of organizational skills based on solid conceptual foundations. The complexity of fundraising and the changing social and economic environments in which it must operate underscore the need for more research into ways to support the profession.

Acknowledgments

Many circumstances and individuals prompted me to write *Principles of Professional Fundraising*. Pure curiosity about why things work stimulated my initial formulation of concepts about the field of fundraising. The advent of an association of fundraisers some twenty-seven years ago provided me with an opportunity to exchange ideas with others. Writing my doctoral dissertation on corporate giving practices inspired more critical thinking about the conceptual bases of fundraising and resulted in my focus on the social exchange theory. Participation in the founding of the Fund Raising School and close work with Henry A. Rosso gave me opportunities to further develop my notions about fundraising principles, and fifteen years' consulting on fundraising with small and large organizations demonstrated the practical value of having a theoretical base for fundraising activities.

Like most authors, I must thank numerous individuals who helped set the stage for the writing of the book. Gloria Segal of the California Arts Council gave me the opportunity to conduct statewide fundraising workshops for local arts organizations and on-site consultations with forty-two county arts councils. Shelly Cullimore of Pacific Bell arranged for Robert J. Apodaca and me to develop and present company-sponsored workshops on fundraising skills and to provide on-site consultations for several hundred nonprofit organizations in California. Both Michael O'Neill, director of the Institute for Nonprofit Organization Management at the University of San Francisco, and Paul L. Terrell, coordinator of academic programs at the School of Social Welfare, University of California, Berkeley, gave me the opportunity to teach courses on fundraising and the management of social welfare agencies.

Not the least of all, Michael O'Neill introduced me to Alan R. Shrader, senior acquisitions editor of the Jossey-Bass Nonprofit Sector Series. Alan's interest in the principles of nonprofit organizations and his guidance and confidence in my work have been an invaluable encouragement. For all these opportunities, I am most appreciative. I also owe a deep debt of gratitude to my wife, Madeline, who donated her valuable time and expert skills to the review of many drafts of the manuscript.

Berkeley, California   Joseph R. Mixer
August 1993

THE AUTHOR

Joseph R. Mixer is adjunct faculty member at the Institute for Nonprofit Organization Management at the University of San Francisco and a consultant on fundraising, board and staff training, and nonprofit organization management. He received his B.A. degree (1943) in economics from the University of California, Berkeley; his M.B.A. degree (1949) from Ohio State University; and his Ph.D. degree (1977) in higher education administration from the University of California, Berkeley.

Mixer's interest in fundraising and nonprofit organizations began at Ohio State University, where he raised funds for the student YMCA. In 1959, as statewide gifts and endowments officer, he became the University of California's first full-time fundraiser. Then, as special assistant to the Berkeley campus chancellor, he established that school's development function and successfully conducted the $15 million Berkeley Centennial Fund during the period of student unrest in the late 1960s. While preparing his doctoral dissertation on corporate giving to higher education, he consulted with educational institutions and social agencies. He is a cofounder of the Fund Raising School and served with Henry A. Rosso as associate director of the school from 1974 to 1981.

Mixer developed and taught the fundraising course in the master's degree program of the Institute for Nonprofit Organization Management and served as chair of the institute's advisory board for six years. He is a member of the trustees' development committee for the University of San Francisco. For the School of Social Welfare at Berkeley, he developed and taught a graduate course on the management of social welfare agencies.

He serves as chair of the Research Council of the National Society of Fund Raising Executives and vice chair of the society's foundation. He is coauthor (1987, with R. J. Apodaca) of *Fundraising Skills Training for Community Agencies.*

PRINCIPLES
OF
PROFESSIONAL
FUNDRAISING

Part One

WHY
PEOPLE
AND
ORGANIZATIONS
GIVE

The central process of fundraising, asking for funds to support needed services, creates relationships between prospects and charitable organizations. The three chapters in Part One identify the elements of these relationships. The key element is a social exchange between the askers and the givers. The discussion also classifies the motivations and influences that cause individuals to give, and analyzes the reasons why people do not give.

The act of asking for funds opens up questions about the underlying attitudes, values, and principles of the persons and organizations involved. The answers to these queries provide a basis for overcoming individuals' negative feelings about asking for money. Recruitment of volunteer solicitors becomes easier when their fears and anxieties can be reduced. The social exchange model illustrates how positive attitudes and satisfactions are created in both solicitors and donors in various methods of fundraising.

Corporate, small business, and foundation giving also fits the social exchange model. The motivations and transactions

1

differ, but the principles are the same. A discussion of the driving forces and decision-making aspects of corporate giving illustrates the process, and an identification of the origin and nature of foundations reveals a rationale for their granting behavior.

One

---■---

The Personal Equation: How and Why People Give

The 1989 Loma Prieta earthquake in the San Francisco Bay area not only shook buildings to the ground and collapsed a double-deck freeway killing dozens of people, it also produced a flood of contributions. Hurricanes, homelessness, and AIDS produce similar outpourings of funds. Yet hunger, poverty, drug addiction, and cultural needs remain unattended and underfunded. What will motivate and influence people to donate to these needs and numerous others?

The challenge to fundraisers lies in finding sufficient numbers of persons who can be motivated and influenced to give, who are capable of giving the requisite dollars, and who can be interested in the purposes and needs to be served. Some people, about 28 percent of our nation, simply do not give, some confine their giving to one or two purposes, and others cover a gamut of interests with their donations. The quest for prospects has become more promising thanks to numerous demographic studies and marketing aids now available to fundraisers; however, sources and techniques of motivation and influence need to be explored more fully. The purpose of this chapter is to provide an understanding of the forces and factors involved in the gift giving process and to show how people become donors.

The discussion examines why people give and describes social exchange as the mechanism that triggers desired responses to fundraising appeals. The basic forces in the social exchange process are the internal motivations and external influences that are involved in all human interactions. Classifying these motivations and influences joins research and theory together in a framework applicable to fundraising. The discussion shows how fundraising can be freed from such pejorative labels as "begging" and "manipulating" and elevated to the same status and value society gives to economic exchange and similar social activities. The chapter concludes with an investigation of the corollary to giving, why people do not give.

People who give to nonprofits represent a market that can be identified, understood, and approached. They are both *prospects* and *donors*. Prospects are those individuals, foundations, and corporations who appear to be potential donors. Most likely, they have already contributed to other nonprofit organizations or to the asking organization. Thus from one point of view, they are donors, while from another, they are prospects for new, repeat, or upgraded gifts. A well-known fundraising axiom states that "your donors are your best prospects." Thus, the terms donor and prospect tend to be used interchangeably by many fundraisers. Hodgkinson, Weitzman, Noga, and Gorski (1992) say that 72 percent of the respondents in a national survey of households made donations in 1991, a finding that suggests a corresponding number of prospects.

Demographic factors, such as location, age, income, and gender, play an important role in indicating who is likely to give and how much they will give. These factors are displayed in detail in studies by the INDEPENDENT SECTOR (IS), a nationwide coalition of nonprofit organizations (Hodgkinson, Weitzman, Noga, and Gorski, 1992; Hodgkinson, Weitzman, Toppe, and Noga, 1992). Certainly, detailed demographic knowledge is necessary to successful fundraising, but it is not sufficient. To begin rounding out the fundraising picture, fundraisers must understand the fundamental question of why people give. That means understanding psychological and social concepts of behavior.

Why Do People Give?

Individuals are vastly complex in their makeup, drives, desires, and interests. Social science investigators over the past twenty-five years have exerted increasing efforts to untangle the web of factors that prompt human action. The work environment in factories and assembly plants was an early focus for research on human motivation and performance. More recently, the philanthropic scene has been examined to determine why people give.

The notion that giving and getting is a social relationship involving interaction between donors and recipients is just emerging (Brittingham and Pezzullo, 1990; Ostrander and Schervish, 1990; Kelly, 1991). It is true that experienced fundraisers who have written about their techniques and donor responses have usually listed a number of reasons why people give (Huntsinger, 1982; Panas, 1984; Schneiter, 1985; Broce, 1986). Their explanations range from religious beliefs and guilt to pride and peer pressure. However, more systematic analyses of donor motivations and conceptual frameworks are needed so fundraisers can carry out their tasks more effectively. The need is especially pressing given the environment of intense competition, an uncertain economy, and reduced government support that faces nonprofit organizations.

Using data collected by the Gallup Organization in 1992, the INDEPENDENT SECTOR has substantiated the widespread view among fundraisers that individuals have multiple reasons for their charitable behavior (Hodgkinson, Weitzman, Noga, and Gorski, 1992). In response to a list of eleven motives for giving funds and volunteering time to nonprofit causes, the largest proportion of respondents (55 percent) felt that those with more should help those with less. Forty-three percent of respondents gained a feeling of personal satisfaction from giving and volunteering, and 41 percent indicated that their behavior met their religious beliefs or commitments.

The eight additional reasons presented to the inter-
viewees received the following responses: giving back to society
some benefits derived from it (39 percent), being asked to contribute or volunteer by a personal friend or business associate
(36 percent), ensuring the continuation of activities or institutions that they or their family benefit from (34 percent), serving
as an example to others (31 percent), fulfilling a business or
community obligation (19 percent), creating a remembrance of
oneself or one's family (17 percent), obtaining tax considerations and deductions (12 percent), and being encouraged by
an employer (10 percent).

Furthermore, the study found that among those who
served as volunteers the leading motives for volunteer participation were the importance of helping others, feeling compassion
toward people in need, and doing something for a cause that
was personally important to the volunteer. Each of these three
reasons was cited by 86 percent or more of the respondents.

An IS/Gallup study conducted four years earlier (1988)
used a less structured approach to investigate individuals' reasons for giving (Hodgkinson and Weitzman, 1988). Researchers
asked respondents the colloquial question, "How was it you
came to give to _____?" The free responses showed a wider dimension to motives for giving. Fourteen percent of the respondents felt that the charity they gave to was a worthy cause, or they
had an interest in the agency. Twelve percent felt that the charity helped the poor and needy, and 11 percent that the charity
did good work or had high quality programs. Ten percent cited
spiritual reasons; 9 percent were asked or responded to an appeal; 8 percent felt obligated or responsible; 7 percent each had
close involvement in or loyalty to the organization, felt the charity provided money for many causes, or cited their personal involvement in the local community; 5 percent felt the charity had
good organization; 4 percent mentioned family tradition; and
2 percent each had been helped when they needed assistance,
referred to the death or illness of relative or friend, or said the
contribution was deductible from their salary.

While it is difficult to draw conclusions about the relative
importance of the major motives in the two studies because of

the different questions asked, the multiple reasons for giving are quite apparent. However, by itself, a survey cannot tell fundraisers how to apply donors' rationales to the methods of fundraising.

Other behavioral characteristics have been found typical of potential prospects and donors. Recent studies (Wuthnow, Hodgkinson, and Associates, 1990; Hodgkinson and Weitzman, 1988, 1990) have found that both religious affiliation and volunteering correlate strongly with giving. Since 70 percent of Americans belong to a church, temple, or other religious institution and 40 percent report attending services every week or almost every week, religion has a major impact on the nation's culture (Wood and Hougland, 1990). The intriguing fact that over half of individuals' charitable dollars go to religious organizations and causes year after year becomes understandable (Kaplan, 1993). However, religious affiliation also promotes giving to secular causes, and Wood and Hougland argue that religious gifts do more than support doctrine and worship. Such gifts also give impressive aid to programs for general human welfare. Homeless shelters, meal services, battered women's secure houses, and counseling programs supported by churches and temples dot the landscape. Also, religious institutions inspire their adherents to volunteer to assist these services and other philanthropic activities in greater numbers than individuals who do not have a religious affiliation.

Of course, not all religious movements inspire their members to give gifts for general human welfare. The notable exceptions are the evangelical sects, which usually focus donors' attention away from worldly causes and disadvantaged groups and toward personal salvation and support of the ministry (Wuthnow, Hodgkinson, and Associates, 1990). Increasingly, these sects are also turning their funds and energy toward local and state politics to elect kindred souls and obtain legislation incorporating sect values.

Volunteering plays a vital role in the propensity to give. In the IS/Gallup study (Hodgkinson, Weitzman, Noga, and Gorski, 1992), households that both gave money and volunteered gave an average of $1,155 in 1991, almost two and one-half times the $477 average contribution from households that did not volunteer. The study estimated the total of adult volunteers to be 94.2 million, a significant number with fundraising potential. Parents coaching Little League, volunteers handling pledge nights for public television's appeals, and members of groups adopting portions of highways for cleanup—all become more responsive to appeals than nonvolunteers.

Other behavioral factors also influence giving. Not surprisingly, households that have worries about money give one-third less than those that do not. Households that claim tax deductions for charitable donations outgive by almost four to one those who do not itemize deductions. People who pledge specific amounts or a percentage of income give larger sums than those whose giving is less systematic (Hodgkinson, Weitzman, Noga, and Gorski, 1992). Religious groups with their regular weekly services capitalize on this phenomenon, reaping a significantly higher harvest of funds when their members make weekly or monthly pledge payment provisions.

Origins of Giving

Gift giving has been traced back to the earliest societies. Many primitive tribes made their first overtures to strangers by placing gifts in a neutral area and withdrawing to await the strangers' gift offerings. People exchanged gifts as a matter of obligation. The refusal to do so, says Mauss, was "the equivalent of a declaration of war; it is a refusal of friendship and intercourse" ([1924] 1967, p. 11). Mauss also sees this obligation as akin to a spiritual bond, stemming from the parties' relationships. Thus, this universal social behavior of giving has aspects ranging from functional altruism to highly pragmatic benefits.

More recent clues to an understanding of individuals' impetus toward charitable giving can be found in the motivational theory that has been developed over the past several decades in the disciplines of management, organizational behavior, and psychology. All contemporary authorities point out the immense complexity of human behavior. Any single act by any person usually results from an array of feelings, perceptions, and reactions in a diverse environment. The challenge is to unwind the intricate interplay of these factors, in order to understand how and why people do such things as making charitable donations. Regrettably, the specific application of these findings to fundraising is just emerging; philanthropy and fundraising have only recently become acceptable academic pursuits (Magat, 1989).

Social Exchange: The Integrative Mechanism

The process of giving involves a circumstance in which individual prospects and donors have needs and desires that can be defined as internal motivations and that can be activated or channeled by external influences. The circumstance also includes recipients—individuals or organizations—with desires and needs that can be met in part by gifts. The transactions between the givers and the recipients are triggered by an argument or case for support, and result in what Blau (1968) calls *social exchange.*

The social exchange process conforms to the concept of *grants economics,* defined by Boulding, a well-respected economist, as a one-way transfer of assets from party A to party B without any economic good returned by B (1973). Boulding asserts that there must be some kind of integrative relationship between A and B that "deals with status, identity, community, legitimacy, loyalty, benevolence, and so on, and of course the appropriate opposites" (1973, Preface). Boulding significantly points out that gifts to the unfortunate provide the donor some "return in the form of status, recognition, or some subtle psychological transfer" (p. 2).

Other economists "view charitable giving as a consumption decision in support of a socially worthwhile cause from which the donor derives some benefit in the form of personal satisfaction or utility" (Auten and Rudney, 1989, p. 77). Still other economists dismiss the reciprocal relationship because no measurable assets or market values can be ascertained for what is returned (Mason, 1984). Yet none deny that some relationship exists.

Sociologists Ostrander and Schervish (1990) believe that "philanthropy is a social relation of giving and getting between donors and recipients" (p. 68), in which "donors have needs to be fulfilled as well as resources to grant, and recipients have resources to give as well as needs to be met" (p. 93). Thus, an exchange of social benefits is clearly indicated. In Blau's conceptualization of social exchange (1968, pp. 452–457), he asserts that "most gratifications of human beings have their source in the actions of other human beings." He defines social exchange itself as "the return of some reward for whatever is given by the first party," and he describes several parameters for this transaction:

1. The parties do not directly specify the return or obligation in advance. The return is left to the discretion of the one who receives what has been given. Thus, social exchange is noncontractual, open, and voluntary with no fixed boundaries or quid pro quo with respect to what is exchanged.
2. The time limit is not fixed; the assumption is that the return will be made sometime in the indefinite future.
3. The transaction must be between two or more parties who have a form of social relationship characterized by trust, especially with regard to the parties' future actions.

Figure 1.1 illustrates how the concept of social exchange applies to individual giving.

The charitable organization or agency presents client needs and services to a prospect along with a request for funds. The manner of presentation varies from an impersonal media message to face-to-face solicitation (see Chapter Two). If the request is favorably received, the prospect responds with a donation of funds and possibly time. To continue the relationship, the recipient provides some form of satisfaction to the donor. This may be as simple as a thank-you letter or as complex as naming a building.

The essence of what is returned to the donor is not a commodity or service that can be used profitably by the giver, but an intangible, psychic satisfaction that relates to the donor's per-

Figure 1.1.   The Social Exchange Model for Giving.

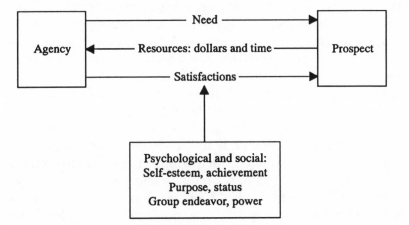

Source: Pacific Bell. Used by permission.

sonal motivations. An enhanced degree of self-esteem, a feeling of achievement, a new status, and a sense of belonging are among the most powerful rewards donors can receive. Giving satisfies donors' fundamental human needs and desires. For example, Leland Stanford Junior University (now Stanford University) came into being because Leland Stanford and his wife wanted to memorialize their deceased son.

Certainly in some charitable exchanges, recipients of donations, or *donees,* have held out promises of tangible, useful, or economic rewards—such as books, records, or price reductions for events or services—but these offers draw the sponsoring agency perilously close to potential revocation of its tax-exempt status by the Internal Revenue Service. Recent rulings require nonprofit organizations to specify the dollar value of a paid event, item, or activity that is nondeductible, leaving only the balance as the deductible charitable gift.

The timing of the donee's response is not formally stated in a charitable social exchange. The expectation, however, is that it will be reasonably prompt. Few donors tolerate the suspense of not knowing if the gift has been received. If the canceled check is not returned with the donor's next monthly statement, doubts arise. Even worse from the donor's point of view is having the canceled check returned before the gift has been acknowledged. The relationship begins to wither as the donor wonders if the gift is appreciated or needed. Therefore, donee responses are often multiple. An immediate acknowledgment serves to assure the donor that the gift is welcomed; other responses, such as ceremonial events and reports on the effective use of funds, usually come later. The timing is a matter of judgment and social custom.

Social relationships between donors and donees take many forms, which range from a donor's personal involvement with a cause to feelings of community and compassion with all human beings. Donors have this sense of community and compassion and feel a responsibility to donate when they learn, for example, of children who are disadvantaged but can be given new opportunities, close friends who have benefited from advice from a health agency, or third-world populations that are starving but can be fed. The more personal the involvement in the cause, the stronger is the relationship. Alumni are more likely to give to their alma maters than to other schools. Geographical proximity stimulates a stronger response than distant needs. The axiom "take care of your own first" has great appeal, but such parochial feelings can be overcome if the more remote need is graphically illustrated. Television broadcasts from distant countries of war refugees, starving populations, flood victims, and earthquake casualties forcefully dramatize urgent needs and always produce an outpouring of gifts.

The social exchange relationship also contains an expectation of some future continuity. For example, a recipient organization will use the donated funds for its stated purpose of counseling and supporting pregnant teenagers, or a gift-supported project such as a new library will be well used. Donors trust organizations to be faithful to their stated purposes, and anticipate some report on accomplishments. Likewise, organizations presume that donors, once having made a commitment, will have a continuing concern for the agencies and their work and will continue giving. A mutual interest and trust underlies the relationship.

Clues to Donor Behavior

Many authorities agree that the stimulus to act comes from both internal needs and desires and from external sources (Herzberg, 1966; Staw, 1976; Leavitt and Bahrami, 1988). Internal motivations arise when something is desired, satisfies a need, relieves tension, or feels good. Research on heart disease may aid the donor's own prospects for survival. Swimming lessons will prevent children from drowning. The new auditorium will increase opportunities for cultural enjoyment.

External influences come from persons, events, or conditions in the environment. Donor names will be etched on a granite facade. A tax deduction will be possible. A golf partner asks for the gift. In addition, when individuals appreciate, reward, or disapprove of another individual's actions, a reinforcement takes place and the likelihood that the affected individual will repeat or modify the action is enhanced. The standing ovation when the donor's gift is announced remains in the donor's consciousness. A simple thank-you note from a disabled child kindles a warm feeling from the donor. The human mind assimilates and learns from these experiences, and expectations develop for future situations.

Not all expectations are positive; fear and anxiety also affect actions. Additionally, people do not exist in isolation, they are dependent on actions of family, friends, workplace associates, employers, government officials, and so forth, and these others can cause disappointments and frustrations. All these needs, desires, and forces swirling within individuals encourage them to strive for stability and balance in the process of living. Emotional reactions to this aspiration frequently prod gift decisions.

All the behavioral factors discerned from theory and research that have been discussed so far can be organized into the following framework, which lists both donors' internal motivations and the external influences that fundraisers can call upon when soliciting gifts. Donors' internal motivations must be appealed to, stimulated, or triggered by these external influences.

Framework for Determining Why People Give

Internal Motivations	*External Influences*
Personal or "I" Factors	**Rewards**
Acceptance of self or self-esteem	Recognition
	Personal
Achievement	Social
Cognitive interest	
Growth	**Stimulations**
Guilt reduction or avoidance	Human needs
Meaning or purpose of life	Personal request
Personal gain or benefit	Vision
Spirituality	Private initiative
Immortality	Efficiency and effectiveness
Survival	Tax deductions
Social or "We" factors	**Situations**
Status	Personal involvement
Affiliation	Planning and decision making
Group endeavor	Peer pressure
Interdependence	Networks
Altruism	Family involvement
Family and progeny	Culture
Power	Tradition
	Role identity
Negative or "They" Factors	Disposable income
Frustration	
Unknown situations	
Insecurity	
Fear and anxiety	
Complexity	

In any effort to categorize human behavior, a caution should be sounded about the difficulty of drawing precise boundaries when many factors are known to interact. Nevertheless, this framework encourages fundraisers to look for and work with the motivations and influences that it specifies. The key questions fundraisers should ask of themselves are, What can I do to satisfy or enhance these factors within my prospects? and How can these motivations and influences be used to activate volunteers and staff?

Internal Motivations

Internal motivations, needs, or drives have three dimensions: personal, social, and negative. These dimensions can also be identified respectively as "I," "we," and "they" factors.

Personal or "I" Factors

Internal motivations are most strongly evident in individuals' concepts of self. Recent studies and theories have focused on this psychological self as the key to understanding human behavior in complex organizations (Goddard, 1988). Donors' personal concerns that are important to fundraising efforts involve acceptance of self or self-esteem, achievement, cognitive interest, growth, guilt reduction or avoidance, meaning or purpose of life, personal gain or personal benefit, spirituality, immortality, and survival.

Acceptance of self or *self-esteem* is closely related to self-identity (Schwartz, 1967) and to the "ego-ideal" that Levinson (1968) asserts is the most powerful motivating force. People desire to like themselves, and this desire encourages them to match their self-images of what they want to be. Donors desire to feel good about their charitable acts. For example, just a few months before her death, movie actress Audrey Hepburn expressed her joy about her work of helping children around the world through UNICEF. In his hierarchy of human needs, Maslow (1973) places the self-esteem need next to the highest need, which is for self-actualization through the use of one's talents, creativity, and full potential.

As a motivation, *achievement* relates closely to self-esteem. In work situations, McClelland and others (1976) and Herzberg (1966) believe that achievement is one of the strongest motivations. Donors want to feel that something specific and worthwhile is accomplished with their funds. Thus, they often place restrictions on their gifts in order to assist specific programs, such as counseling teenagers or providing services to the elderly.

Cognitive interest lies at the core of motivations for giving. If people are not mentally attracted to a nonprofit organization's purpose, work, or clients, very little can be done directly to command their attention and funds. For example, the widow of an electronics manufacturer had no interest in electrical engineering scholarships, but she endowed a studies program in philosophy to satisfy the interest in that topic that she had acquired as a student. Indirect methods using prospects' peers or other external instrumentalities may be helpful to arouse interest. An important customer can stimulate the interest of a supplier in the customer's favorite charity.

Growth reckons in both Levinson's and Maslow's theories of motivation. Psychologists and sociologists view people as complex, unfolding, and maturing organisms passing through physiological and psychological states of development (Goddard, 1988). This growth is believed to result in individuals' looking beyond their own immediate welfare to the needs and concerns of others. Older persons donate more than younger ones, and that phenomenon tends to substantiate the notion of psychological growth.

Guilt reduction or *guilt avoidance* ties in with self-esteem. Individuals feel their self-regard or self-image is undermined when they do not respond to accepted values or standards of action. This burden of real or potential guilt weighs most heavily on people when the values and standards in question are entwined with the individuals' own expectations. Charitable acts appease many guilty feelings. Consider the case of a conservative industrialist who led a campaign for the development of a minority youth center with a million-dollar gift from his company. This happened after he had alienated his son, who had participated in the civil rights movement and later worked with disadvantaged youth.

People often crave a sense of *meaning* or *purpose in life*. A chronic complaint in the modern work environment is the lack of this sense; work has been fragmented, and its meaning has become lost (Sievers, 1986). Much of the unrest and resulting social movements in the 1960s and 1970s sprang from this lack of meaning. Many gifts accrue from desires for more meaningful actions and relationships. People often find this meaning or purpose by affiliating with a cause or institution that they feel is larger or more important than themselves or their current situation. The desire for meaning and purpose stimulates many gifts to world peace agencies.

Unquestionably, *personal gain* or *personal benefit* motivates many so-called charitable acts. An individual or family may have previously benefited from the services of a nonprofit organization, and wishes the services to remain available. Many fundraising promotions appeal to the idea of some personal gain. The implications of hospital solicitations, for instance, are that services and beds for donors and their families will be available when the need arises.

The prevalence of religious affiliation reflects the strength of *spirituality* as a motivation. Religious teachings almost always point to the needs of others and urge philanthropic acts. Spirituality also affects individuals' sense of purpose and meaning of life.

Desire for *immortality* derives from several other needs and feelings: spirituality, permanence, stability, self-image, ego-ideal, and survival. Motivations to establish endowed memorials range from selfishness and egocentricity to family honor, religious values, and transcendental beliefs.

Survival is our most basic drive. Gifts to deter crime, alleviate hunger, and prevent other hazards to life manifest this primary motivation. While their intent may seem charitable in relieving threats to others, often donors want to prevent those hazards from affecting themselves and their families. Donations to Holocaust remembrances come from survival impulses.

Social or "We" Factors

Donors' internal motivations are also bound up in feelings toward others. We are social beings. Our condition of dependency, experienced from birth and infancy through adolescence and into adulthood, forms the basis of our social drive. Social relationships with others are a manifestation of our dependency. Satisfaction of social motivations also helps to satisfy many personal or "I" factors. The social factors of motivation include status, affiliation, group endeavor, interdependence, altruism, family and progeny, and power.

Status invoked by such forms and symbols as titles, authority, honors, and salary helps individuals clarify their standing in relation to others (Blau, 1986; Maslow, 1973; Herzberg, 1966). People desire acts of recognition and approval from others to satisfy their strongly felt need for status. The conveyance of titles such as "chair," "honorary chair," "trustee," and "benefactor" meets this motivation. Gift clubs that assign names to donors descriptive of dollar amounts of donations and the hierarchy within the nonprofit organization work on this principle. A ballet company has established donation levels of "dancer," "choreographer," "director," and "producer," with increased dollar amounts for each rung up the ladder of prestige and authority.

Affiliation builds on individuals' status and involvement with others in an organization. McClelland and others (1976) include affiliation with achievement and power as the most powerful motivations. Membership and involvement in philanthropic organizations can meet individuals' need to belong and to be a part of some social activity. While individuals' sense of status can encourage affiliation, that status can also be enhanced by affiliation. Support groups, such as Tradewomen—an organization for blue-collar females in occupations fraught with sexual harassment—meet affiliation desires. Religious institutions provide affiliation opportunities while also satisfying needs for spirituality and immortality.

Group endeavor describes the drive to actively realize social cravings. McGregor (1960) reported the importance of this motivational attribute, asserting that humans have a strong

need to join with one another to accomplish tasks. Working together in such endeavors as helping the poor, training youth in
citizenship, and fundraising satisfies the group endeavor yearn-
ing. Donors' joy at participating in the victory celebration that
concludes a successful campaign springs in part from the group
endeavor motivation.

Interdependence is closely associated with the other social
factors (Kotter, 1985). The complexity of modern society with
the many threads of relationships woven through its fabric attests to interdependence's criticality. Individuals sense the need
for interdependence keenly, especially when their current relationships are breaking down. Their feelings of loneliness and
abandonment open the door for their gifts to such charitable
activities as hospitality centers, support groups, and international welfare agencies.

Altruism is a much debated motivational factor in giving
and volunteering because researchers question whether it is
truly separate from self-interest. Smith (1981) asserts that "there
is literally no evidence to justify a belief in some 'absolute' form
of human altruism, in which the motivation for an action is ut-
terly without some form of selfishness" (p. 23). He feels that
people receive at least psychic rewards from their charitable actions and that these rewards contribute to a positive self-image
or ego enhancement. Nevertheless, concern for the welfare of
others is often cited by individuals as a strong impulse for giving.
Altruism may rarely be pure but it still exists. Altruism is bound
up with people's feelings about interdependence, group endeavor, and human moral principles.

Because families are individuals' primary social units, the
motivation of *family* and *progeny* influences many acts of charity.
Donors' desire to aid and protect personal family members in-
duces giving to organizations such as family service agencies that
serve or potentially benefit children, parents, and relatives. Donors often view these gifts as means to preserve the family unit.
In addition, donors' lack of family has inspired broad support
for children's home societies across the United States.

Power is a social phenomenon and motivation with great
allure. Its existence and exercise require the presence of others.

Power may be defined as one's ability to influence others toward the realization of one's goals, the control of scarce resources (money, land, water, minerals) needed by others, or the ability to get things done (McClelland and others, 1976; Kotter, 1985). In nonprofit organizations where the use of volunteers is critical for fundraising, policy formulation, planning, and even service delivery, the ability to influence others, especially when formal authority over them is minimal, makes the difference between success and failure. For donors, the power to influence the nature and scope of helping others creates a strong incentive for philanthropic giving. People like to point out that their giving caused good things to happen. However, when nonprofit organizations motivate donors and volunteers with power, the organizations must exercise some care to avoid such personnel problems as the retired corporate executive who used the board and operations of an impaired persons agency to satisfy his cravings for power to the detriment of funding efforts. Subsequently, another leader contributed funds for a consultant who analyzed the situation and made recommendations for change, resulting in increased funding.

Negative or "They" Factors

Individuals' motivations do not consist solely of positive factors. Negative feelings and drives abound, arising out of frustration, unknown situations, insecurity, fear and anxiety, and perceived complexity. In an effort to protect or enhance his or her concept of self, an individual may ascribe a problem or crisis to others. "They" cause or may cause difficulties; "they" are to blame, not the individual, even when the situation is of the individual's own making.

Frustration comes from denial or obstruction of the fulfillment of desires and needs. Donations can be a means for actually or symbolically overcoming blockages in given situations by fostering some action. For example, an individual can overcome lack of status in a group by making a major gift. In one capital campaign, an ignored volunteer came forth with a five-figure gift, much to the surprise and admiration of the volunteer leaders. The volunteer was alleviating the frustration of being over-looked.

Unknown situations create vast negative feelings of insecurity, fear, and anxiety (Wilkinson, Orth, and Benfari, 1986). For many people, the threat of an unknown situation is one of the most powerful behavioral influences. People conjure up all forms of frightening difficulties that might be encountered: loss of memory from disease, destruction of a favorite wilderness area, a child led astray. Philanthropic giving can be interpreted as a means by which people counter such threats or seek answers to such current uncertainties as the causes of cancer, the violence of gangs, and the rise of the drug culture. In another sense, gifts can be viewed as means of relaxing tensions by transferring a threat to someone else for solution.

Insecurity develops when individuals feel unable to cope, understand, or act when threatened (Spread, 1984). Stability and balance in life seem illusory when individuals face a rapidly changing world. Insecurity may arise from both unknown and known situations. *Fear* and *anxiety* operate similarly and center around a perceived inability to control outcomes positively (Sievers, 1986). The *complexity* of life and the many demands made on people adversely affect the stability and balance that people seek. Pressures from all these negative motivations build up until individuals find a release, which may take the form of aggression or a fight or flight response. However, donations also offer an opportunity for people to "do something" about offending problems and feel a sense of relief.

External Influences

People are influenced by a host of activities and experiences that originate outside themselves and condition or cause action. Individuals' responses to these environmental factors may be immediate and easily identified, or their actions may be delayed and the actions' sources obscured. In either case, the external influences interact with the existing state of the individual, who is conditioned by past experience and current internal needs and desires. Thus, the effort to identify and classify external influences cannot be considered precise and must be treated with the same caution suggested for internal motivations. Yet three main categories of influences show promise as aids to fundraisers: rewards, stimulations, and situations.

Rewards

Rewards fall into three overlapping types: recognition, personal, and social rewards.

Gifts and volunteer assistance from individuals produce a variety of donor *recognition rewards* from organizations: special introductions of donors at annual meetings, invitations to elite gatherings, feature articles in newsletters, and so forth. The effectiveness of the response depends on how well it satisfies the motivations that prompted the donor's original action. The greater the perceived significance of the rewards to the donor, the stronger the reinforcement of his or her giving and volunteering behavior. Time is of the essence here; prompt rewarding produces greater effect. Also, a single action is rarely induced by a single motivation. Thus, rewards may have to be multiple and applied judiciously.

Personal rewards range from immediate thank-you letters to telephone calls from leaders and officials, awards, membership in elite groups, and peer acknowledgments. A school teacher of modest means expressed great joy about her inclusion in a "Chancellor's Circle" after her gift to establish a scholarship fund for aspiring teachers.

Less tangible, but quite significant, *social rewards* for donors include the development of new personal relationships, an increased sense of community and status, and a new awareness of group cohesion. A feeling of power as a reward is being provided by over 180 United Ways that allow donors to designate the specific charities that will receive their gifts (Millar, 1991a). When donors are shown that their gifts make a difference in meeting a human need, their reward comes from a sense of both achievement and power. Economists who discuss the role of voluntary donations in society stress that personal rewards from giving are important because they complete the exchange transaction (Steinberg, 1987). However, the profusion of rewards to sway donors in today's competitive fundraising environment have caused Dunn (1988) to assert that "the crux and challenge of today's creative fund-raising is finding tangible rewards that will stand out in a very crowded field" (p. 10).

Stimulations

Some actions taken by fundraisers and others to influence prospects' giving behavior can be readily categorized as direct stimulation. These actions include proving human needs, making direct requests, presenting an attractive vision, promoting private initiative, stressing efficiency and effectiveness, and offering a tax deduction.

Foremost among fundraising techniques is the demonstration of the *human needs* that can be met with donors' gifts. Because people are interdependent and have grown up through a period of dependency, the appeal of others in need is very effective. Creating an awareness of the need is a crucial step in the appeal (White, 1989), and the responsibility to educate donors about the need for giving and its benefits lies squarely with the fundraisers (Burchill, 1990). E. C. Dorsey, chairman of the INDEPENDENT SECTOR, recommends that donors make first-hand visits to see where the need is being met and "not just see, but feel the need and develop a sense of interrelatedness and connectedness" (p. 2). Board members who were reluctant to raise funds for a newly established homeless shelter, for example, got "the message" when they saw children and parents being cared for at the facility.

Asking, making a *personal request*, is also one of the strongest ways to stimulate giving. While this seems like such an obvious fact, volunteers, immobilized by their fear of asking, refuse to acknowledge it. The 1992 IS/Gallup survey reports that individuals who are asked are more than twice as likely to give than those who are not asked (Hodgkinson, Weitzman, Noga, and Gorski, 1992). The sheer presence of another individual, presenting the need and demonstrating the value of the gift, compels a positive response. The success of personal asking arises from the fact that people are naturally social. As the process of asking becomes more impersonal, its strength diminishes. (This point is developed further in Chapter Two.)

Challenging prospective donors with the *vision* of what can be done, what the organization should be, and the part that the donor can play strongly influences giving. When the organization goes a step further and involves the prospect in planning future actions, a tight bond develops that creates a sense of ownership and responsibility in the prospect. A wealthy donor who was carefully consulted at each step in the planning of a major marine research facility became so enthused that he increased his gift substantially. Expectations that arise from looking to the future create fundamental psychological drives (Leavitt and Bahrami, 1988) that involve many of the personal and social motives discussed above, especially self-esteem, achievement, status, and group endeavor.

Expectations and visions of the future are conditioned by the personal and social value systems that individuals hold. For example, some people distrust government, resist the welfare state (Ostrander, 1985), and therefore, respond to *private initiatives* to solve problems. Other people are attracted to nonprofits that demonstrate *efficiency* and *effectiveness*. A recent study showed that a significant increase in giving occurred when nonprofits' perceived efficiency (defined as the percentage of funds actually reaching clients, in contrast to administrative costs) rose above 60 percent of total income (Harvey and McCrohan, 1990). Prospective donors resist solicitations when they believe that administrative costs are excessive and client needs are left unmet. United Way agencies across the nation suffered significant declines in gifts for several years after widespread publicity about the extravagant expenditures and personal gain of United Way's national chief executive at the time.

Tax deductions for gifts are powerful incentives that affect the amount of gifts more than the decision to give or not give. Hodgkinson and Weitzman (1990) found that "respondents who intended to claim a charitable deduction gave more than the average contribution to charity and two and one-half times the percentage of household income as those who intend not to

[handwritten note:] Unclear. Those who itemize are richer. Is the "2½ x" skewed by super-rich? Otherwise, a 25-33% incentive doesn't jibe with 250% increase in donation.

itemize" (p. 166). In addition, higher tax rates have a positive effect on giving. The tax deduction stimulus lies not only in the lower cost of gifts to the donor because the donor saves the amount that would otherwise be paid in taxes, but in the donor's power to allocate tax savings to purposes that he or she chooses. A taxpayer, on the other hand, has no power to direct where taxes are used.

Situations

The circumstances in which people find themselves influence their giving, whether the situations arise from individuals' own actions or are created by others. Situational factors include personal involvement, planning and decision making, peer pressure, family involvement, tradition, networks, culture, role identity, and disposable income.

Personal involvement in charitable nonprofit organizations ranks as one of the most effective means of generating contributions. Involved people are usually the most generous (Hodgkinson and Weitzman, 1990). By participating in any form of organizational activity, individuals soon find themselves identifying with organizational goals and requirements. They feel they are a part of the agency and their bonding extends beyond their concern for the human needs served. Participation in agency *planning* and *decision making* results in strong feelings of ownership and concern for the organization. As a consequence, gifts flow readily from this involvement.

Peer pressure is an important influence both within and without organizations. When people see friends and associates donating, they are hard pressed to refuse, especially if they want to maintain their status and self-esteem. In particular, peer pressure manifests itself strongly when committees and other groups are formed to achieve financial and organizational goals. At a board meeting of a local YMCA that had not previously had a major gift club, the volunteer development chair introduced the gift club idea with a personal gift several times larger than his previous gifts. Members of the development committee immediately stated their similar intentions. The gift club became a reality, and board members who had not given or were giving only modest amounts joined the club at the requisite level.

In addition to creating formal organizations, individuals form numerous *networks* with others based on shared interests, demographics, and social structures. The giving practices of others in a network impel many contributions. Here again, the motives of self-esteem and status are operative.

While concern for one's family is an internal motivation, the fact of *family involvement* with organizations and their services can be considered an external influence and one that inspires many gifts. Health, education, and social service organizations benefit markedly from family involvement. Parents and children who have received treatment or services prompt their grateful relatives to donate.

An organization's *culture* exerts great leverage on its participants. A 1981 national study of organizational norms and values that expected corporate managers to be involved in community work found that managers' attitudes and behavior corresponded to these norms and values (Christenson, Hougland, Ilvento, and Shepard, 1988).

Traditions and historic values, especially those based on religious principles and teachings, instigate giving. Religious organizations are particularly forthright in expecting members to give, and the success of this traditional expectation is demonstrated by the preponderance of gifts they receive from individuals (Wuthnow, Hodgkinson, and Associates, 1990). Secular organizations are recognizing the impact of such formalized giving traditions as tithing by overtly creating their own "traditions." Their success arrives when they establish a "climate of giving." The INDEPENDENT SECTOR, for example, promotes its national Give Five program, which asks all individuals to donate 5 percent of annual income and five hours a week of volunteer time to the charities of their choice. IS conveys its message through public service announcements on television and radio and in print media, and it encourages charitable organizations to bring the Give Five concept to their constituencies.

Role identity plays a key part in social and organizational situations. Role can be defined as the behavior a person is expected to exhibit when occupying a given position in an organization or social setting (Katz and Kahn, 1966). Role identities are formulated in part by the individual and in part by the social structure involved (Callero, 1985). The greater the convergence between the individual and social aspects, the more positive is the behavior. A person who makes a token gift usually does not perceive himself or herself as having the role and status of a donor, particularly in an environment such as a major gift campaign where high levels of giving are emphasized. However, when the first and then the next "token" gift is coupled with rewards and reinforcements from others, the individual begins to accept and learn the donor's role. This phenomenon explains in part the fundraising axiom that "small gifts precede big gifts," and donors of large gifts frequently admit that they began with small gifts to the same agency. Initially, therefore, a person's attitude may not encompass making a major gift, but the act of giving and the environment in which it occurs changes the person's views (Leavitt and Bahrami, 1988). The new attitude of giving and the newly found role of being a donor abets additional, larger gifts.

Disposable income counts as a critical factor in donors' giving decisions (White, 1989). When asked why they give, many individuals respond, "Because I have the money." While this behavior seems patently obvious, it shrouds the finding that lower-income households ($20,000 and under) give a greater percentage of their income than do more affluent ones. Hodgkinson and Weitzman (1990) found that people who had no worry about having enough money in the future gave an average contribution 50 percent higher than those who did worry. Again, the finding seems trite, diverting our attention from the challenging fact that people stressed over money do give to causes important to them.

[handwritten marginalia: acc. to them? This seems to have been said above. If NOT, then the author doesn't understand detachment.]

Why People Do Not Give

Approximately twenty-seven million households (28 percent of all households) do not contribute to any nonprofit organization, according to the IS/Gallup 1992 survey (Hodgkinson,

Weitzman, Noga, and Gorski, 1992). Furthermore, approximately sixty-nine million contributing households give the majority of their contributions to religious organizations with the balance spread thinly over eleven other categories containing tens of thousands of agencies.

Two basic questions arise from these data to face fundraisers: Why do so many people not give any funds? and more pointedly, Why does my organization not receive funds from the 75 percent who do give? The answers are not readily apparent because of insufficient research on this topic. However, the foregoing discussion suggests that many people are not asked or they believe their household incomes to be insufficient or they lack convincing external influences. Further reasons for people's failure to donate time or money are suggested in the following discussion, along with some reasons why a particular organization may fail to attract funds.

When questions about giving practices are posed in household surveys, some investigators are faced with a "mushiness of response" that White (1989) attributes to prospects' not telling the truth. Individuals are not able to respond to all requests, so they forgo the truth to get rid of requests, or they understate donations to evade being included on "hit lists." The overwhelming direct mail appeals that jam many home mailboxes result from donors' names being added to numerous rented mailing lists.

Hodgkinson, Weitzman, Noga, and Gorski (1992) found that household respondents who had stopped giving to a particular charity (17 percent of the total sample) had the following rationales: lack of money (25 percent), lack of trust in the charity (24 percent), charity's misuse of funds (17 percent), disagreement with the charity or lack of similar beliefs (7 percent), the charity's fundraising tactics or "pestering me" (6 percent), gave to another organization (5 percent), don't know (4 percent), and other miscellaneous reasons (17 percent). (Scores total more than 100 percent because some respondents gave multiple reasons.) These findings suggest categories fundraisers could use to evaluate prospect resistance and improve subsequent donation performance. Other explanations for people's failure to give can be found in an absence of positive motivations, a denial or frustration of internal motivations, or an absence of external influences.

The statements in the following framework were provided by several thousand participants in over one hundred fundraising workshops. They were asked for their opinions on why people did not give. The rationales they mentioned for not giving were clustered around four problems of donor/donee relations: personal characteristics and situations, communication, reactions to solicitations, and organizational image.

Framework for Determining Why People Do Not Give (* indicates most frequently mentioned)

Personal Characteristic and Situation Problems

Personal preferences
Higher priorities*
Not concerned
Not interested*
Not involved
Stinginess

Contrary beliefs
Disagree with mission
Don't agree on policies*
Don't believe in cause*
Don't like programs
Different work ethic

Finances
Can't afford to give*
Fear of reciprocity
Economic conditions
Tax rates

Situations
Complexity of life
Competition
Changing environment
Outside local area

Communication Problems

Lack of information
Mission not known
Organization unknown
Others not supporting
Need not shown*
No record of service
No real case
No results seen*

Ineffective communication
Negative publicity
Publications too slick
Unclear need
Promotion too costly

Reactions to Solicitations	*Organizational Image Problems*
Manner of asking	**Perceptions of poor**
Asked too often*	**organizational behavior**
Asked wrong way	Active mistrust
Manipulation	High administrative costs
Too many mailings*	Agency too rich
	Bad experience
Solicitor	Poor reputation
Don't like the asker	Services cost too much
No obligation to asker	Duplication of services
Used paid solicitors	Government involvement
Wrong person asking*	Taxes pay for services
Relations with prospect	**Management**
No personal contact	Misuse of gifts
No recognition	Poor policies and rules
Not appreciated	High fundraising costs
Not asked*	Poor management
No tradition to give	
Timing	
Already gave	
Asked too late	
Wrong time	

Personal Characteristic and Situation Problems

Personal preferences, beliefs, finances, and situations account for many of the reasons people do not give.

Among their *personal preferences*, individuals often have other interests or higher priorities. The purposes or clients of a given nonprofit organization just do not hold much concern for them. Their cognitive interests have shifted or lie elsewhere, and they are content to let others support the agency. At one time, public weariness with homeless people in the San Francisco Bay area rose to such a point that donations declined dramatically for some agencies. The phenomenon was labeled "compassion fatigue" (Fagan, 1990) because donors were numbed by street mendicants and saturated with television and direct mail appeals. More often, however, it is lack of contact, stimulus, or involvement that underlies peoples' disinterest. No organization has taken the time to engage their attention. Other individuals are not accustomed to making gifts because they lacked examples of giving during their childhoods, and a few persons are so self-centered or devoted to acquiring material wealth that they cannot bring themselves to part with their money.

Contrary beliefs play an important part in refusals to give, especially to specific organizations. An organization's philosophy, mission, cause, policies, program, or activities can run counter to a prospect's established perceptions of what ought to be. A strongly held work ethic can militate against support for the unemployed. Agencies ministering to AIDS victims encounter prospects who have negative attitudes toward those whose sexual preferences are different. Conflicting attitudes and beliefs resist solution because they are based less in rational factors than in deeply ingrained emotions. Unless individuals who hold conflicting views are essential to the success of a particular project, the practical course is to involve others who are more compatible. Where necessary, conflict resolution techniques can be employed.

Personal *finances* affect many decisions not to give or to give less money. The 1992 IS/Gallup survey (Hodgkinson, Weitzman, Noga, and Gorski, 1992) showed that approximately 61 percent of the respondents that did not give in 1991 cited lack of money. Additionally, the study found that people who worry about having enough money in the future give a significantly lower proportion of their household income than those without such worries.

The economic health of the nation sways decisions about contributing. Both recession and inflation can become excuses as well as realities. In 1991, a recession year, the number of households contributing to charity dropped by 3 percent from 1989, and the average household contribution declined by 20 percent (after allowing for inflation). Fear of reciprocity also enters the picture because some donors feel that if they give to one charity they will be asked to give to similar ones by their friends and associates. Some individuals refuse to give unless they see a business return or some other quid pro quo.

Tax rates affect levels of giving, particularly among the affluent. When the tax benefit of a gift decreases owing to a lower marginal tax rate, wealthy donors feel less inclined to give generously. The Research Institute of America, for example, found a significant drop in the average size of charitable contributions made by high-income taxpayers between 1987 and 1988 when the U.S. marginal tax rate dropped from 38.5 percent to 28 percent (Williams, 1991). Average contributions decreased by as much as 25 percent.

Foremost among the *situations* that enter into personal decisions not to give is the complexity of people's lives. They feel too busy or face so many other demands that they cannot focus their attention on nonprofit causes. The multitude of appeals most people receive compounds the problem. The easy solution is to ignore all appeals or use some excuse not to give. In addition, individuals' particular social, political, and economic environments can create values and practices that prompt decisions against giving. Liberal causes find little response in conservative neighborhoods. Appeals from outside a locality often suffer from hometown competition. A "let's take care of our own" philosophy shuts the door on many requests.

Communication Problems

Nonprofit organizations may make errors and omissions in the process of communicating with prospects. The leading error is a failure to make up for prospects' *lack of information.* Prospects may know little or nothing about the agency. The purpose or mission is obscure and no record of service is apparent. The results and benefits from gifts seem remote. The case for supporting the organization is not transmitted to prospects. In this case, prospects simply have insufficient information on which to base their giving (White, 1989).

Closely related to lack of information, *ineffective communi-*

cation leaves many prospects cold. Publications may appear too slick and expensive in relation to campaign goals and sponsoring organizations' needs. Apparent unwise use of promotional funds deters support. Frequently, the urgency and severity of the need to be met fail to make an impression (Harvey and McCrohan, 1990). Negative publicity results more often from the manner in which problems are reported than from the events themselves.

Reactions to Solicitations

No more critical time exists than that during the process of asking the prospect. Negative responses can be generated by the manner of asking, the character and conduct of the solicitor, the quality of the organization's relations with the prospect, and the timing. All these problems can be overcome by careful attention to the principles of solicitation discussed in Chapter Two, but the surprising fact is the extent to which effective practices are ignored.

The *manner of asking* produces many different complaints. Chief among them is the frequently heard "I don't like being asked so often." Other variations include "too many mailings," "asked for too much money," and even "asked for too little money." Some people feel that they are being manipulated, that the quality of the presentation is poor, or that the organization's expectations are unrealistic.

The *solicitor* for the charitable organization may incur negative reactions. On the one hand, employment of paid professionals raises prospects' questions about the potential use of their money and the true costs of the fundraising. On the other hand, volunteer solicitors can have personality characteristics that do not blend with prospects' characteristics or that actively offend prospects. Sometimes prospects sense no obligation to the solicitor or no peer relationship. The status of the solicitor may seem too unimpressive for the amount of money being asked or the stature of the prospect. A blue-collar worker faces difficulty in asking an executive to give, not to mention the problem of getting the appointment to solicit in the first place.

Relations with the prospect often produce adverse reactions.
Most obvious and quite common is the failure to ask for a gift.
Volunteers and staff may be guilty of "protecting" the prospect
until "the right moment comes along." The right moment may
never occur for a variety of reasons, but the usual reason is a lack
of proper cultivation and involvement. Prospects welcome being appreciated for their qualities and abilities and not just for
their money. Donors value reasonable recognition for their gifts
of time and treasure. Misspelling and mispronunciation of
names quickly turn off many prospects. Using the title "Mr." in
a letter to a woman conveys lack of care and undermines the
validity of the request for funds. The frequent absence of common courtesies ruins many donor/donee relationships. Also, if
those immediately concerned with an organization's affairs and
services are not giving, less-involved prospects begin to question
why they should give. The lack of a tradition of participant giving discourages prospect response. This problem increases dramatically when board members avoid giving.

The *timing* of a solicitation affects results. Negative variables encompass prospects' lack of involvement before they are
asked, personal problems, schedule conflicts, and temporarily
reduced cash flow. A recent gift by a prospect usually rules out a
subsequent gift unless some intervening organizational activity
supports the new request. New information, change in the need
being served, and public events are examples of intervening
activities.

Organizational Image Problems

A negative view of a nonprofit organization discourages many
donations. Even when there is little or no factual basis for the
negative opinion, the effect can be ruinous. Negative views tend
to cluster around perceptions of poor organizational behavior
and management problems. *Perceptions of poor organizational behavior* can arise from individuals' bad personal experiences with
the agency or from individuals' believing the perceptions of others. The complaints range from active mistrust to charges of in-
efficiency and duplication of services. The multitude of appeals
from similar agencies in fields such as health, welfare, and the

environment causes donors to question what portion of their gifts supports the expense of solicitations.

High fundraising costs, whether perceived or real, discourage donations. Studies by Greenfield (1991) and Levis (1992) indicate that the costs of different fundraising methods vary widely, from $1.25 for each $1.00 raised from new donors to $0.05 for each $1.00 donated in large capital campaigns (fundraising costs are discussed further in Chapter Four). However, when the costs of all methods are combined, the overall bottom-line percentages range from 15 to 20 percent throughout the nation. These amounts are well within the 35 percent reasonable cost standard specified by the Philanthropic Advisory Service of the Council of Better Business Bureaus. Unfortunately, these figures and their rationale are not well understood by the donating public.

The *management* of nonprofit organizations can cause prospects to withhold gifts. Negative reputations arise from misuse of gifts, lack of accountability for performance, no evidence of results, apparent overstaffing, and news stories of scandals or mistreatment of clients. Administrative costs are frequent targets of management concerns, along with perceptions that an organization charges too much for services. Salaries and perquisites perceived to be excessive damage claims of financial need. Witness the periodic publicity about the top executive compensation paid by national charitable organizations. The public perception that these organizations are too rich follows easily. When policies, procedures, and style of leadership do not fit the situation, management is perceived to be incompetent. Consequently, that management's ability to make effective use of donations is called into question. Governmental involvement can also produce negative reactions. Some people eschew organizations that have governmental participation. Other people use the excuse that taxes pay for these organizations' services, thus relieving any private obligation to give funds.

Conclusion

All the reasons that people do not give pose serious enduring challenges to fundraisers and their organizations. Careful analysis of giving trends and random sampling of former donors can cast light on the specific practices that deter giving to a particular organization. Continuing attention to this area is vital for every fundraising organization's survival.

Fundraising is becoming both more prevalent and more sophisticated. Tens of thousands of new charitable organizations seeking funds appear each year (Internal Revenue Service, 1991). The search for those who will give has become more intense and professional. The solution to this competitive pressure lies in more effective use of the motivations and influences that stimulate giving. The social exchange model of the charitable transaction provides a rationale that elevates the practice of fundraising and gives impetus to both parties, the donors and the recipients, to perform well. The next steps for nonprofits are to apply basic principles and create productive social exchanges.

---◼---

Two

The Dynamics
of
Asking People
for Money

Since individuals are the largest source of charitable funds, averaging over 81 percent of all gifts for the last five years (Kaplan, 1993), an understanding of the process of asking them is essential for nonprofit organizational survival and growth. The goal of all asking activities is to create social exchanges that benefit both parties by producing funds for the organization and satisfactions for the donors.

Fundraisers ask prospects through several different methods: face-to-face meetings, telephone calls, letters, special events, and television programs and other electronic media. Most factors in the asking process are the same regardless of the method used because prospects go through similar intellectual and emotional steps to arrive at decisions to give no matter how they are asked, although some steps may be foreshortened or extended, depending on the attributes of the method employed and on the desired results. For example, face-to-face solicitation is the most time consuming and difficult process of asking, yet it has the highest positive response rate.

This chapter explores the process of asking individuals by drawing out the underlying concepts and essential activities involved and by developing procedural models from those concepts and activities. The analysis focuses first on the stages prospects experience, then on the persons doing the asking, and finally on process variations.

The Asking Process

The asking process has three essential stages:

1. Prospect cultivation, or preparation
2. The act of asking
3. Completion of the social exchange

However, the steps within these stages are not necessarily linear, nor of equal weight. This is particularly true when the persons to be asked have been involved in some activity of the asking organization or have previously given. A complete cultivation stage may be unnecessary because the prospects or donors have served as volunteers on a project for which funds are sought, yet the other two stages will remain essential. Furthermore, prospect/donee interchanges through such modes as meetings, events, letters, awards, telephone conversations, and projects are seldom confined to one of these modes. Instead, multiple interactions take place through a variety of modes, yet each mode contains similar principal elements: communication, involvement, and reinforcement.

Prospect Cultivation

The cultivation stage makes the prospect aware of the need for the services that donated funds will support. Ideally, this awareness gives the prospect an emotional feeling for the cause and the need to be met. Awareness begins when the prospect becomes linked to the organization through communications from the organization, knowledge of someone already linked to the organization, a personal relationship, or participation in an organizational activity.

The nature of the need is conveyed through a variety of vehicles: personal participation or contact, newsletters, brochures, news stories, television, radio, video and audio cassettes, facsimile transmissions, and direct mail. The substance of the communication determines the viability of the emerging relationships. Rational arguments should accompany the transmission of the more effective emotional appeals (Leavitt and Bahrami, 1988). United Ways throughout the country frequently use an attractive but disadvantaged child as the centerpiece of their campaigns. The aim is to establish an emotional bond with potential donors by vividly displaying a vital need that they can meet. But in addition to the emotional appeal, the rationality of giving is substantiated by reports from United Ways of success in helping disadvantaged children and meeting other needs.

The prospect's cognitive interest in an agency's clients or service ranks as a fundamental prerequisite in the process of building awareness. The prospect must be interested in youths, elderly persons, students, research, health, or whatever the issue is. When an asking organization proceeds with the cultivation process, it assumes that the prospect has this cognitive interest. If a person is not interested in the people involved or in the work to be done, an exchange will be unlikely because of the great difficulty of getting that person's attention and commitment.

However, a further assumption can be made that when the needs and desires of prospects are sufficiently identified, these attributes can become vehicles for creating interest. For example, prospects with elderly parents face potential problems of home care, dementia, and terminal diseases; because of these prospects' concerns, organizations can often interest them in such proposed solutions as senior service agencies. A marketing principle described by Kotler (1982) is that determining what the target population needs and wants precedes the asking function. Once needs and wants are determined, the thrust of the appeals can be adjusted to the prospects' concerns. As a result, the initial message will relate to donor motivations and imply the return of personal and social satisfactions.

As a typical next step, prospects become identified with

or involved in the organization. They see that the organization shares their concerns for a particular problem, cause, or services, and they feel aligned with the organization. The relationship becomes especially strong if the organization's vision for the solution of the problem is conveyed effectively (Leavitt and Bahrami, 1988). For instance, youth development agencies like the scouts or the YMCA capitalize on the promise of the growth and maturation their services provide youthful clients.

When an organization makes prospects and donors feel involved, it also rewards these individuals' involvement through satisfying their social motivations. When they are asked through direct mail or in a meeting for their opinions on an organization's direction and goals, they experience affiliation and status (Zander, 1985). Reports and briefings, particularly if made personally, strengthen the social relationship. Formal membership in the organization gives status, enhances self-esteem, and meets affiliation needs. Participation in fundraising events develops bonding. Serving on committees and task forces creates similar satisfactions. Invitations to join such special groups as giving clubs organized by level of gift further donors' sense of involvement and strengthen donor/donee relationships.

A major challenge facing federated campaigns, such as the United Way, is the psychological distance created between donors and needy recipients by the intervening fundraising organization (Brilliant, 1990). Not only is the service delivery agency separated from the prospect, but the persons to be helped are even further removed. Consequently, donors do not feel involved. Many United Way organizations seek to resolve this remoteness by encouraging their donee agencies to establish agency communication programs with United Way donors.

As the donor/donee relationship develops, the individual accepts the organization as the vehicle to meet the need that is being presented, and realizes that the organization will be asking for support. The knowledge that others are supporting the organization also legitimizes the forthcoming solicitation (Cialdini, 1984).

The sequence of cultivation activities can vary considerably. Friends or social activities may start the process before a prospect senses or learns of a need. Personal acquaintances may suggest that the individual could have an interest in or should be aware of the good works that an organization undertakes. Invitations to special events attract attention. Strong personal motivations such as a keen desire for status can often shorten the cultivation process and lead to a gift before the prospect internalizes the need. For example, a person may notice the names of valued friends or customers on a list of donors and decide to join them before developing an appreciation of the need.

Once individuals are involved in an activity, they usually feel compelled to go along with the role expectations that surround their chosen levels of participation (Cialdini, 1984). In recent years, for example, nonprofit board members have been recruited with the explicit understanding that they are required to donate and to seek donations. The same expectation holds true for other positions of responsibility in nonprofit agencies. When program volunteers become aware of the fundraising done by board members, they sense that they also should give and get funds to enable their projects to thrive.

Cold lists contain names of people not known to have connections with the requesting agency. Direct mail solicitations that use cold lists suffer because the prospects have not been cultivated before the request reaches them. The limited response rates for such mailings, hovering around 1 percent, underscore the problem. However, solicitations for funds to help victims of natural or human catastrophes that are the subject of widespread news stories are an exception to the rule. Large-scale disasters abridge the preparation or cultivation phase, and direct mail letters and brochures elicit outpourings of gifts.

The Act of Asking

Asking begins with presentation of the request to the prospect through one or more methods. (The unique aspects of each method are discussed later in this chapter.) To respond to the request, the prospect has to feel the importance and urgency of the need. As Payton (1989) states, "Philanthropy, after all, is the product of persuasion, not of logical demonstration" (p. 41). A poignant illustration of the persons who can be helped, such as homeless people or starving children, serves this persuasive aim.

The capability of the recipient organization to meet the need must also be clearly shown. Further, the prospect wants to know that the requested gift amount will be effective. Prospects frequently express this concern by asking, "How can my small gift be of real value?" An allied question is, "Will my donation be consumed by high administrative costs?"

During the presentation, doubts will arise in the prospect's mind. Some of the tensions that prospects experience when they are asked to give correspond to the reasons presented in Chapter One for people's decision not to give. Suitable reassurances and additional information are required in response to these concerns so that the donor feels comfortable with the request. Examples include offering a convenient pledge payment plan if the amount suggested appears too high, describing what other gifts have accomplished, or citing the satisfactions that other donors have experienced.

As the beneficial attributes of the proposed social exchange are shown, the prospect moves closer to the giving decision. A listing of donor names, for example, implies status, pictures of projects in progress suggest achievement, and photos of volunteers give a sense of group endeavor. The basic conditions the asker is working to achieve are the realization of the social exchange potential and the development of trust between the donor, the person asking, and the organization represented. Frequently, endorsements, testimonials, and leadership by respected persons or known authorities can abet this trust. Former President Jimmy Carter and President Bill Clinton when he was still a candidate gave substantial impetus to the funding of low-income housing by driving nails on a construction project.

Completion of the Social Exchange

The final stage of the asking process occurs when the donor feels that a reasonable social transaction has taken place, with satisfaction of some internal donor motivations and accommodation of external influences. An immediate acknowledgment of gratitude for the gift from official sources starts the completion process. Other types of personal and social rewards must follow in forms suitable to the contribution. The closer in time the reward is to the act of giving, the more effective it is.

Psychological research has demonstrated the importance of reinforcement to assure continuation of desired activity (Leavitt and Bahrami, 1988). All the varieties of donor involvement described earlier in this chapter can provide a significant portion of the necessary reinforcement. Recognition also ranks as a preeminent social exchange element. All forms of recognition produce the desired effect: thank-you letters, awards, honors, use of donor names in newsletters, facilities named for donors, peer acknowledgment, and so forth. However, the form and degree of recognition must appear to be reasonable or appropriate to the size and nature of the gift. Otherwise, the credibility of the recognition deteriorates. Success in sustaining donor interest depends also on the quality and frequency of the feedback the donor receives about what was accomplished with the funds raised. Efficient administration of gifts reinforces donors' decisions to donate.

Ideally, the developing relationships between donors and recipient organizations are interactions of ever-increasing bonding. The various activities that make up the relationships should bring donors ever closer to the core of the organization, increase their commitment, and raise their level of giving, as illustrated in Figure 2.1. Individuals may participate in the whorl of involvement at any point as a result of shifts in their peer connections, personal interests, finances, or other factors.

Initially, donors are just names about whom very little is known unless they are found in membership rolls of churches, museums, alumni groups, or other constituencies with clear

Figure 2.1.   Progressive Donor Involvement.

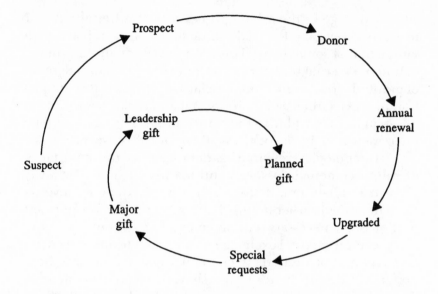

common characteristics. The names come from mailing lists, public documents, publications, other donor lists, and personal referrals. Fundraisers frequently call these persons *suspects* until additional information about them is uncovered by research or by their response to a fundraiser's initiative. Communication begins with the nonprofit organizations' newsletters, bulletins, invitations to events, and low-level mail appeals. Positive responses from prospects are reinforced, and increased levels of participation and commitment are invited.

Bonding between donors and requesting organizations develops as donors realize that they have a special status as annual givers. As donors' involvement increases and their financial capacities enlarge, their potential to make bigger donations increases. Studies of donors at large universities show that prior giving is the biggest factor determining who will give major gifts in the future (Lindahl, 1991). Ultimately, some donors who have been continuously involved will make a final gift of part or all of their estates to the agencies with which they have had a close, rewarding relationship marked by social exchange. However, Lindahl also points out that in his case study at Northwestern University some prospects who made bequests and planned gifts had not had a strong history of giving but became donors for personal reasons that were not always known to the donee, such as financial and beneficiary advantages. Presumably, these donors had other forms of university linkages and involvement than gift giving.

Face-to-Face Solicitation

All effective solicitations contain four stages that are based on the psychological motivations and influences discussed earlier.

1. An introduction in which social amenities and relationships between the parties are covered
2. A dialogue that allows the prospect to express his or her personal views regarding the need, the agency, and his or her individual values
3. A description of the needs to be met and the benefits for the prospect and the asking of questions that can be answered positively
4. A conclusion in which a gift is requested

A similar solicitation model was developed by the Fund Raising School (1977), from a model developed by Preston McCoy (1977) and other sales trainers.

The exact format for a solicitation will vary with the characteristics of the persons involved. However, to produce the desired results, the content of the four stages must satisfy the donor's personal motivations, present suitable donor stimuli, and cite potential donor rewards. The following sections describe how the four stages apply to face-to-face solicitations.

The setting for face-to-face solicitation usually involves two persons, the prospect and the asker, although when a major gift is expected a second asker may be present and the prospect's spouse or trusted advisor may sit in. The prospect knows either directly or indirectly that a request for funds will be made. This message is conveyed during the telephone call for the appointment or in mailings sent in advance. The amount of the request is not announced but is left to be introduced strategically during the presentation.

Introduction

In a very brief time, the solicitor should establish a rapport with the prospective donor by discussing existing relationships, mutual involvement with the agency, and shared values. The purpose of the visit is clearly stated: to talk about the prospect's interest in the need to be met and the opportunity for the prospect to be a part of the solution. A brief assertion of the agency's capacity to deal with the need reassures the prospect. In a minute or so, by following this format, the asker can reduce the prospect's concern over any unknown factors by stating the nature of the visit and encouraging the prospect to concentrate on the message instead of on questions about what is going to happen. The recitation of common affiliations reinforces the social bonds between the asker and the prospect.

Dialogue

Since a social exchange is the desired result of the meeting, a discussion must ensue to determine the prospect's knowledge, feelings, and interest about the need and the organization working on it. Low-key questions posed to the prospect serve this end. By encouraging the prospect to express his or her views, the solicitor helps mutual understanding and common concerns to evolve. Furthermore, the solicitor can draft a mental road map of the points he or she should cover in the subsequent description.

The dialogue portion of the meeting ends with the solicitor's summing up the areas of agreement and asking the prospect if the points are correct. The dialogue process is based on psychological studies that demonstrate the importance of a person's ventilating concerns and feelings before another person suggests a change in behavior (Lewin, 1948). In this case, the desired behavioral change is from taking no action to making a donation. Additionally, the prospect's assent to the correctness of the summation begins the vital process of encouraging the prospect to agree with the solicitor's statements (Cialdini, 1984). This getting-agreement strategy is further enhanced when the solicitor asks the prospect if the solicitor can proceed to talk about some of the agency's accomplishments in meeting the need at hand.

Description

Before making a decision to give, prospects want reassurances that their money will achieve a worthwhile end and not be wasted. They want confirmation that the organization can carry out the proposed project. Thus, the solicitor must have in mind several agency project examples that match the interests and feelings the prospect cited during the dialogue. Recitation of the ways agency work has benefited individuals or improved situations causes the prospect to sense the potential personal power, status, and achievement that can result from a donation. At this point, the solicitor can reinforce the prospects' feelings by mentioning some satisfactions the donor will receive. Again, the solicitor employs the principle of getting agreement by asking the prospect if the service or plan of action seems to be a good idea. Once two or three activities have been described, along with their client and donor benefits, and once confirming questions have been asked and answered, the prospect will be stimulated to wonder what the bottom line is, what is expected in the way of a donation. Any delay in satisfying this curiosity will disrupt the conditioning that has taken place.

Conclusion

The effective donation question is worded to address internal motivations and to incorporate external influences as well as to state a specific sum. For example, a solicitor could say, "Because of these benefits, would you join with me in making a gift of $1,000 to help these people do X?" or, "Would you become a part of this effort [or plan, or activity] to achieve these benefits by making a gift of $1,000 along with me?" The effectiveness of these questions lies in their intimation of achievement ("do X"; "achieve these benefits"), affiliation ("become a part"), status and group endeavor ("join with me"), and self-esteem. If the presentation has touched on other personal, social, or negative motivations felt by the donor, added leverage is obtained. With a commitment in hand, the solicitor thanks the prospect, reassures the person that positive results will occur, and leaves promptly.

Defusing Objections

Rarely will a solicitation proceed as smoothly as this outline shows. Objections and concerns arise quite naturally in prospects' minds as the individuals process a request for action that may or may not have been anticipated. Reactions can include such defensive tactics as temporizing or stating a need for more information and rationales. Prospects who do this are striving to preserve their sense of self-worth by fending off perceived invasions of their images of themselves. Initially, they may consider the idea of making a gift as a threat, a move into the unknown, or an additional frustration. To a prospect these feelings are real; the solicitor who denies the feelings increases the prospect's negative reactions.

The solution to this defensiveness requires that the asker acknowledge and empathize with the objection. The prospect must clearly feel the asker's consideration and feel that the asker is truly listening to the prospect's concerns. Such empathy allows the existing rapport to continue and grow. As the emotional aspect of the concerns is being addressed through empathy, the cognitive aspect can be handled in several ways. A frequent prospect objection is lack of money. The asker can express sympathy, not rejection, and build on the objection by suggesting that he or she has faced a similar situation and found the answer in pledging a donation on a monthly or quarterly basis. Other objections may center around dislike for a particular program, personality, or seemingly unjustified need. In these cases, the solicitor can switch the topic after sympathizing with the prospect. This technique allows the solicitor to intro-duce, for example, a new agency activity to occupy the prospect's mind, thus removing the disliked activity from the prospect's attention and easing the tension, or the expression of sympathy for the prospect's concerns can be followed by a supposition of what could happen to clients, programs, or agen-cies if there were no support to correct the situation. These two responses to objections are less stressful and more constructive than direct confrontations.

A more forceful tactic is to ask the prospect a direct ques-tion. This is particularly effective when the person has no inter-est in the need presented or states interest only in another field. A pertinent question at this time is, "What would it take for you to become interested in this project?" This question causes the prospect to provide more information about his or her values and feelings, which the solicitor can then address. If the pros-pect voices a particularly vehement objection, another helpful tactic is to ask the person to repeat the statement. Usually, indi-viduals find it difficult to sustain an emotional outburst a second time. Also, the repetition can help the prospect recognize that the statement was unrealistic or inappropriate.

An additional method of dealing with strong concerns is for the solicitor to rephrase the objection with a slight overstate-ment or emphasis. For example, in response to a prospect's worry that an agency is not well equipped to deal with the need, the solicitor might say, "As I understand it, our agency does not have any solution to this problem?" The slight exaggeration prompts the prospect to clarify the objection and, in doing so, to gain a better perspective on what is at issue. This procedure helps defuse emotion and focuses the prospect on the value of the services to be supported. Also, when the solicitor restates the objection, it is important that he or she avoids attributing it to the prospect. Otherwise, the prospect will feel compelled to defend the objection rather than enabled to step back and look at it objectively.

The handling of any objection requires judgment and discretion to adapt the remedy to the rapport existing in the relationship. Harsh responses stiffen opposition. As already mentioned, objections to requests for funds frequently take the form of delaying tactics. Prospects may say, "I need more time to think about this," or "I need to consult with my wife [or husband]." An empathetic response by the solicitor and further dialogue softens the objection and allows rapport to develop further. If the delaying tactic cannot be overcome, the solicitor should establish a definite time to return, bringing back the pledge card and one or two new pieces of literature. The return visit appears more necessary and comfortable to both parties when the solicitor has some new items to show and discuss.

Choosing the Face-to-Face Solicitor

One of the most well-known axioms espoused by fundraisers asserts that "people give to people." The experience from which this statement is drawn demonstrates that prospects are reluctant to donate to faceless organizations. A person must represent an organization if the organization is to inspire confidence in the purpose and use of contributed funds. Thus, the axiom is frequently modified to state that "people give to people with causes." This axiom holds true in all methods of asking, face to face or by mail, telephone, or television. Attendance at a nonprofit's special event is enhanced by an invitation from a specific person, usually a leader or well-known personality. An exception to this rule may be claimed for the public's response to dramatic catastrophes such as floods, famines, or earthquakes. However, in these situations the afflicted people themselves are prominently shown or reported.

Therefore, selection of the right asker is critical for successful results. When the method for asking is impersonal, as it is in direct mail for example, the person chosen to make the request must have higher name recognition and leadership status than other solicitors typically need in more personal situations. Known names and leadership status induce confidence and trust in the organization the person endorses, while they also reduce subtle anxieties or fears about unknown conditions surrounding the gift. The stature of the person selected usually conforms to the scope of the fundraising campaign. Nationwide solicitations require nationally known figures. Local solicitations can use local leaders effectively.

In face-to-face solicitations the criteria for solicitor selection arise from the asker and the prospect's relationship. The ideal solicitor has some linkage or connection with the prospect, is at least the prospect's peer, and may even have higher status than the prospect. The ideal solicitor also has status and a recognized role in the nonprofit organization. Underlying this matching of solicitor to prospect is the factor of trust built on the two parties' mutual experiences and individual reputations. The most effective peer is a person who has contributed an amount equivalent to that being asked of the prospect and who has similar social and economic status. These factors strengthen the bond between the prospect and the solicitor.

The larger the expected gift, the greater is the importance of these criteria and the greater the consideration that should be given to the parties' personality types. Both Gerard (1985) and McClelland (1987) found that matched personality characteristics facilitated relationships and more effective outcomes for the purpose of a meeting. Askers can be tested for their personal qualities, but prospects would find such measures offensive and unwarranted. However, prospect profiles can be compiled from staff and volunteer assessments of a prospect's behavior, comments by known associates, and research in public records. While this procedure lacks the reliability of personality testing, it results in more effective solicitations than blind matching.

When no suitable volunteer solicitor is available, the question arises whether it would be appropriate and effective for staff to solicit the gift. The frequency of this quandary increases with the size of the expected gift. An organization may have a prospect capable of making a ten thousand dollar donation, but no donor who has yet given that sum. A board member or volunteer who also has this capability and qualifies as a social or economic peer might be unwilling to ask because of personal dislike for soliciting or fear that the donor might make future reciprocal demands.

Besides their availability, staff have the advantage of their detailed knowledge of the organization and the needs to be served, plus the prestige of representing the organization and its accomplishments. Chief executive officers are the most effective staff solicitors because of their positions of power and influence. Yet there is a limit on the time they can spend on soliciting, even though some nonprofit executives, such as private college presidents, reportedly devote a majority of their time to fundraising.

Staff solicitation is most frequent in larger institutions where gift expectations are higher and in smaller agencies where capable, willing volunteers are not available. (The relative effectiveness of using staff and volunteer solicitors for colleges and universities is addressed in Chapter Nine.)

Negative factors in nonprofit organizations' using staff typically include staff's lesser social and economic status, lack of outside power and influence, and appearance of asking for personal gain in that the funds might be used for their own salaries. An additional detraction is that when a prospect refuses the request of a staff member the prospect is, in effect, turning down the whole organization; no other solicitor for that organization can effectively ask until a year or more has passed or a different need is proposed. Conversely, when a volunteer solicitor is unsuccessful, another can soon ask because the social linkage and refusal was made to the peer person and not to the organization as represented by its staff member.

Volunteers can and do ask for gifts larger than their own, but their efforts here are less effective than prospect peer solicitors' efforts because of the asker's implied lesser status. However, if the prospect feels that the volunteer's gift was generous or at least appropriate for the volunteer's economic status, the volunteer's position is equalized, and the influence and power necessary in a solicitor are reasserted.

Principles of Recruiting and Training Solicitors

One of the greatest obstacles to recruiting solicitors is the lack of persons willing to undertake the assignment. Many are approached, few are willing, most are reluctant, and a few absolutely reject the task. The low level of response indicates that many of the internal motivations and reasons for not giving are operative. Solicitors' status and self-esteem are threatened by cultural values which denigrate solicitation as a form of begging. Fear of the loss of social standing or credit with the prospect and other peers, coupled with the potential obligation to recipro- cate, prompts negative reactions. Fear of failure and the conse- quent loss of respect by others frightens many volunteers away from soliciting.

In addition, many individuals have been taught from early childhood not to ask, even though many continue to do so. Asking for help can be seen as a sign of weakness. The histori- cal ethos of the United States as the land of opportunity rein- forces achievement motivations and devalues persons perceived to be unsuccessful. A high regard for individualism and self-re- liance depreciates welfare activities. All of these attitudes and beliefs together cause volunteers to avoid asking for funds.

The solution to the problem of recruiting and subse- quently motivating solicitors lies in the application of theories of *group dynamics* and *organizational psychology*. Changes in behav- ior and attitudes occur most readily in group settings and in re- lation to role expectations and visions created by organizations (Zander, 1985). Therefore, organizational training of volun- teers to ask provides the vehicle through which behavior can be changed. Face-to-face soliciting demands the most attention to sound principles of asking, followed closely by telephone solic- iting. Such fundraising methods as direct mail and videocas- settes require mainly staff work, but they too must adhere to recognized principles for generating commitment and action.

A strong organizational commitment to fundraising is fundamental to successful volunteer recruitment and training. When specific needs and opportunities to meet those needs are spelled out and fundraising leadership by board and staff is readily apparent, a positive environment for recruitment and training is created. Individuals coming into an organization quickly adapt themselves to the prevailing climate and practices because of their natural drive toward affiliation (Zander, 1985). If the task of fundraising is an acknowledged responsibility of board members and volunteers, new participants will feel a strong compulsion to take part in this task, even though they may have many of the reservations just described. When agencies lack such a pervasive commitment, the core leadership has the responsibility to instigate commitment by careful planning and management of goals, policies, and behaviors (board responsibility for fundraising is discussed further in Part Two).

An organization preparing volunteers to solicit should follow accepted training principles. Tasks and techniques are most effectively taught through a combination of description, demonstration, and role-playing—all undertaken in a motivational frame of reference. The stages of prospect readiness and commitment are explained, along with the strengths and weaknesses of the agency's case. Learning the concept of social exchange will help trainees to feel more comfortable about their forthcoming task and its value. Success stories from experienced solicitors will increase confidence and motivation. Positive peer pressure is applied to timid volunteers when leaders who have little fundraising experience are trained alongside the other volunteers.

Because of the fear and reluctance of some candidates, trainers must know such behavioral change tactics as Lewin's concepts (1948) of behavior modification. In Lewin's theory, change occurs in three stages. First, there is an *unfreezing* of currently held views and attitudes. This occurs when the learner recognizes that a problem exists that must be resolved. Second, new solutions give the learner an opportunity to *move* away from old behaviors. Third, the learner adopts a new mode of behavior that is then reinforced and *refrozen* through group support and endorsement.

To apply Lewin's theory to the modification of fundraising behavior, trainers can first ask volunteers to list reasons why people do and do not give. This exercise allows many positive and negative feelings to be expressed, shared, and released. Next, trainees can be asked to give the reasons why they do not like to ask for funds. This exercise allows them to ventilate their solicitation problems and fears.

Typically, their greatest concerns center around attitudes

about fundraising being like begging and fears of failure or rejection. The act of summarizing these views allows them to recognize their problems, to unfreeze. It also sets the stage for solutions. The social exchange model sets the begging concern to rest, and effective models for soliciting relax fears of rejection or failure. Once trainees' attitudes have been changed, the new attitudes are refrozen as the trainees role-play solicitations and discuss what those playing the donors' roles feel are the most convincing arguments and benefits. Corroborating views from experienced volunteers reinforce the new attitudes and behaviors.

Additional Means of Asking

All means of communicating with individuals hold promise for eliciting financial support. Face-to-face solicitation remains the most effective. However, means such as group activities, telephone calls, and letters have also produced funds for decades. Newer means embodied in electronic media are evolving rapidly as prospects become accustomed to videocassette recorders, facsimile machines, and computers in both their business and personal lives. While each medium has dedicated advocates, success in soliciting through all these media depends on nonprofits' understanding the advantages and disadvantages of each and, most importantly, fitting the form of communication to their organizational environments. An expensive-looking video production from an agency with a small budget will appear wasteful to prospects, who will wonder how much of the expected gift will simply be spent on more fundraising.

The following discussion of communication media focuses on their impact on prospects and those prospects' responses. (Other strategic aspects of these media are discussed in Chapter Four.)

Group Activity Solicitation

When organizations sponsor gatherings of prospects, donors, members, and friends, they are employing the social and psychological principles of group dynamics in order to enhance these individuals' feelings of personal involvement, status, achievement, self-esteem, and personal gain from affiliation. Implicit in people's agreement to participate in nonprofits' organizational activities, special events, or benefits is the knowledge that a portion of the cost of attendance is a donation for charitable purposes. Event announcements and invitations convey promises of status and affiliation through the forthcoming association with peers or celebrities, imply or assure a pleasurable experience, or even suggest satisfaction of a cognitive interest. The initial attraction, however, lies in the presumption of personal gain or benefit (Cialdini, 1984). Something of value to the participants will occur. Outstanding entertainment, door prizes, silent auctions, raffles, and party favors substantiate this impression.

The value of a group activity derives not only from the desired number of people attending, which signals a "success," but from participants' obtaining satisfaction for their personal and social internal motivations. The atmosphere of the event plays a key role in the fulfillment of participants' expectations. A warm reception, acknowledgment of participants by peers, and other reinforcements are important to participants' feelings of fulfillment. Follow-up reports to donors on the financial success of the occasion and the good use of the proceeds add an altruistic and charitable dimension that enhances the donors' self-esteem and reduces any vestiges of guilt about their personal gain from the event.

Telephone Solicitation

People are accustomed to talking to both acquaintances and strangers on the telephone. The instrument acts as a partial screen between conversing parties, reducing some of the pressure on prospects found in face-to-face encounters. The size of gift expected is usually less than in face-to-face asking, and the amount of time spent in the conversation is considerably shorter.

Still, the fundamental principles of successful asking

must be observed as completely as the conventions of the medium will allow. The reduced time people expect to spend on this kind of telephone conversation requires that the purpose of the call and the solicitor's linkage to the prospect be quickly conveyed and that some indication of what is expected be given early in the conversation. Otherwise, the prospect is thinking more about the unknown reason for the call than about absorbing the presentation. After this introduction, the solicitor can open a dialogue to establish rapport and allow the prospect to express interests and concerns. The balance of the presentation has to move quickly, allowing the prospect to comment and agree while the caller describes needs, cites solutions, and asks for the commitment.

Direct Mail Solicitation

The basic concepts for convincing a person to give also apply to the letters used in the direct mail packages that inundate every household. A relationship and rapport have to be established between the reader and the signer of the letter. The more personalized the salutation, the stronger is the bond that is created. Using the word "you" one or more times in the first sentence strengthens this relationship. Additional use of "you" throughout the text reinforces this feeling. However, a single author who uses "we" conveys a sense of separation and pomposity.

The need to be met has to be demonstrated in graphic human terms, usually by describing a person with a problem. The opportunity for the prospect to help must seem reasonable and effective, applicable to the person described, and generalizable to others with similar problems. Listing specific amounts of gift dollars to be considered removes prospect uncertainties about what amount is appropriate. A request to act immediately commands attention. An expression of appreciation for the action to be taken reassures the donor of the gift's importance.

Brochures, brief flyers, and other items in the direct mail package augment the message of the letter. The contents of these additional elements can give donors a sense of power and achievement by spelling out opportunities for specific remedies. The implied rapport and relationship with the signer convey status, affiliation, and self-esteem. The assumed interdependence between people suggests that if the donor has some future need for service, others will help.

A current drawback to direct mail soliciting is that prospects are expressing increasing dissatisfaction with the volume of appeals that they find in their mailboxes. They express their dissatisfaction by discarding the appeals unopened, thus lowering response rates and increasing nonprofit mailers' costs. Unfortunately, even accepted and previously supported agencies find their requests ignored.

Electronic Solicitation

The use of television, radio, videocassettes, audiocassettes, electronic mail (E-mail and facsimiles), or even computer diskettes follows the same principles of motivation, influence, and social exchange as are found to work with other media. However, the perceived high cost of producing messages in some of these media raises questions from some prospects, particularly older people who have not grown up with these devices. These individuals may reject some electronic messages because the individuals are unfamiliar with the medium or feel that their contributions will have to pay for costly production and distribution expenses.

Televised solicitations have the distinct advantage of visually portraying human needs and the satisfactions that donors can obtain from meeting those needs. Prospects feel that they are being addressed personally. The combination of sight and sound stimuli leaves a powerful impression of the needs to be met. Real-time presentations (that is, live productions such as telethons) that use well-known personalities for the appeal enhance viewers' sense of relationship, authenticity, and urgency. Making telephone numbers available, so that donors can call volunteers and staff immediately, fosters the dialogue and interaction that encourage commitment. The ease of credit card payment facilitates giving and partially overcomes the lack of action cards and reply envelopes that are included in direct mail packages to encourage a decision to give. However, the response rate for acquisition of new names is much lower for real-time televised presentations than for direct mail. Television's cost effectiveness may increase in the future as nonprofit organizations make greater use of cable television's specialized programming and greater audience segmentation.

Radio solicitations convey a low-cost image while providing real-time presentations. Talk shows focusing on client and community needs can stimulate listeners' interest by encouraging dialogue that leads to commitment and action. Radio appeals have to overcome the lack of action cards and reply envelopes in ways similar to television programs. The ease and modest cost of preparing and broadcasting public service spot announcements makes radio an attractive medium for nonprofit agency messages.

Videocassettes are somewhat less personal than real-time presentations but still convey strong, direct messages supported by visual effects. Videocassettes are used more frequently for such large-scale fundraising projects as capital and endowment campaigns than for other projects. Some large organizations now use them to renew and upgrade substantial annual gifts. Videocassettes require either transmittal letters or individual solicitors to explain their use, provide a means for returning a check or pledge, and justify the appropriateness of this more expensive medium for selected prospects. Timid solicitors find videocassettes most helpful to bolster their interviews. When agencies use videocassettes for group presentations, the expense decreases. Large volume production of videocassettes and employment of local or in-house talent also greatly reduce the cost and help satisfy donor objections to costly solicitations.

Audiocassettes have less impact than videocassettes because only the spoken word is involved. Still, the vocal message creates a personal impression, especially if the speaker addresses prospects as individuals and appeals to their motivations. The lower cost of audiocassettes lessens prospects' concerns about expenses; thus these cassettes require less justification.

Electronic mail and facsimile (fax) messages are similar

to direct mail letters and follow the same principles; however, the lack of accompanying promotional material or response items (pledge card and reply envelope) somewhat limits the effectiveness of electronic mail. Fax transmissions can provide response items, and as reproduction technology improves, the visual image and message will also create more persuasive solicitations. Initial appeals face potentially negative reactions from recipients who have their fax lines tied up by organizations with which they have no prior linkages. However, faxes' current novelty commands attention and tends to offset their limitations, although the novelty is rapidly disappearing with millions of fax machines sold each year.

Conclusion

This chapter considered the effects of various solicitation means and media on prospects. The underlying concepts that explain why various tactics work were discussed in order to present models for asking. The basic model has three stages: preparation, or cultivation of the prospect, the act of asking, and completion of the social exchange. The model for the act of asking has four stages: the asker's introduction in which the parties develop a rapport, a dialogue in which the prospect can express his or her personal views about the charity and its cause, the asker's description of the charity's activities and donor benefits, and the asker's conclusion in which a gift is requested. The success of these models is based on the principle of developing and establishing personalized linkages or bonds between donors and donees through communication and involvement processes. The methods of applying the principle in organized settings are discussed in Chapter Four.

Three

◼

Understanding
Corporate
and
Foundation
Giving

Corporations and foundations interact with nonprofit organizations in a number of significant, highly visible ways from donating funds to providing services, personnel, and gifts-in-kind. Because these corporate and foundation actions influence the direction and services of charitable agencies, the purposes and motives behind them, even though less visible, are no less significant to fundraisers, who must understand these purposes and motives in order to increase corporate and foundation giving. This chapter examines the relationships between charitable nonprofit organizations and corporations and foundations in order to lay out the relevant theoretical concepts. Central to the discussion is the social exchange that interorganizational transactions reveal. The elements of this exchange show what corporations and foundations want from nonprofit agencies and what the latter want and have to offer in return.

While corporations and foundations share such characteristics as being sources of large donations, having formal granting procedures, and having identifiable interests, different motives and rationales usually drive their exchange processes. Corporate foundations, however, can be considered direct agents of their sponsoring firms. In most cases, only corporate personnel serve as corporate foundation board members. And in reporting corporate contributions, the Conference Board, a recognized source for corporate giving statistics, combines corporate foundation grants with direct corporate gifts (Klepper, 1992). Thus, the following discussion of corporations encompasses their foundations also.

Following some general observations about organizational philanthropy, corporate giving is analyzed, small business practices are examined, foundation activity is described, and to conclude, the conceptual factors important to grant making are outlined.

The Nature and Scope of Organizational Philanthropy

During each of the last thirty-five years that comparable records have been kept, donations from corporations and foundations have ranged from 10 to 14 percent of the total annual gifts to U.S. charitable, nonreligious organizations; the remainder of the gifts come from individuals and bequests. Organizational donors' small percentage of total contributions may seem to diminish these donors' importance, but several factors increase these gifts' value. The size of corporate and foundation grants relative to the budgets of the nonprofit grantees makes these grants important sources of support to those particular nonprofits. Organizational donors are also easily identified targets for solicitors. Information about them is readily available from the directories that publish corporate and foundation giving policies, fields of interest, grant-making procedures, key contact officials, and dollar ranges for gifts. Also organizational donors' interests cover a broad spectrum of activities and services (see Tables 3.1 and 3.2).

Many large foundations have a particular interest in funding the kinds of innovative services and programs for which the newer small nonprofit organizations have difficulty attracting sufficient support from individuals. Corporations are beginning to be more adventurous, but usually their interest in innovation is confined to those fields they deem amenable to company purposes and acceptable to their peers and such groups as business and trade associations.

Corporations rarely give to religious organizations, and foundation grants to religion are only approximately 2 percent of foundations' total distributions. Since individuals give more than half of their donations for religious purposes, the gifts by foundations and corporations are proportionally more important to secular agencies than the small total amount that corporate and foundation contributions would suggest. However, nonprofit agencies do not view organizational donors as willing or able to meet their increasing financial needs. Moreover, organizational donors' values and goals direct organizational giving to specific interests that are not necessarily the grant seekers' preferences (Wood and Hougland, 1990).

The different giving patterns of larger corporations and foundations are shown in Tables 3.1 and 3.2. The dollar amounts and percentages of total dollars given to each field of interest present a general picture of corporate and foundation giving based on averages over three-year periods; however, these data are only estimates and should be used with caution. Larger

Table 3.1.   Distribution of Corporate Contributions.

Field of Interest	Averages of Leading Firms: 1988–1990	
	Dollars (in thousands)	Percent
Education	701,003	38.1
Health and human services	513,791	28.0
Civic and community	240,056	13.0
Culture and art	209,467	11.4
Other	174,761	9.5
Total	**1,839,078**	**100.0**

Note: Averages are drawn from 356 firms in 1988, 333 firms in 1989, and 330 firms in 1990. These figures include contributions from corporate foundations. More recent figures are not available in identical categories.

Source: Adapted from Klepper, 1992.

Table 3.2. Distribution of Foundation Grants.

| Field of Interest | Averages of Largest Independent and Community Foundations for 1989–1991 | |
	Dollars (in thousands)	Percent
Health and human services	1,319,961	31.7
Education	1,025,882	24.3
Arts and Culture	591,958	14.1
Public/society benefit	436,069	10.3
Science and technology	247,440	6.0
Environment and animals	201,604	4.8
International affairs	159,629	3.8
Social sciences	125,935	3.1
Religion	76,085	1.8
Other	4,799	0.1
Total	**4,189,362**	**100.0**

Note: Averages are drawn from 472 foundations in 1989, 872 foundations in 1990, and 846 foundations in 1991.

Source: Adapted from Foundation Center, 1990, 1991b, and 1992b.

corporations and foundations are more visible targets for grant proposals than smaller businesses and foundations, and data on them are more accessible. Complete data on the distribution of funds to more specific fields of interest are beyond the scope of this presentation; indeed, some details of this giving are not currently available.

Nevertheless, based on data that are available, it appears that corporations consistently favor education over other areas of interest. Health agencies and human services also attract substantial support, because of employers' concern over the cost of employee health care and the value to employers of services that reduce absenteeism and aid greater productivity. Next, civic and community needs command support because community goodwill toward business protects and legitimates the corporate presence. Culture and art are close behind due to their importance to both executives and employees.

Foundations put health and human services considerably ahead of education in their allocation of grants. Following these two areas come cultural activities and public benefits. Foundations show their broad range of interests with sizeable contributions to science and technology, environmental concerns, international affairs, and social sciences; the least amount of support is directed to religion. (The rationales for these allocations are discussed later in this chapter.)

Each year, every private foundation is required by law to pay out "an amount equal to five percent of its net investment assets in the form of qualifying distributions" (Edie, 1987, p. 14). Actual gifts have exceeded this legal minimum. In 1992, some 32,400 grant-making foundations gave grants totaling $8.33 billion, which looks like a substantial increase over the $2 billion dollars they gave twenty years earlier in 1973 (Kaplan, 1993). However, when the 1973 dollars are converted to 1992 dollars, they equal $6.92 billion, indicating only a modest yearly gain in the purchasing value of 1992 contributions. In terms of 1992 dollars, foundation giving dipped to a low of $4.91 billion in 1979, then began a steady rise to the 1992 level.

In addition to understanding foundations' interests, fundraisers should be aware that fluctuations in economic conditions affect the value of foundations' stock and bond investments and therefore the income available for distribution. However, the impact of economic cycles is usually delayed because foundation grants tend to cover one- to three-year periods. Variations in fields of interest occur in response to regional, national, and international conditions. In recent years, the need to address problems resulting from the Gulf War, the AIDS epidemic, and the Eastern European economic crisis revealed by the Cold War collapse has influenced foundations' giving programs.

Corporations are under no legal compulsion to give unless they have established corporate foundations, which are subject to the 5 percent rule. However, pressure to give is exerted on corporations by many of their stakeholders and peer organizations. Additionally, steadily increasing human needs and declines in government support have increased the volume of funding requests from nonprofit organizations. Both these factors have resulted in a gradual growth in corporate philanthropy.

For tax purposes, corporations are legally allowed to deduct contributions amounting to 10 percent of their pretax income. In the 1970s, corporate giving averaged less than 1 percent of pretax income. In the 1980s, giving reached 1.66 percent, and in the 1990s, it increased to 1.96 percent of pretax income. Over the twenty years from 1973 to 1992, corporate annual giving rose from $1 billion ($3.46 billion in 1992 dollars) to $6 billion (Kaplan, 1993). In the last five years, corporate donations dipped slightly in comparison to earlier rapid growth. Tax laws that encouraged corporate debt in the l980s, and mergers and acquisitions, and the recession in the early 1990s all retarded expansion in corporate giving (Harvey and McCrohan, 1990). While this kind of overview based on available statistics clarifies some dimensions of organizational giving, it does not reveal the underlying factors that prompt corporate and foundation support of nonprofit agencies. These underlying factors are the subject of the following sections.

The Bases of Corporate Giving

Corporate giving is essentially a transaction between two kinds of organizations, profit and nonprofit, that have different missions and operational goals but similar ultimate goals of survival and growth. These organizations conduct their activities in overlapping operational or task environments that affect each other. For example, corporate employees have health, educational, and cultural needs that nonprofit organizations address. Nonprofit organizations have financial, personnel, and management needs that corporations can provide. Thus, the two kinds of organizations enter into exchanges in order to manage their environments more effectively and assure both organizations' functional success. Nonprofit agencies seek money from corporations to fund their programs and personnel and meet other costs. Corporations provide these funds because the corporations perceive that the nonprofits can create a more favorable corporate operating environment. This favorable environment may be one that directly benefits corporate employees and families or one that is expected to produce a general atmosphere of favorable public opinion in corporate marketing areas.

The common characteristic of these organizational transactions is social exchange in a form similar to the exchange that
occurs between individuals and nonprofit agencies. Thus, this
exchange is not an economic or formally contractual one with
specified items or services of value and a fixed time limit for
transfer or completion. Social exchange is noncontractual,
more open, and less bounded by time commitments and specified returns than a contract agreement, but it does assume that
something of value accrues to each organization. Even though
there is typically no direct advance specification by the parties
of an exchange's value, nature, or obligations, underlying assumptions and expectations of returns or benefits from the exchange do exist. While no time limit is set, the longer the
interval of response between the parties, the weaker the relationship becomes. Also, some form of interaction such as duplication of personnel, overlap of task environments, interaction
between members, or recognition of mutual interests must exist between the two parties before a social exchange can occur
(Mixer, 1977).

The relationship between corporations and nonprofit
institutions fits a widely accepted theoretical view of organizations that has them functioning in an *open system* context (Scott,
1987). No organization is self-sufficient, all must enter into exchanges with the environment. They are dependent on inputs
or resources from outside their boundaries for their operations,
and they produce outputs of goods and services that must be
consumed by others (Pfeffer and Salancik, 1978). Thus, organizational boundaries are permeable, open to a constant flow of
items, services, and information that affect organizational goals
and objectives. As these effects are fed back to management and
employees, efforts are made to adjust conditions to the most
favorable status. This feedback mechanism causes organizational learning, self-regulation, and adaptation.

The environment itself is characterized by rapid change
and turbulence in social, economic, and political conditions
(Emery and Trist, 1965). In geographic scope, it ranges from
local neighborhoods to national and international arenas. Business cycles reverberate around the world. The knowledge explo-

sion, coupled with efficient, instantaneous communication, invades all organizations and compounds their environmental interests and problems. Furthermore, as Scott (1987) notes, the "positions, policies, programs, and procedures of modern organizations are enforced by public opinion, by views of important constituents, by knowledge legitimated through educational systems, by social prestige, by laws, and by the definitions of negligence and prudence by the courts" (p. 115). In other words, corporate giving is embedded in a complex, interconnected environment. Hosts of networks and subsystems affect the giving process, determining the nonprofit agencies supported, amounts of funds and equipment given, and services rendered.

The *political economy* concept of organizations views them as arenas in which inside and outside interest groups who possess resources needed by an organization compete in order to optimize their values through that organization. Hazenfeld (1983) states that "organizational processes are based on exchange relations established between different interest groups that compose the organization and on the power each exercises in controlling and influencing these relationships" (p. 45). When it comes to corporate giving, internal executives, employees, unions, and stockholders voice their opinions about giving, often without reference to the needs that exist, while external customers, suppliers, competitors, civic leaders, and government regulators also express their opinions about giving in order to advance their interests.

The nonprofit environment, too, has its share of complex influences and structures that affect corporate giving. Federated campaigns place restrictions on corporate solicitations and prospects. Member agencies of United Way are prevented from soliciting corporations during campaign periods and even in the rest of the year in some communities. Coalitions of agencies such as Independent Charities of America, United Negro College Fund, and various environmental protection groups are formed to raise their members' visibility and command corporate support. Corporations and foundations frequently press nonprofit organizations to create joint venture projects or merge operations to reduce perceived duplication. Volunteers from the business community serving on agency boards and committees exert internal influences and value judgments on programs, projects, funding requests, and sources of support.

Driving Forces for Corporate Giving

The overall case for corporate giving lies in the concept of social exchange. However, fundraisers can better understand how corporate giving decisions are made by examining specific driving forces that operate within and on corporations. Given corporations' ultimate goals of survival and growth and the profit motive encompassed by these goals, a number of situations and needs stimulate corporate actions to reach these goals. These corporate aims affect corporate giving; however, they do not operate in unison. Local business climates, national economic conditions, competition, industry growth and decline, and the profitability of individual firms create different forces at different times. Thus, the corporate selection of contribution programs to meet corporate needs illustrates *contingency theory,* which holds that there is no one best way to arrange tasks or manage an enterprise (Carlisle, 1973). An assessment of the primary factors in the situation dictates the choice and employment of available options. The ability of executives to scan their environments and become aware of current and future conditions impinging on their corporations determines the degree to which their firms will engage in social exchange with nonprofit organizations (Mixer, 1977).

Reduction of Uncertainty

In a complex, rapidly changing environment, corporations seek to reduce the uncertainties they may encounter. Executives realize that they cannot completely regularize their turbulent environments, but they prudently seek to moderate environmental influences and create more stable operating conditions. McElroy and Siegfried (1984) found corporate executives viewed charitable contributions as aids to long-term profits because nonprofit agencies provide such critical services as medical assistance and educational and cultural activities, which encourage stable employment and reduce corporate expenses. Other scholars argue that contributions are a form of social control to achieve certain political and economic ends (Davidson, Timmer, and Eitzen, 1982). Thus, nonprofit agencies perceived as favorable to corporate interests are selected for grants while others are ignored.

Strategic Planning Benefits

Most large corporations (and well-run nonprofit agencies) require management to assess future conditions and anticipate new developments by undertaking strategic planning. The process usually includes a determination of the impact of many driving forces inside and outside the corporation. Typically, the lead time in planning is five to ten years with annual reevaluation of changing conditions; although some authorities recommend much shorter time spans (Peters, 1987). Early detection of new situations is crucial to organizational survival and success. For instance, research findings, technological innovations, management improvements, and new processes and materials can radically change companies' competitive environments. Contributions to universities and research institutions provide an early entrée to these developments (Mixer, 1977). Future market conditions and competitive positions concern executive planners. If other corporations are making inroads in public acceptance of corporate products and services because of the high visibility of charitable corporate gifts, some managers alter their own giving plans to meet the challenge.

Provision for Necessary Resources

A major cause of uncertainty is that many organizational resources lie outside the organization (Pfeffer and Salancik, 1978). Milofsky and Romo (1988) concluded that resource exchanges with the environment are important causes of organizational behavior. Suppliers, competitors, governments, economic conditions, and innovations can change conditions rapidly. For example, adequately prepared personnel are key resources that come from educational systems. In the last few decades, corporate giving focused on college and universities to ensure the supply of qualified graduates, especially M.B.A.'s in the 1980s. Grants to elementary and secondary school systems were rarely made. Then, in the late 1980s and early 1990s, attention and support shifted to this ignored sector because employers began to realize that entry-level employees were poorly educated and unable to meet business requirements (Bailey, 1990b; Weber, 1991).

Creation of Market Acceptance of Products and Services

A firm's image in the minds of present and future customers plays a key role in the acceptance of that firm's products and services. Corporate gifts to such worthy projects as sports events for the handicapped and cultural exhibits enhance a firm's image and add to the acceptability of the firm's products and services. The dramatic rise in corporate giving during the early 1990s by Japanese firms doing business in the United States has been assessed as a drive for public acceptance and an accompanying market penetration, particularly since such giving is not the general practice in the firms' homeland (Greene, 1991; Millar, 1991). Tobacco firms try for greater public acceptance by sponsoring cancer research undertaken by nonprofit institutions. Cause-related marketing seeks product and service acceptance by giving gifts to charitable agencies when the public purchases certain items—witness the flurry of offers by American Express, VISA, and MasterCard to give donations to charitable projects in a ratio with individuals' credit card use (Moore, 1990). Steckel (1989) cites numerous examples of corporate partnerships with nonprofit agencies, ranging from donations of a percentage of raisin bran cereal sales to agreements to pay museums licensing fees for reproducing items in their collections for public sale.

Promotion of Institutional Growth and Development

Continual upgrading of management and employee skills and the use of new methods are essential for profitable operations.

Conferences, seminars, and training events conducted by non-profit organizations receive corporate support to enable key corporate personnel to gain this expertise. While some of these activities are viewed by corporate controllers as an operating expense borne by participating firms, they are often a conduit for corporate grants to host institutions to further cement the beneficial relationships. New Ways to Work, a nonprofit agency advocating shared jobs, flexible work schedules, and other innovative employment practices, receives support from corporations interested in finding new work practices that will add to employee productivity and stability.

Establishment of Legitimacy

Corporate existence and operation is dependent on society's acceptance and approval. Public opinion swings and related governmental responses can seriously affect corporate operating environments through regulations and taxes. Corporate giving contains a strong element of self-justification, returning benefits to the society that allows free enterprise and profits. Researchers have documented the "halo effect" of corporate giving in a detailed study of major gifts to the Public Broadcasting System by some of the largest corporations, mainly oil companies (Ermann, 1978). Corporate support for the good works of nonprofit agencies helps abolish public images of previous corporate transgressions such as antitrust violations (Harvey and McCrohan, 1990).

Establishment of Corporate Social Responsibility

The extent of corporate social responsibility receives continual discussion and debate in academic and civic circles and to some extent in the business sector. As external influences surrounding corporations affect corporate value systems (as observed by Scott, 1987, in the generalized case of all organizations), more acceptance of external values develops among business leaders. Thus, Unseem and Kutner (1984) noted a growing endorsement of social responsibility by senior managers, who imbued giving with a "noble purpose" (p. 94). However, the strength of this drive toward corporate social responsibility is not fully documented or accepted. Galaskiewicz (1985) found moral obligation or social responsibility was the ostensible rationale for contributions reported by two-thirds of firms studied, yet the real motivation uncovered was a desire by senior officers for the prestige that peers and community leaders could bestow as a result of the officers' decision to make a corporate gift.

Acceptance of Enlightened Self-Interest

Corporations strive to enhance their operating or task environment by improving some aspect of society that benefits both them and society. Dienhart (1988) cites the long-term project by B. Dalton Booksellers to reduce illiteracy. The project creates a more productive pool of workers while also ensuring a market for the firm's products—books. Many corporate grants require that beneficiaries include minorities in the services rendered. This strengthening of ethnic groups increases the number of potential workers who can help corporations meet their affirmative action goals. Redevelopment and urban renewal projects get financial support from nearby corporations that see such improvements adding to quality of the physical environment and fostering goodwill and greater productivity. Health, education, and welfare projects operated by nonprofit groups increase the ability of project clients to function more effectively and raise their incomes, a direct contribution to increased purchasing power for corporate products and services. Ecology and conservation projects attract contributions from corporations wishing to alter an environmentally poor image or maintain a good one. Chevron's sponsorship of National Geographic television specials is a notable example.

Production of Executive Satisfactions and Employee Benefits

Personal interests elicit corporate support. Galaskiewicz (1985) found that business leaders gained status with their peers and the social elites in their communities by contributing to selected charities. This prestige factor so predominated in the giving motivations that product and service market objectives were not a factor in the metropolitan area Galaskiewicz studied. An opposite phenomenon was reported by Sproull (1982), who found that some executives gave principally to abate pressure from peers, or as the executives put it, "to get them off my back." As mentioned earlier, employee benefits arise from corporate support of community programs that provide medical services, cultural activities, and recreational opportunities, which add to quality of family life and a stable employment pool (McElroy and Siegfried, 1984).

Reinforcement of Values and Norms

Through gifts, corporations can foster their own values and norms in the larger community. Many corporate contribution programs also support technical assistance to nonprofit organizations to improve the nonprofits' management skills, efficiency, and accountability. Some grants encourage nonprofits to engage in entrepreneurial activities, emulating business practice in order to produce needed revenues. Other grants are designed to help clients of nonprofit agencies develop skills and competencies that will enable them to become more self-sufficient and productive. Beyond this, corporations have an interest in effecting change in the views and attitudes of the larger community so these views correspond with corporate values, and this interest affects corporate gifts. Corporations see that if more of society holds values compatible with business interests, the opportunities for corporate survival and growth increase immeasurably.

Further Factors in Corporate Giving Decisions

Decision making in corporate giving depends on a number of factors and determines which nonprofit organizations get what kinds of grants and amounts in social exchange transactions. The basic elements in this decision making are the driving forces just discussed, the return values expected, the decision makers involved, and various external influences.

Expectation of Return Values

Beneficial returns accrue from contributions that satisfy the driving forces described in this chapter. In making grants, decision makers assess several dimensions of these returns: ability and accountability of the recipient agencies, feasibility of program assessment and evaluation, lapsed time for results to appear, businesslike style of operation in terms of efficiency and effectiveness, short- and long-term gains, and the extent to which results will gratify the driving forces. Nonprofit agencies succeed in their grant requests to the degree that they can project their ability to fulfill these dimensions.

Increased Professionalism

Expertise in the corporate decision-making process for corporate giving became the norm as the size of contribution budgets increased, the numbers of corporations making grants expanded, knowledge about techniques and methods of grant making spread, and the influx of trained administrators (usually from foundations) grew in the early 1980s (Unseem and Kutner, 1984). These professional administrators developed policies, regulations, and procedures that encoded the desired results and also created bureaucratic structures.

The standardization of processes carries on even during the current decline in total giving by corporations. Standard processes reduce the decision-making arena and, in large firms, allow decentralization within fixed authority limits to subsidiaries and divisions. However, the role of the chief executive officer remains crucial. This person typically spends a preponderance of time in the external environment, which abounds with supplicants and peers advocating support of various causes. Chief executives develop personal interests that influence policies, selection of agencies and programs to be supported, and types and amounts of grants.

Influence of Coalitions and Associations

Interorganizational activity makes an impact on corporate giving. In most metropolitan areas, professional administrators
have created formal and informal networks of peers to exchange
information on giving practices, needs of local communities,
unwarranted appeals, and shady nonprofit operations. Unseem
and Kutner (1984) reported that over 50 percent of the firms
surveyed viewed other corporations' gifts as the most important
single external influence on their giving. The mimic effect of
grantors' following the precedent of other corporations was also
documented by Galaskiewicz and Wasserman (1989). They
found that a firm is more likely to give to a nonprofit organization when that nonprofit has also been funded by companies
whose chief executive officers or contributions officials are
personally known to their counterparts in the firm that is
considering a gift. Similarly, support given to nonprofit agencies
by wealthy individual or family contributors in a community
power structure positively influenced corporate donations.
Galaskiewicz and Wasserman also observe that more gifts are
given by a corporation to nonprofit agencies that share directors
with the corporation.

Influence of Corporate Employees

An increasing volume of specific giving decisions within policy
guidelines is coming under the influence or control of company
personnel. Acting on management theories that encourage
greater employee participation in decision making and greater
delegation of authority, corporations form committees composed of employees and lower-level managers to review and ap-
prove or disapprove funding applications presented to them by
the professional administrators of corporate giving programs.
Employees are also often encouraged to volunteer their services
to nonprofit organizations, both with and without paid leave.
Some corporations, such as Levi Strauss, provide automatic annual grants to agencies that have their employees serving on the
nonprofit agencies' boards. Significant volunteer participation

by employees of a corporation in the activities of a nonprofit organization usually result in a higher level of contributions to that agency. The resulting grants also strengthen the employees' influence in agency operations. Overlapping membership provides various degrees of co-optation by corporations and facilitates the desired return values discussed earlier.

Influence of Business and Trade Associations

Grant making is often influenced through the information, suggested policies, and standardized practices distributed by industry groups. Specifically, the Conference Board promulgates carefully drawn guidelines for corporate giving (Klepper, 1981; Klepper and Mackler, 1986). Also, the Council on Foundations (1982, 1983) makes its concepts of appropriate administration of grants programs available for corporate use. The significant number of former foundation executives now staffing corporate giving programs abets this transfer of policies and procedures. Other business-oriented organizations such as think tanks, political action committees, ideological groups, and data-reporting agencies sway giving decisions. Advocacy of certain economic, political, and social values can favor or disfavor particular nonprofit organizations. Specific nonprofit agencies may not be cited by such advocates, but generalized descriptions can produce the desired effect of directing funds to certain kinds of nonprofits and excluding others.

Importance of Elements of Exchange

The various types of support that can be applied to perceived needs influence giving decisions. Money, which is easily reported, commands the most attention, but gifts-in-kind of products, equipment, supplies, and property amount to a sizeable portion of total values exchanged by corporations and nonprofits. The mutual benefit of such transfers make these exchanges attractive (Koch, 1979). Nonprofit organizations frequently get more valuable goods than they can afford to buy. Corporations can promote their products through an agency's use of the products or empty corporate warehouses of unused equipment, receiving a tax deduction as a result.

Services such as printing nonprofit agency publications, providing meeting space, and placing free advertising on grocery bags lower beneficiaries' costs with a minimum outlay by the donors. Underwriting public events conducted by nonprofit organizations functions like a corporate contribution, but the specific source of the funds is often the donor firm's advertising and public relations budgets, because of the benefits of such sponsorship to corporate products and services. Automobile and beer company sponsorships of events are prime examples. In addition, the monetary value of the volunteer time and talent rendered by managers and employees working for nonprofit agencies amounts to a considerable yearly sum; the nonprofit coalition INDEPENDENT SECTOR estimates that the dollar value of all volunteer time exceeds the total dollars given annually ("Facts and Figures on the INDEPENDENT SECTOR," 1991).

Importance of Conditions Attached to Exchange

Finally, funding provisions that provide additional values for corporations influence giving decisions. Gifts with matching provisions add leverage, publicity, and morale value to corporate monetary commitments. The popularity of firms' matching employee gifts grew from matching employees' alumni gifts to their alma maters to matching employees' contributions to a wide range of nonprofit agencies. Employers enjoy increased goodwill from their employees for the additional support given to these selected charities. Generally, matching funds go for unrestricted use. However, these unrestricted matching programs have also inspired programs that match contributions to projects favored by corporations (Knudsen, 1985). Matching ratios range from one dollar for each additional dollar from other donors to one for two, or one for three dollars. Occasionally, a reverse ratio of two dollars for every one from other parties is offered, depending on the value of the project to the corporation.

The exchange process may also include forms of bargaining and coercion to achieve corporate ends. Grantors are often in a position to change the nature, objectives, and scope of projects proposed for support; thus, bargaining takes place in which the potential grantee has to weigh the advantages and disadvantages of the corporation's offer and bargain for the most favorable terms. The negotiations become coercive when financial pressures force the donee to accept unwanted alterations to proposed activities and client services.

Small Business Philanthropy

The charitable activities of small businesses have been overshadowed by the interest in large corporations whose giving habits are publicly documented. Very little research has been undertaken on the small business segment of the charitable economy despite the large numbers of such businesses. Their relatively limited individual capacity to give and their less visible impact on social needs and charitable organizations have deterred widespread investigation.

One exception to this lack of information is a study of seventy-five small businesses in San Francisco (Wiltsek, 1990). Wiltsek found that 95 percent of the firms studied made charitable contributions, and that "the majority of companies surveyed (almost 90 percent) make annual contributions of less than $10,000; half of those give $2,000 or less. Not surprisingly, pretax net income is positively correlated to total contributions" (p. 2). The chief executive officers of these firms are the sole arbiters of who gets what and when. The rationales for giving are a desire to be involved in the community (cited by 96 percent of the contributing firms), public relations (76 percent), and tax benefits (34 percent). The stimulus for giving came from a request by a friend or colleague (64 percent), familiarity with the beneficiary (60 percent), and the fact of having made a previous donation (53 percent). Beneficiary agencies were in the fields of human and social services (46 percent), health (20 percent), the arts (20 percent), and education (14 percent).

In view of the chief executive officer being the sole decision maker in small business gift decisions, the social exchange

rationale described for individuals applies more readily to small
business charitable behavior than it does to the more complex,
professionally staffed giving programs of large corporations.
The small business owner's involvement in the community
through contributing satisfies both his or her personal and social motivations, particularly the sense of achievement, self-esteem, status, and affiliation. Public relations benefits relate to
the motivations of rewards and personal gains as well as to
power and interdependence motivations.

Origin and Nature of Foundations

Foundations arise out of the political economy of society. As
political entities, they operate under state and national governmental authority. The chartering and inauguration of foundations rest with state governments, which are showing increased
interest in the charitable intent and behavior of these tax-exempt organizations through regulations and reporting requirements. Still, the federal government exercises the greatest
control through its criteria for tax-exempt status and submission
of annual operating reports. Further conditions are encoded in
the Tax Reform Acts of 1969, 1976, and 1986. These acts seek to
restrict the random behavior of foundations and refocus their
purpose and activities on charitable works (Odendahl, 1989).
The resulting regulations established by the Internal Revenue
Service define and restrict the tax deductibility of funds and
property given to establish and increase foundation assets. Unrelated businesses, operating expenses, and political activities
are circumscribed. All this governmental intervention attests to
the foundations' vulnerability to political power and pressure.

Odendahl (1989) asserts that such governmental actions
discourage the wealthy from creating new foundations. However, the Foundation Center's yearbook (1992a) shows a steady
increase in the total number of foundations since 1975, and its
Directory of New and Emerging Foundations (Foundation Center,
1991a) states that 3,029 new foundations were established from
1985 to 1989. Still, community foundation executives report an
increasing use of "donor advised funds." This device allows individuals making donations in excess of fifty thousand dollars to

establish a fund with the foundation and direct the charitable use of the fund's income and sometimes of the corpus itself. For example, the San Francisco Foundation received a gift of a former residence from a woman who wished to direct the proceeds from sale of the house to organizations that assist women trying to enter nontraditional jobs in the trades.

As economic entities, many foundations come into being as a result of individuals' or families' having at their disposal accumulations of capital assets. These foundations can be contrasted to corporate foundations, which are usually instigated and supported out of corporate income and rarely from capital assets. The vast majority of existing foundations, some 28,700 out of 32,000, are independent or family foundations, and most of them have assets under five million dollars (Foundation Center, 1991a). As the name family foundation implies, many of these smaller foundations carry out the personal charitable interests of families, with the preponderance of operations actually conducted by family members. Although the larger general purpose and special purpose foundations, which distribute the majority of funds, were also created by individuals and families, their operations are administered by professional staff.

Foundations can also be viewed as social functionaries. Their overt political activities are narrowly restricted, and they are not economic in the sense of being for profit, but they do provide an integrative function by reallocating assets (or, more precisely, mainly income from assets) for the betterment of society (Boulding, 1972). They have a profound effect on the quality of society through their innovative grants, which push for redirection of social and economic life. Voter registration drives and the civil rights movement received substantial support from foundations, much to the annoyance of Congress, which reacted with restrictive legislation on reporting requirements and conduct of foundations (Jenkins, 1989).

Founders' Rationales

Foundations come into existence for the fundamental reason of enacting the donors' values and preferences, which include both idealistic influences and pragmatic concerns. Odendahl

(1989) found that "foundation donors were motivated by a cluster of 'altruistic' variables including a concern for the welfare of others, a religious heritage, a belief in social responsibility, and a family tradition of giving" (p. 172). Typically, such values are incorporated in foundation charters, which also contain generalized statements of purpose that encompass the fields of interest, such as education, health, welfare, arts, science, or social sciences. The founders subsequently promulgate specific directions for the use of funds, directions that are restrained only by the underlying wide-ranging statements of charitable purpose and the absence of personal financial gain.

The pragmatic values and preferences of donors typically center around control over the dispensing of capital assets and income. Initially, there is a strong preference to avoid taxes that would accrue if personal estates were passed on to others. Closely allied with this motive is the donor's desire to prevent the government from making allocation decisions, through expensive governmental administrative procedures, about moneys obtained from taxes on the income and estates of these individuals (Odendahl, 1989). Founders feel strongly that federal and state governments cannot or will not carry out their values and preferences. Another motive for some founders is to avoid distribution of capital assets to children and other family members. These relatives may have been adequately provided for by other means, or may be estranged from the founder.

In a more positive vein, founders wish to improve society in accordance with their viewpoints. Their intents may range from assisting handicapped persons, because of some personal association with these people or their problems, to promoting entrepreneurial activities that will alleviate welfare dependency. Frequently, these donors feel that society has misallocated resources and that they want to correct these misallocations: the poor may not have been helped in ways the donors deem appropriate, health concerns may not have been addressed adequately, or education may not be producing the results desired.

Individuals and families who create foundations often feel that no other agency, governmental or private, can do what they desire: namely, to stimulate, encourage, sponsor, or develop change in the conditions they deem important. While not often expressed, a common underlying motivation is legitimation of the capitalistic society (Odendahl, 1989). This legitimation can be achieved, so donors feel, by the donors' returning to society some of the donors' monetary gains that were sanctioned by the capitalistic system. Such returns are felt to offset complaints about exploitation, and at the same time make society more humane.

Social Exchange Behavior

Foundations operate like corporations and individuals in their social exchange behavior. Foundation grants are provided to nonprofit agencies in exchange for activities that satisfy the interests of founders, trustees, and managers. A grant to fund an innovative program in education that will train teachers to instruct students in entrepreneurial activities provides satisfaction to foundations and their donors that are interested in promoting the free enterprise system. Support for battered women's shelters enables women and their children to change the harmful pattern of their lives and gain security and self-confidence. Such support provides a remedy for conditions that the person who set up the foundation may have experienced.

In other words, foundation grants work to improve social situations that concern the foundation founders, thereby satisfying their intrinsic personal and social motives as well as relieving some of their negative perceptions of social and economic conditions. Providing funds for creative activities and innovative solutions gives the provider a strong feeling of power, status, prestige, and self-esteem, which economists characterize as benefits in the form of personal satisfaction or utility (Auten and Rudney, 1989).

Like the founders, foundation trustees and managers have values and preferences that seek satisfaction. These needs gradually permeate the direction of the foundation, particularly as foundation originators grow older and lessen their influence and interest in detailed operations of the institutions. A 1990 survey of 723 leading foundations revealed that two-thirds of the trustees were white males and a quarter were white females (Boris and others, 1990). These institutions own about half of all assets and make about 40 percent of all grants. Most of these leading foundations (86 percent) have paid staff, in contrast to only 10 percent of all foundations. Staff members are preponderantly (80 percent) white middle-class professionals and 57 percent of all staff members are women. The professionalization that occurs principally in these larger foundations tends toward increasing bureaucratization, similar to that encountered in large-scale corporate giving programs. Policies and procedures become standardized and reflect the value systems of the key decision makers.

Why Foundations Give

The concepts behind the actions of larger foundations in making grants are remarkably similar to the concepts found in gift giving corporations. Both organizations move to institutionalize their grant making, decrease the randomness of allocations, and carry out the broad goals of their existing power structures. These goals, however, may be quite divergent because of foundations' and corporations' different values: typically, corporations desire to control their operating environment (maintain their economic freedom and the free enterprise system) while foundations move more concertedly toward improving the lot of all society. The similarity of the giving process in large corporations and foundations arises in many cases from the recruitment of experienced professional foundation administrators to manage corporate giving programs or foundations. Small businesses and foundations, particularly family foundations, respond more readily to the personal views of their owners and founders. They generally confine themselves to precedents of giving to lessen the burden of decision making. Nevertheless, the granting activity of all these donors can be understood better by applying some of the concepts derived from *organizational behavior theory*.

Rational System Perspective

Foundations may be viewed as *rational systems* created to accomplish desired ends with means (monetary resources) and a formal structure (Scott, 1987). As indicated earlier, their declared purposes range from generalized statements to designated fields of interest. The guiding philosophy is to achieve goals and objectives set forth by founders, trustees, and staff. The goals provide sets of preferences that inform decision making about how the organization will operate, what staff will be hired, and how resources will be allocated. This behavior is further modified by the rules, authority, directives, performance standards, and other constraints that are typical of rational organizations.

Operating or Task Environment Perspective

The physical, geographical, and functional areas of organizations, including input and output transactions, are considered to be organizations' operating or task environments. The vast majority of foundations typically confine their grants to the geographical areas in which they are physically located, as do corporations. Community foundations operating under restrictions to serve their identified localities are a particular example. Family foundations with their smaller size, limited or nonexistent staff, and family connections typically restrict giving to local entities or to local branches of national organizations. The family members know the community, its needs, and its charitable organizations, so decision making restricted in this way becomes less burdensome. Usually the family's assets were developed in the same locality, producing strong relationships with local economic, social, and political entities. Larger foundations reach out beyond their immediate locations because the sizable amount of dollars available for administration and grants enables them to expand the scope of desired projects. The largest foundations, like Ford, Kellogg, Lilly, and Johnson, not only react to proposals from nonprofit organizations but also frequently stimulate requests from nonprofit agencies that function in the areas of the foundations' interests.

Promotion of Nonprofit Capacity

The development of management, planning, and evaluation skills enables organizations to be more effective in achieving their goals and objectives, hence their capacity is enhanced. Most foundations are concerned with the efficient use of their funds and with obtaining demonstrable results. In addition, the rapid increase in the number of new small nonprofit organizations in the last decade has caused foundations to give greater attention and support to management and professional capacities in this burgeoning sector. Foundations' efforts to promote sound management practices in their grantees also reflect the values of many founders, trustees, and staff. The development of fundraising skills in nonprofit agencies is seen as a means of enlarging donor bases, providing greater self-sufficiency, and lessening demands on organizational grantors. Thus, a grant to improve management skills in a youth agency that serves families and children in the local area produces double benefits: services to needy persons and effective use of funds. These grants, known as *technical assistance*, are becoming more prevalent.

Natural Systems Perspective

In the *natural systems* concept, the behavior of individuals in organizations is viewed as more important than formal structures because "participants within formal organizations generate informal norms and behavior patterns: status and power systems, communication networks, sociometric structures, and working relationships" (Scott, 1987, p. 55). Thus, formal structures bend to the influence of the informal arrangements. For foundations interested in bettering human conditions, this perspective suggests the benefit of focusing on the human interrelationships, cooperative systems, and individual preferences that affect the functioning of society through human organizations. This perspective stimulates grants to help people relate to social conditions, solve conflicts, and accommodate a variety of interests.

Diffusion of Innovation Benefits

A central thrust of organizations public and private since the turn of the twentieth century, and one that has received increasing attention from managers in the last few decades, is *diffusion of innovation* (Rogers and Shoemaker, 1972). A concern with diffusion of innovation focuses individuals and organizations on factors that encourage or inhibit innovative processes, their transfer and adoption, and their organizational acceptance. In this vein, the development of solutions to society's problems is a major goal of foundations and, more recently, of corporations. Foundations are notorious for their desire to be the first wave on the beach and to develop new practices and innovative programs, sometimes at the expense of the new projects, which may be left high and dry after the initial grants subside because the foundation has finite funds and other innovations are now the attraction. However, the criteria for grants imposed on potential grantees often ask for demonstrations that projects are replicable, so that the grantor may assist in spreading the innovation and bask in the glory of the diffusion.

Change Management Perspective

The diffusion of innovation is closely related to *change management*: the "conscious, deliberate effort to improve the operations of a system whether it is a self-system, a social system, or cultural system, through the utilization of scientific knowledge" (Bennis, Benne, and Chin, 1985, p. 3). Frequently called *planned change*, this process receives considerable support from foundation executives who believe progress in human affairs is possible only with positive change in how people relate to each other in organizations and the broader systems of society. This belief calls for projects seeking to change people's attitudes, prejudices, and ignorance by introducing newer methods of group dynamics, consciousness raising, and learning. Within agencies, the same process is identified as *organizational development*. It attempts to free up communication, interpersonal relations, and individual growth. The techniques employed include team building, conflict resolution, and problem-solving skills. Thus, requests for funds to maintain steady states in agencies attract little interest.

Conclusion

This chapter described the various theories and concepts of how individuals and organizations function in order to explain the panorama of organizational giving in U.S. society. Different forces and circumstances produce different responses, but these forces and circumstances can be identified and analyzed. The task of fundraising professionals is first to understand these theories and concepts. That has been the goal of this chapter. The second task of fundraising professionals is to use the concepts and theories to plan, organize, and manage an effective development program. That is the topic of Part Two.

Part Two

■

MANAGERIAL
AND
ORGANIZATIONAL
STRATEGIES

Fundraising is carried out in an organizational environment, and the principles and concepts of management and organizational behavior can be useful in understanding how fundraising works. The chapters in this section focus on planning, organization, and management as strategic processes. Strategic planning concepts are adapted to fundraising's need to create effective development plans. Situational analysis and the SWOT model (strengths, weaknesses, opportunities, and threats) are discussed in terms of nonprofit organizations' awareness of environmental influences and internal conditions (Steiner and Miner, 1977). Strategic criteria for fundraising are examined and applied to specific methods.

Organizational principles and theories help fundraisers build effective fundraising structures. The basic elements of structure are related to fundraising activities. Factors influencing organizational form are considered including the impact of departmentalization and integration.

Strategic management requires planned change and

adaptive leadership styles to meet the demands of the rapidly changing fundraising environment. Four possible leadership styles are discussed in this chapter. Planned change interventions that improve the behavior of individuals and their organizations so they can more rapidly attain organizational missions and goals are described.

Four

---■---

Strategic Planning: Giving Direction to Fundraising

Planning in nonprofit organizations takes many forms, ranging from almost no planning (except to cover increased costs) to comprehensive long-range projections based on all available data. Ideally, the planning process examines the purpose or mission of a nonprofit organization in the light of internal and external factors and develops concepts and proposals, including fundraising programs, to achieve it. Thus, the planning process reaches rational decisions, based on the elements affecting the organization, that will solve critical problems and direct future actions on programs, finances, and administration. Strategic planning, in particular, focuses on the organization's obligation to accomplish its purpose in the context of external forces.

Fundraising is a central topic in strategic planning for a charitable organization to the extent that the organization depends on private gifts and grants. The selection of programs and services to achieve organizational purposes requires consideration of potential funding. Thus, strategic planning processes

91

and decisions affect fundraising structures and methods. In large nonprofit institutions having extensive, highly evolved fundraising programs, strategic planning processes are also applied to the development office to determine its mission, goals, and objectives (Lindahl, 1992). Smaller agencies without differentiated structures for fundraising centralize the planning process.

A key result from strategic planning is a statement of the case for securing financial support. The case consists of all the reasons that will be effective in convincing individuals and organizations to contribute (Rosso and Associates, 1991). These arguments or points are developed from the human needs that the organization will address, the organization's mission, goals, and objectives, and the organization's capacity to undertake the planned endeavors. A summary of these arguments, usually known as a *case statement*, can then be used as the copy platform for the fundraising organization's promotional activities and publications.

Planning is most valuable when it involves the organization's leadership, has widespread participation from organizational members and other constituents, and incorporates the expertise of staff and volunteers. An appropriate planning process can engender enthusiasm, cohesion, and responsibility throughout the organization. These results are especially critical for motivating the volunteers and staff members who are raising funds.

In the following examination of strategic planning concepts and their impact on fundraising, the emphasis is on the capabilities of an organization to address present and future environmental forces and on the direction that should be taken, particularly in obtaining gifts and grants. The criteria and strategies for the selection of fundraising methods are also discussed.

Background and Nature of Strategic Planning

The concept of formal organizational planning evolved in the early 1900s as a means for budgeting and controlling organizational performance. In the 1920s, formal planning patterns evolved further, becoming a means for organizations to anticipate growth by taking a long-range view of trends. At first these trends were assumed to be rather stable; however, the realization by managers and scholars in the 1960s that organizations operated in turbulent and complex environments produced an interest in predicting the changes and new trends that would affect organizational goals and objectives. Analytical techniques emerged to enable executives to make rational choices about desired directions and performance; strategic planning had arrived (Benner, 1984). It had also begun to penetrate fundraising planning.

Strategic planning is founded on *open systems theory*, which states that organizations are composed of sets of interdependent parts; have basic needs to adapt, survive, and maintain themselves; and take actions based on cybernetic principles of communication and feedback (Weiner, 1979). An essential part of this theory is that organizations are embedded in larger economic, political, and social systems that affect organizational operations. Because nonprofit organizations, like all other organizations, appear to function as this theory states, they must look at and anticipate the environments in which they are embedded. They must assess their current positions and future options, particularly their potential funding. The way they do this is through strategic planning.

Strategic planning is vision oriented, market driven, and concerned with clients, resources, and competition (Garner, 1989). It asks these obligatory questions: What should we be? Where should we be? Where should we go? Where should we seek funds? These questions about the future supersede the older typical questions about the present: Where are we? What are we? Where do we want to go? Who are our prospects? (Benner, 1984).

Strategic planning differs from two other common styles of planning: incrementalism and long-range planning. *Incrementalism* seeks to adjust specific problems, make minimum adaptations, or attend to the "squeaking wheel." Existing aims and direction are assumed to be appropriate. Budgeting and controlling receive major emphasis, and the time span considered is the next twelve to eighteen months (York, 1982). Examples of incrementalism in fundraising are plans to increase membership campaign goals by a few percentage points or to send additional mailings to donor lists. Questions about the validity of the membership structure or the case for the appeal are not asked.

Long-range planning focuses on five-, ten-, or twenty-year periods. All available data on internal operations, performance, personnel, and structure of an organization receive thorough analysis. However, the purpose and mission of the organization are assumed to be predetermined and justified—growth is assumed to be continuous (Benner, 1984). Many capital campaigns are based on long-range planning rather than strategic planning assumptions.

Strategic planning differs in that it looks both internally and externally for the unexpected, examines changing demographics, technologies, and service requirements, and analyzes present and potential funding sources (Unterman and Davis, 1984). As economic and social conditions in the organization's market area vary, the needs and interests of clients, members, and donors will change, affecting the purpose and fundraising capability of the agency. Competing organizations will arise or alter their services. Government regulations, programs, and grants will change, forcing adjustments in services and funding efforts. In view of this rapidly changing environment, strategic planning is most effective if the time span projects no more than three to five years. Some authorities suggest shorter time periods and annual reassessments in order to avoid being caught off guard by especially rapid changes (Benner, 1984). In order to answer the obligatory strategic planning questions, planners must undertake a careful reassessment of the organization's mission, purpose, and basic values, its capabilities, and its overall performance. The agency's future orientation and vision come under scrutiny.

Although effective strategic planning is largely a rational process based on objective facts, intuitive judgments still enter into the process (Steiner, 1979), reflecting the participants' predispositions, value interpretations, and inability to handle quantities of data. Hazenfeld (1983) elaborates on this phenomenon by suggesting that decision making can be likened to a garbage can into which four independent streams pour: problems, participants, choices, and solutions. He implies that organizations need a collection point or can for the various data and views that must be assembled for subsequent consideration, sorting, and decision. The three factors that influence those streams are the organizational structure, which affects the arrival and departure of each stream, the cultural and normative contexts of the organization, which create biases, and the personal attributes of the participants, which shape and influence the contents of the can. Volunteer leaders and staff members have independent notions about who will donate, how much can be raised, and what the best fundraising methods are. Thus, individuals' ideas and opinions must be considered even as the planning team works to develop a systematic strategic approach.

The Strategic Planning Process

Board, staff, and volunteer members require a manageable, coherent process if they are to handle the many variables involved in strategic planning and understand the data and issues. Therefore, they first need a plan to do the planning. The elements to be considered are commitment, leadership, participants, planning time, appropriate scope and depth of consideration, and costs.

Planning efforts come to fruition only if a positive commitment by the board and administrative staff is made and a top staff leader is designated to manage the process (McLaughlin, 1986). In small organizations, the chief executive officer bears this responsibility. In larger organizations, a senior officer may be designated, but the interest and participation of the top executive must be obvious, otherwise board members, staff, and volunteers will see the planning effort as unimportant. A small planning team representing the board members, staff, volunteers, and sometimes clients, oversees the process. The volunteer leader and staff member responsible for fundraising belong in this core group. They have the responsibility for a two-way communication process. They must bring the issues and concerns of development personnel to the planning team, and they must inform their volunteers and staff of the procedures and principles involved in strategic planning.

Since the final plan will affect the entire organization, provisions to seek advice and consent for plan elements from all influential members augur for success. The scope and depth of the planning must be commensurate with the size of the organization and the issues that it faces. Smaller agencies may have less complex problems to resolve, fewer participants to consult, and a more circumscribed environment, whereas larger organizations with regional and national operations face geographical differences and multiple stakeholder groups with varying needs and influence that must be considered. The essential principle to be applied here states that the planning exercise must fit the organization. Planning must not be an arbitrarily applied fixed regimen (Bryson, 1988). Funding considerations are also central to realistic planning outcomes.

An outline of a strategic planning process that can be adapted to fit the needs of either large or small organizations is illustrated in Figure 4.1.

This process leads rationally from data analysis and conclusions to identification of critical issues and their impact on the mission, and then to strategic choices of goals, objectives, and action steps. In his widely used book on strategic planning, Barry (1986) estimates that smaller organizations can complete the planning process in eighteen to twenty hours of meetings over three months while larger organizations may accomplish their more extensive planning in 60 hours of meeting time over nine months. Costs of staff time and data gathering play a part in determining the extent of the process. Outside consultants may be needed to help formulate the process, but carrying it out remains the responsibility of the core planning group designated by the board. Turning the task over to support staff also undermines the effectiveness of the effort. The *principle of participatory planning and decision making* remains key to success (Mayer, 1985). Those parties most affected by the plan will give

Figure 4.1.   Strategic Planning Process.

Source: Pacific Bell. Used by permission.

it greater support if they are consulted and involved during its creation. In addition, all plans should be subject to evaluation for their effectiveness. The planning teams should schedule quarterly progress reports and annual reviews for this purpose of matching results to expectations. King (1979) points out that planning should be made part of the organization's culture if it is to have any significant impact

The relationships between all the planning elements discussed here, the data to be collected, and subsequent decisions that organizations make in strategic planning are described in the following section.

The Situational Analysis

The data and reports collected for the planning team's analysis require a structure that will focus the attention of the decision makers on critical issues, problems, and the choices to be made. Too much data can overwhelm the core group; too little can lead to inadequate conclusions. In response to this need,

Steiner (1979), a leading advocate of strategic planning, proposed a conceptual framework that embraced the principal concerns. These concerns are the organization's internal *strengths* and *weaknesses* and its external *opportunities* and *threats* (or *problems*). To describe the framework, Steiner and Miner (1977) coined the acronym WOTS UP, standing for weaknesses, opportunities, threats, and strengths under planning. Other authorities (Barry, 1986; Bryson, 1988) group the concerns more simply as SWOT or SWOP, with the last letter indicating either threats or problems.

Internal Assessment of Strengths and Weaknesses

Organizational strengths and weaknesses reveal themselves through the planning team's examination of operational performance, established policies, organizational elements, financial resources and restraints, and current trends. Pivotal questions about these topics include, How well are we doing? Is there a proper balance? Can improvements be made? Are we pursuing our mission effectively?

The *operational performance* analysis deals with client loads and outputs or results, market share, productivity, management capabilities and growth, volunteer and staff development and performance, and the degree of innovation and change. The *established policies* of an organization provide guides to its actions and frame its identity, image, and basic thrust. The *organizational elements* to be analyzed consist of internal structure, personnel, tasks, and culture.

The effectiveness of an organization's structure can be judged by the ease and efficiency with which tasks are accomplished. Personnel issues to be looked at center around leadership style, expertise, skills, training, staff and volunteer attitudes, and morale. The work load in nonprofit organizations overwhelms many staff members and volunteers. Careful scrutiny of personnel issues can detect what needs to change. An organization's culture determines how things are done in that organization. Ingredients such as decision-making style, degree of openness, acceptance of risk taking, sense of mission, and normative values create the culture (Ott, 1989).

Financial resources and constraints to be examined include all sources of income and allocations of expenditures, ratios of services to costs, actual cash flows versus organizational needs, and budgeting effectiveness. Review of the fundraising function's *current trends* requires the team to analyze several factors: costs and returns of fundraising programs, reliability of donor and prospect lists, volunteer and staff time expended, and growth of fundraising activities.

The internal assessment suggested here provides board and staff leaders with the status and current trends of the entire organization and highlights where strengths and weaknesses lie so that changes can be made. However, actions to change internal conditions should not be proposed without consideration of the external forces that are also at work. These external forces can lead to the decline and obsolescence of even well-considered internal changes.

External Assessment of Opportunities and Threats

Opportunities and threats are disclosed in surveys of immediate market conditions, environmental trends, actual and potential competing agencies, and service group status. Key questions regarding outside elements are, What is the need for our services? What do our present and potential constituents (clients and prospects) want from us? What changes are taking place? What forces are at work? What possibilities are open to us? How should we adjust to these conditions?

A planning team's understanding of marketing theory can play a vital role in this part of the planning process (Kotler and Andreason, 1991). The *immediate market survey* should build on information developed from the internal assessment to look for potential changes in clients, members, and donors in terms of their characteristics, needs, incomes, and motivations. Segmenting these factors into distinct clusters facilitates analysis and proposed action.

Environmental trends embrace demographic changes (age, ethnicity, family, and socioeconomic status), economic conditions (disposable income, the effects of recession or growth, and regional variations), governmental acts (taxes, expenditures, funding programs, and regulations), cultural attitudes (orientations toward spending or saving, helping others or self-centeredness), and technological innovations (computers, facsimile machines, videocassette recorders, and electronic media). *Competing agencies,* actual and potential, influence market conditions by their size, effectiveness, programs, resource demands, and future directions.

Organizations are usually grouped by the type of service rendered such as education, cultural activities, or human welfare. *Service group status* analysis identifies the trends in growth, support, saturation, and declines of the focal organization's group in comparison with others. For example, environmental organizations grew rapidly in the last decade, and health agencies expanded significantly on the wave of interest in personal health care. These trends affect public awareness and the amounts donors allocate to various service groups.

Critical Issues and Organizational Mission

The SWOT framework for internal and external assessments allows critical issues and problems to be identified and discussed and solutions proposed. For example, the concerns of the various political and economic factions within the organization will surface and seek resolution (Hazenfeld, 1983). Faced with increasing demands for services, program managers will likely press for expansion. In response, financial development staff often estimate the strength of the case for support, the extent of likely donor response, and the fundraising costs of the added effort. Through such deliberations, organizational recognition of the severity and impact of each issue develops, and people take positions about priorities. Problem-solving techniques may be needed to reach accommodations and achieve consensus (Fox, 1987; Tropman, 1980).

As critical issues are debated and emotions heat up, an effective leadership technique for aiding resolution is to raise the discussion to a higher level of abstraction. For example, when seemingly intractable arguments arise over which service or program should be emphasized for fundraising purposes, asking the question, What is this agency trying to accomplish? allows participants to bring the mission and purpose of the organization into play as decision-making tools. A fundamental review and adjustment takes place when people address the obligatory question, What and where should we be? As a result, the mission may remain the same, be slightly revised, or be greatly changed once the planning team has viewed the external threats and opportunities and understood the internal strengths and weaknesses. In the process, the participants become conscious of the critical issues and these issues' relative importance and priority.

Criteria for mission statements vary. Some authorities believe that mission statements should contain feasible ends and means; others believe that only inveterate ends must be stated while means are expressed in goals and objectives; and still others state that a preamble about the causal conditions for the mission should be included. Such a preamble describes briefly the broad human need to be served and the values underlying the service that the mission embodies.

From both a fundraising and an organizational perspective, a mission statement is most effective when it inspires those who must apply it, addresses an enduring human need, espouses the values and philosophy of the organization, and gives a positive direction with the ends broadly stated (Drucker, 1990). For example, the statement of purpose of the Children's Home Society of California declares the society's commitment "to the fulfillment of every child's right to a secure home, loving and responsible parents, and the opportunity for healthy development" (Children's Home Society of California, 1992, p. 6). This statement focuses on the society's vulnerable clients, creating an appeal that motivates volunteers and staff and empowers them to present the case for funds effectively.

Strategic Planning Decisions

The specific programs designed to pursue a mission often change as environmental factors change and internal capabilities alter. For instance, the alarming rise in teenage pregnancies

has prompted youth agencies and educational institutions to
instigate such new services as sex education workshops, contra-
ceptive advice, and the dispensing of contraceptives to cope with
the problem. The agencies' missions to help youth have not
changed even though the needs and programs have changed.
To formalize an agency's direction, volunteers and staff must
define and select the strategic alternatives that show the optimum potential for organizational survival and growth. Some
alternatives will indicate new or expanded services that can attract private funds. Others will indicate reductions or elimination of existing programs where grants and contracts have
terminated. Still others will indicate changes in administrative
capabilities and funding resources (Mayer, 1985). By casting the
selected alternatives into goals and objectives, the planning
team stakes out the path the organization should take. Goals
express what is desired for the organization, while objectives
highlight what is feasible (Steiner, 1979). Figure 4.2 shows the
steps planning teams use to set strategic direction.

These steps are expressed in terms of questions about
needs, mission, goals, objectives, and finally, action steps. The
answers to these questions will affect organizational structure,
staffing, facilities, and fundraising. The descending order of the
items in the figure indicates decreasing abstraction and increasing specificity, ending with the insertion of action steps on a
time line for completion.

Accepted definitions of goals and objectives remain
mixed, but the trend is toward the predominance of the *management by objectives theory*, which defines goals as long-term aims
and objectives as short-term, specific activities (Jones, 1981;
Odiorne, 1965). Thus, goals reduce the broad concepts in the
mission statement to challenging ends that are attainable in
three to five years. By encoding values and providing direction,
goals enable organizations to enlist the support of donors and
volunteers. Goals expand on the mission statement by citing in
broad, general terms the service programs, organizational structures, personnel capabilities, and financial resources including
fundraising programs that are to be attained by the end of a
current plan. Since it is often easier to change goals and objec-

Figure 4.2. Strategic Decision-Making Questions.

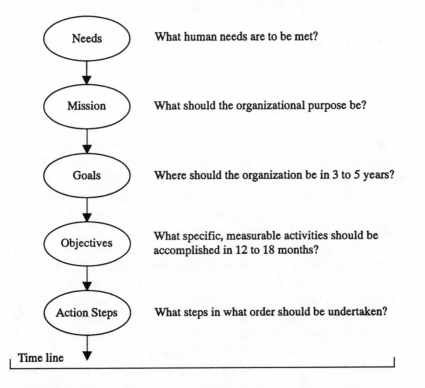

Needs	What human needs are to be met?
Mission	What should the organizational purpose be?
Goals	Where should the organization be in 3 to 5 years?
Objectives	What specific, measurable activities should be accomplished in 12 to 18 months?
Action Steps	What steps in what order should be undertaken?

Time line

Source: Pacific Bell. Used by permission.

tives than to change a mission, instigating new programs through changes in goals and objectives rather than changes in mission helps organizations maintain flexibility and relevance.

It is useful to define two categories of goals. Master or organizational goals have the broadest scope, are closest to the mission, and affect the whole organization. Operational goals relate to principal organizational functions (Hardy, 1984). For example, expansion of services typically requires additional staff and facilities. Before such increases can take place, more funds have to be raised. A master goal for this new program might state, "Improve and expand counseling services for homeless families." The related operational goal might state, "Increase

corporate and foundation funding to match expansion needs."
(Note that goals are always stated in the imperative mood, as a
directive to action.)

Objectives describe activities that are specific, measurable, and can be accomplished in a fairly short time, usually
twelve to eighteen months. Typically, each goal has several objectives related to it. Fulfilling all the objectives results in attain-
ing the goal. In turn, each objective has a number of specified
action steps that must be laid out and taken during the designated time span. Action steps describe specific functions and
tasks that must be accomplished to fulfill the objective. In the
preceding example, the related objectives might state, "Employ
and train three additional counselors within twelve months,"
and "Increase foundation grants by 10 percent and corporation
giving by 5 percent during the first year."

In large organizations, departmental staff in consultation
with volunteer leaders prepare the goals, which are then discussed and adopted by the board of directors. Smaller organizations achieve the best results when a mix of board members,
staff and volunteers prepare the goals and gain consensus on
them before presenting them to the board for formal adoption.
Some large organizations (for example, Girl Scouts of America)
require departmental staff to prepare objectives-based goals
approved by the regional boards or councils, submit them for
adoption by the appropriate governing body, and carry them
out, with volunteers reporting to staff for performance. Other
organizations prefer a structure in which volunteers report to
volunteers up to the board level, and staff assist in setting both
goals and objectives.

A final function in strategic planning decision making is
a periodic evaluation of progress that allows adjustments to be
made. Three-month reviews of action steps ascertain progress
and problems in meeting objectives. Early detection of changes
in the environment and organizational capabilities allows cor-
rections to be made easily and quickly. These reviews are carried
out by staff, who must analyze and adjust as necessary. Observations and comments by volunteers often stimulate changes. Serious deviations from the plan are reported to executive staff

and the board, with recommendations for modifications to the plan. Annual reviews of the objectives and their success in advancing the organization toward its goals also permit adjustments and realignment of efforts. These reviews are usually the responsibility of the staff, but the original planning team may be involved. Significant alterations in conditions experienced and unanticipated delays signal the need for a review of assumptions underlying the goals and objectives. For example, foundations frequently change their fields of interest, thereby causing income shortfalls among local agencies that have come to expect renewals of the foundations' one- to three-year commitments.

Severe changes such as economic recessions or a principal employer leaving the market area can abruptly increase client loads and reduce donations. These extraordinary problems mandate repeating the full planning process to develop new strategic options.

Regardless of conditions, the ideal review model calls for goals and objectives to be reviewed annually, with full-scale planning undertaken every third to fifth year. The process described here from initial planning through review stages produces a reasonable, orderly strategic plan with high potential for success.

A girls organization in a community with a population of 150,000 undertook this strategic planning process and developed several new programs. The external assessment revealed a new potential client base of minority girls, the needs of existing clientele for self-esteem development and early career exploration, and a parental concern for more after-school activities. New goals and objectives were established through a rigorous group process. New funding possibilities from local businesses, parents, and area foundations were uncovered and pursued with success. Annual reviews produced modifications that increased participation, both by the girls and the funders. A thorough evaluation at the end of the third year confirmed the value of the programs and the availability of continued financial support. In contrast, a small performing arts organization attempted the strategic planning process without success. The problem lay in the lack of board commitment to the process and its refusal to support the directions chosen. Board members participated halfheartedly in setting goals as a reaction to overly ambitious aims of the artistic director. The new goals required the board to undertake fundraising for which they had no interest, desire, or experience.

Resource Planning

Because nonprofit organizations are critically dependent on resources, especially financial resources (Pfeffer and Salancik, 1978), consideration of these resources takes center stage in planning. All forms of income enter the deliberations: fees for services, product sales (including cause-related marketing), unrelated business income (for-profit, taxable enterprises), governmental payments, endowment proceeds, and of course, gifts and private grants from fundraising efforts. Gifts of materials and services are also considered. Prudent resource planning seeks to balance income sources so that organizational dependency and risk of significant change are evenly distributed among them. When resources are diversified, organizational autonomy increases and dependency decreases. The large cutbacks in federal funding during the last two decades emphasized the importance of organizations' maintaining a balance among resources, and the 1990–1991 recession reinforced it. Fluctuations in costs of goods, services, personnel, and facilities also create resource-related problems.

Resource planning decisions rest on several factors: stability of the source, known policies of source fund allocation, costs of obtaining funds, impressions created by the source, ethical values, expertise and time of staff and volunteers to manage nontraditional enterprises, and the resultant effect of these enterprises on the agency's mission and public relations. Product sales, cause-related marketing, and for-profit subsidiaries create public images that often detract attention from an agency's charitable purposes. Further, the staff time and energy required for such operations obscure staff's true mission and purpose. In contrast, fundraising activities can be planned strategically to address income needs while fostering the philanthropic nature of the organization.

A resource planning process proposed by Lindahl (1992)

allows organizations to select various fundraising methods based on statistical relationships among the methods' costs, resulting income, and the degree to which the method enhances institutional and fundraising missions. Historical fundraising data and the combined judgment of key staff members about each method's potential income are applied to a mathematical model that includes a multiplier determined by the value of the method to the institutional and fundraising missions. Planners can then make decisions about the resources to be allocated to each method in relation to the method's projected income and institutional value.

Because so many factors affect fundraising efforts, the selection of income sources should be based on *contingency theory* and planning. Since no one method or combination of methods is forever durable or universally applicable, this theory argues for the usefulness of decisions that are based on current and future variables (Carlisle, 1973). Situations change and methods of fundraising must be contingent on the new circumstances. It is especially important for an agency's fundraising programs to be well-planned and executed because poorly planned and organized programs create negative reactions internally and externally for the agency, leaving it without sufficient support to pursue its mission.

The Development Plan

The development or fundraising plan contains goals, objectives, and action steps for securing private funds and is an integral part of the overall strategic plan. Strategic decisions about mission and master or organizational goals influence the development plan's formulation. Depending on the capacity of the organization, the need for funds, the availability of resources, and other external factors, fundraising methods are selected for implementation at designated times and in coordination with each other to achieve the desired results. These elements constitute the development plan. For instance, a typical master goal in the development or fundraising area could assert the aim of the organization to reduce dependency on governmental funds and substantially increase private support. A connected operational goal would be to achieve maximum potential return from the selected fundraising activities by the end of the specified plan period. Related objectives would specify which of the fourteen fundraising methods shown in the listing that follows would be used to achieve the dollar amounts or percentages of total income specified in the objective. For example, an annual campaign might have an objective to increase donations by a fixed percent during the first year.

The market research undertaken by the planners during the external assessment for the strategic plan provides the critical data that determine the feasibility and strategic choice of individual fundraising goals and their objectives. The fundraising case also comes from the external assessment and describes the needs to be served, the most cogent arguments to enlist support, and the most likely prospects. At year-end, the results of the plan are examined and new objectives set for the second year.

Fourteen basic methods are employed to raise funds. The effectiveness of these methods requires careful consideration of strategic criteria plus aspects unique to each one.

- Annual campaigns
- Personal solicitations
- Gift clubs
- Membership drives
- Phonathons
- Direct mail
- Special events
- Neighborhood canvasses
- Small business solicitations
- Corporate and foundation solicitations
- Project funding
- Capital campaigns
- Major gifts
- Planned giving

Strategic Criteria for Fundraising Methods

One set of criteria that affects the selection and use of fundraising methods are the ways in which prospects and donors react to different methods. These ways were set forth in Chapter Two. A second set of criteria reflects an organizational view. These organizational criteria are the purpose of funds; appropriateness of the fundraising case; sources of funds; cash flow needs; related time, effort, and costs; frequency or scheduling requirements; personnel requirements; and integration and coordination factors.

Determination of the *purpose of funds* to be raised will involve consideration of the kinds of funds that are needed and donors' reactions to different purposes. Unrestricted funds permit allocation to the most needed uses, while restricted funds limit management options. Funds sought for organizational uses such as facilities, capacity building, and institutional enhancement require more intense justification to donors than do funds for obvious needs of clients. A counseling program for abused children commands more empathy than an administration building or a strengthened public relations program. Overhead costs have little or no attraction. However, a plan to serve additional needy clients with a new facility carries a strong appeal. Opportunities to personalize giving, such as naming a new building for the donor or a beloved official, overcome mundane usages.

Appropriateness of the fundraising case is an issue because the method of fundraising must be aligned with the need described by the organization. Membership drives do not relate well to special purchases of equipment. A lavish celebrity banquet to raise funds for starving refugees appears incongruous and raises questions about managerial judgment.

In many instances, a proposed *source of funds* will determine the selection of fundraising methods. Individuals with little or no connection to an agency rarely give to capital campaigns until those individuals have been sufficiently cultivated. Corporations and foundations respond to grant proposals, but not to ordinary membership solicitations. Special "affiliate" or sponsorship schemes attract corporations that see an advantage in joining. Planned giving programs are directed only at individuals.

The *cash flow needs* that will be required from the fundraising are determined by the anticipated expenditures. Operating expenses such as salaries and services require steady income while long-term needs for new facilities or endowment can await the results of periodic campaigns. Short-term special projects, which include pilot programs, specialized equipment, or emergency services, need one-time inputs of funds.

The *related time, effort, and costs* of the various fundraising methods influence selection. A planned giving program takes a minimum of three to five years to produce commitments (even longer to produce usable funds) and entails costs for skilled staff, computer programs, and suitable literature. Direct mail solicitations of cold-list prospects to acquire donor names for future mailings produce returns of 1 percent and cost as much as the dollars received in the first year. Capital campaigns demand great effort, up-front money, and considerable expertise.

Frequency or scheduling requirements determine whether the fundraising effort will be undertaken continuously through such methods as ongoing major gift campaigns and planned giving programs, or whether efforts will be made periodically through such methods as special events and project funding.

Personnel requirements apply to board members, volunteers, and staff who will be needed for a successful fundraising effort. Direct mail uses only staff, except in small organizations where volunteers may be recruited for such clerical work as addressing and stuffing envelopes. Personal solicitation requires extensive use of volunteers and board members for whom training in how to ask is essential and entails costs.

Integration and coordination considerations concern the effect each fundraising method has on other methods. A direct mail appeal to a major gift prospect invites that person to make a final giving decision in favor of a small donation. Similarly, a gala special event with a large gift component gives a donor an excuse to refuse a near-term personal solicitation. However, annual campaigns prepare donors for future capital campaigns by establishing commitments and, therefore, subsequent strong motivations for consistency (Cialdini, 1984).

These criteria form the basis for strategic planning at the operational level of nonprofit organizations. When applied to the strategic aspects of fundraising methods, they facilitate effective decision making that augurs well for the success of the development plan.

Strategic Aspects of Fundraising Methods

The principles of organizational, group, and individual psychology play a crucial role in fundraising activities. In the context of organized fundraising methods, the internal motivations and external influences involved in individual giving, as discussed in Chapter One, trigger desired donor actions. The response of prospects and donors to the several means of communication, as explored in Chapter Two, enters into the selection and coordination of solicitation methods. The present discussion focuses on behavior that the fundraising or development department must consider in developing a strategic plan for funding.

Group dynamics play a principal role in the planning, organizing, and execution of all fundraising methods. For example, when a few strong personalities in a planning team or organizing committee commit themselves to high-level gifts, the other members feel an active compulsion to emulate them. The cohesion of a group inspires dedicated action and impresses other individuals and groups to act similarly. Even in major gift solicitations and planned giving programs, where the individual donor receives the attention, groups of volunteers participate in prospect identification, cultivation, and organization. These phenomena support the familiar cliché that fundraising is a psychological exercise.

The following discussion of fundraising methods focuses on the unique aspects of each method and the operative principles that underlie it; detailed steps are left to the many excellent how-to fundraising books available from booksellers and libraries.

Annual Campaigns

Annual campaigns involve several fundraising methods repeated yearly in an organized, leveraged fashion. *Systems theory*, which highlights the interdependence and feedback of sequential events, supports the validity of this arrangement of multiple methods. Personal solicitation, gift clubs, membership drives, phonathons, and direct mail make up a typical annual campaign. The order in which these methods are listed here shows the principle of leadership by example at work. Bigger gifts are solicited first to leverage the dollar amount of subsequent donations. In addition, organizational leaders including officers, board members, volunteers, and top staff must demonstrate their commitment to fundraising by leading off the campaign with gifts commensurate with their economic and organizational status.

When the core leadership group shows high relative effort, even though the absolute sums may be small, potential donors feel justified in making large gifts in line with their financial ability. In addition, success at the top of the asking hierarchy is a dynamic that elicits the energy and enthusiasm of volunteers during the broader-based solicitations.

The usual time span for annual campaigns is the calendar year because market research reveals that most individuals and businesses plan their finances and tax reporting on this basis. Educational institutions' campaigns are a notable exception because students and alumni are conditioned to the traditional school year starting in the fall and ending by summer. Again, the principles of leadership and leverage dictate the scheduling of deadlines, "kick-off" meetings, and reporting schedules.

Difficulties with annual giving campaigns are typically due to the repetitive nature of the asking, which can cause disinterest and burnout. The tendency to slide along, building incrementally on last year's effort, thwarts creative plans. Each year, leaders and other volunteers have to be recruited and trained, fresh themes and program highlights developed, prospects and donors evaluated to set appropriate goals, and new campaign materials prepared. Sustaining interest and success becomes the principal challenge.

Personal Solicitations

Personal solicitations, as discussed earlier, embody the most effective fundraising as volunteers and staff meet face-to-face with potential donors to present the need, the opportunity to help, and the request for funds. Starting with the largest gift prospects, volunteers and staff members move through the prospect lists to visit personally as many individuals as time and the number of solicitors permit. In this method also, the size of initial gifts and percentage of participation set an example and leverage the gifts of others during the balance of the campaign. Gift-range charts elevate giving by showing the number of gifts of specified amounts necessary to meet goals. Prospects are influenced by this systematic plan for potential success, the scope of the expected participation, and the roles they see they can play.

Gift Clubs

Gift clubs are groups of donors organized by gift dollar amounts. The rewards and recognition given to these groups encourage prospects to enlarge their gifts in order to become group members and prompt current members to continue their annual donations. For group members, giving confers a special or elite status. Additional psychological incentives occur if the names of various clubs identify donors with a hierarchy within the organization. For instance, in order to create extra donor incentives, a business school admits donors to the "managers' club" for $500 gifts, the "executives' society" for $1,000 gifts, the "presidents' club" for $2,500, and the "chairmen's circle" for $5,000. Personal solicitation, direct mail, and phonathons are used in gift club solicitations, with the caveat that the larger the expected gift the more personal the solicitation should be. The unrestricted purpose, size of gifts, and effective annual renewal make this form of solicitation highly desirable for the sponsoring organization.

Several problems can arise with gift clubs, however. Members, motivated by a desire for consistency, tend to stay in their same dollar categories year after year, despite rising costs and inflation. Prospects and donors may opt for low dollar levels and resist being upgraded. Recognition devices become outworn and ineffectual. The steady state syndrome becomes burdensome for volunteers and staff members.

Membership Drives

Membership drives provide the broad base of constituents so necessary for sustained annual, unrestricted income and for demonstrating to other funders the legitimacy and acceptance of the organization. Agencies with little or no membership face prospects' doubts about the agencies' charitable character and purpose. By providing membership opportunities, agencies capitalize on individuals' need for affiliation and group endeavor. This method often features various combinations of personal solicitation, gift clubs, phonathons, and direct mail. Membership drives face problems similar to those of gift clubs; they must cope with the never-ending difficulties of sustaining donor interest and reaching new goals.

Phonathons

Phonathons, using banks of volunteers or hired personnel, enable organizations to reach large numbers of prospects with personally tailored messages. In annual campaigns, telephoning reaches prospects missed during the personal solicitation phase and also broadens the number of prospects who receive a personalized request for funds. Organizations with few available volunteers design their phonathons as stand-alone events that secure wide coverage. The short, intense two- to four-week calling period enables management to know quickly the amount of funds that will be available. Phonathons are also employed as follow-ups to direct mail efforts. Costs when using volunteers and donated office space remain low, and the response rate is generally greater than when using hired personnel. Also, prospects feel comfortable talking to volunteers, who are devoid of motives of personal gain and are making charitable donations of their time as well as their money. An exception to this principle occurs when colleges and universities hire students to call. Prospects still feel at ease talking to these students, and the students' obvious linkage to the benefiting institution explains this experience.

The training of telephone solicitors and subsequent calling is generally done in an office with a phone bank. Group reinforcement takes place when multiple persons work at the same task. The enthusiasm and energy of team spirit, the immediate application of the training, the opportunity to handle any difficulties easily and quickly, and the recognition of successful solicitations all combine to reduce the time and effort of training.

Phonathons can experience difficulties because affluent residential markets are easily saturated by commercial firms' extensive use of telemarketing along with other nonprofit phonathons. Residents object to interruptions on their evenings and weekends. The attraction of television adds to this problem; viewers do not feel kindly toward unannounced disruptions of their programs. Fundraisers can counter this obstacle by mailing personalized letters, attractive cards, or other suitable notices that alert the prospects to the impending call and set forth the case for support. Finding, recruiting, and adequately training volunteers year after year causes some phonathons to flounder. Few agencies have clients that can be hired to replace volunteers as colleges do.

Direct Mail

Direct mail appeals seek a range of gifts: small gifts from people not previously involved, renewals and increases from annual supporters, and even large sums from well-cultivated donors; large national and regional organizations such as Amnesty International, Common Cause, public television stations, and the Sierra Club can attract sizable donations through direct mail. This method is used in conjunction with annual campaigns, membership drives, and phonathons to reach the people who slipped through the net of the other approaches.

A solicitation letter requires the assent of only one volunteer, the signer. Good fundraising practice requires that the person be a prominent individual well known to most of the prospects or, at least, one whose name will be recognized by them.

Cold-list direct mail solicits persons who have not previously been involved with the organization but have some target market characteristics such as kindred interests with the agency, membership in similar organizations, or the same socioeconomic status as existing donors. These lists are purchased or are exchanged with comparable organizations to use in expanding the donor base. New and small agencies find this method helpful in quickly generating a donor base.

Direct mail's advantage is its ability to reach large numbers of prospects and donors over wide geographical areas quickly and systematically. Since only staff need be involved, this method eliminates the burden of volunteer recruitment, training, and supervising. The process can be performed in-house or contracted out to firms that will handle some or all of the details.

The disadvantages of direct mail programs are the low response rate, hovering around 1 percent for cold lists, diminishing returns on renewals, and start-up costs amounting to thousands of dollars without any assurance that the campaign will break even the first year. Legitimate appeals arrive in household mailboxes lumped together with junk mail, catalogues, and spurious solicitations. This competition contributes to the repeated lowering of response rates. In addition, if the individual selected to sign the direct mail letter has strong opinions on writing style, the content and form may not agree with tested principles of mail solicitation. Subsequent negotiations to mediate differences frequently result in letters that fail to get cost-effective responses.

Recent trends to overcome declining response rates and the impersonal nature of direct mail solicitations include follow-up telephone calls, requests for reader views on pertinent topics, ballots on key issues, special appeals sent to specific market segments, and messages adjusted more precisely to fit prospects' status and interests. Once a person has given, follow-up cultivation techniques establish the donor as an in-house prospect or member with a higher renewal rate and a considerably lower cost of solicitation. In addition to charitable needs, the appeals can emphasize past gift support from the recipient, stimulating a consistency motivation and feelings of affiliation and group endeavor.

Special Events

Special events, or benefits, provide organizations the opportunity to involve large numbers of prospects in pleasurable activities that produce net income after expenses are met. Such events attract many nondonors by offering entertainment, products, prizes, and other quid pro quo amenities. The limitless variety of such events challenges the creative energies of enthusiastic volunteers. The positive effects of group dynamics cultivate prospects and bind them closer to the organization, making later solicitations more productive. Volunteers working on the events develop additional loyalties (unless poor management creates excessive workloads and burnout).

Liabilities accrue when the character of the event obscures the organization's charitable purpose, or the event produces no net income. Further, public tastes change, and the popularity of fancy dress balls may be overtaken by demand for rock concerts or walkathons as fundraisers.

Telethons

Telethons are a particular type of special event that exploits the visual medium through the use of celebrities, vivid demonstrations of the need to be addressed, and sense of personal audience involvement. The success of telethons hinges on securing large gifts in advance of broadcast deadlines to give momentum to the campaign and stimulate commitment from viewers. Sizable production costs limit this method to large regional and national organizations, unless an agency is extremely well financed. Public television stations are an obvious exception to this limitation because they own television production facilities and use large numbers of volunteers. One hazard of the method is that events tied to a particular celebrity may be harmed by a sudden change in the individual's popularity or his or her interest in the cause.

Neighborhood Canvasses

Neighborhood canvasses of residents permit new, smaller, or less well-known agencies to present their case directly to new audiences. Upper middle class neighborhoods are prime targets. Known enclaves of socially minded residents are also productive. Established organizations such as national health agencies and youth organizations have used such canvasses effectively for many years. However, in urban areas, rising crime rates have forced agencies to abandon this method. Residents are unwilling to answer their doorbells, and it is difficult to recruit volunteer canvassers. Agencies resorting to paid canvassers to overcome the lack of volunteers find costs running from 30 to 50 percent of funds collected, which deters both donors and the agencies. Turnover in paid canvassers, who almost always work on a commission, runs high due to the rejection and resentment of fearful residents and the low dollar level of gifts.

Small Business Solicitations

Small business solicitations share the characteristics of canvassing and personal solicitation. Volunteers and sometimes paid personnel call on business proprietors with appeals that stress local needs and imply increased sales through the goodwill generated by the gifts. The rationale for small business philanthropy was discussed in Chapter Three. Gifts-in-kind are the more frequent donations from small businesses, unless the solicitor knows the owner or has some potential business reciprocity to suggest. Dollar amounts are usually low and depend on the local economic conditions. For organizations, the value of this method lies in the way it relates local needs to local sources, builds a broader donor base, and obtains quickly needed support, either cash or usable goods and services.

Small businesses, and retailers in particular, are obvious targets for solicitations. However, because they respond to appeals with low-cost gifts-in-kind or donated services, they have limited power to alleviate nonprofit agencies' cash flow needs.

Corporate and Foundation Solicitations

Corporate and foundation solicitations, as described in the previous chapter, provide relatively large sums of money with minimal use of volunteers. In this method, volunteers' main role is to establish relationships and open doors for staff to solicit. Grantsmanship has become a well-established practice demanding ever-increasing skills and sophistication. Yet foundation officers report that only a small percent of the huge number of proposals they receive get funded. This low success rate raises the cost of grantsmanship in terms of salaries for proposal writers and time consumed by program personnel to develop attractive projects and substantiating data. The changing interests of grantors noted in Chapter Three create uncertainty about the continuity of any agency programs that they fund.

When a grant is made, it becomes evidence of the credibility of a program and its sponsoring organization. Nonprofit organizations seek grants for stand-alone projects or as part of annual and capital campaigns. Grants often fill critical dollar categories on gift-range charts for both annual and capital campaigns; this is especially true for small organizations that do not have suitable major gift prospects. The grant funds give leverage to matching efforts directed at other sources.

Project Funding

Project funding relates closely to grantsmanship because most grants support specific projects or programs. It stands in contrast to annual and capital campaigns, however, because it describes an organized, short-term solicitation effort to fund a particular project or program from various sources. The timing of project funding usually falls outside the schedules for other campaigns. The purpose may be to purchase specialized equipment, remodel a small facility, or cover start-up costs of a new program. The value of project funding is that it permits the targeting of sources who have a special interest in the designated purpose.

Drawbacks of this method include the stand-alone project itself, which limits the scope of appeal and the number of prospects. Within the requesting organization, the project may compete with other interests or be ignored by key constituents. Potential funders may perceive this isolation and give the funding a low priority. Enthusiastic support by the chief executive is the quickest means to erase any internal or external doubts about the project and its funding.

Capital Campaigns

Capital campaigns fund capital needs such as buildings, large-scale technological improvements, or endowments. Many big institutions such as universities expand their capital campaigns to include institutional operating costs and services during the period of the campaign. The sizable goals demand careful, intensive preparation and organization to achieve success. Capital campaigns marshall high levels of attention, dedication, and commitment from board, volunteer, and staff members. The renewed spirit lifts the organization to new heights of performance and generates cohesion among the many stakeholders involved. The large goals raise donors' sights regarding the level of their gifts, both during and after such campaigns. As a consequence, successful capital campaigns typically increase the level of giving to subsequent annual campaigns if follow-up efforts are maintained.

The downside of intensive capital campaigns comes from subsequent exhaustion among agency personnel and the diversion of board and staff attention from other pressing needs. All too frequently, once the pressure and expense of the campaign is past, the organization will cut its staff and the donor maintenance programs in development departments. Multipurpose capital campaigns frequently end with one or more projects underfunded or not funded, causing disruption of financing, construction, or projected services. Overly ambitious goals founded on poor market research or unwarranted judgments cause serious, lasting harm by the failure they incur. Depression among personnel and infighting by staff and volunteers follow such failures.

Major Gifts

Major gifts solicitations traditionally occur during capital campaigns. However, recent trends indicate that this type of asking also transpires systematically outside of these campaigns (Altizer, 1992). Large gifts form an increasingly important segment of fundraising efforts and financial results. Once confined to large institutions, major gifts solicitations have also become a key function of smaller agencies. Potential big gift prospects may turn up during continuing research of likely markets. Rather than wait for a major campaign, staff and volunteers will begin the cultivation process promptly and pursue prospects with proposals appealing to their identified interests. In addition, donors with big gift potentials may not be ready to make a commitment during a campaign, but with continuing, additional involvement, they become ripe for proposals. The willingness of the organization to negotiate and adjust its needs to the interests of prospects makes positive giving decisions more likely. Large contributions relative to agency size and gift history inspire other donors, boost morale, and thrust programs forward.

On the negative side, the long lead time for securing major gifts increases fundraising staff costs and occupies time of other officials, principally the chief executive officer and one or two other top-level officers. Strategic plans containing programs waiting for these gifts to mature may suffer delays and alterations.

Planned Giving

Planned giving covers all situations in which the commitment to give a gift is made currently, but the gift itself is available to the agency only in the future after some critical event such as the death of the donor or the termination of a legal trust. Bequests are the most prevalent and simplest form of planned giving, but irrevocable legal commitments are rapidly gaining in volume. These arrangements provide lifetime transfer of assets with the income from the assets payable to the donor or closely related beneficiary until that person's death. Endowments evolve most readily from this type of giving. Planned giving entails sophisticated planning and preparation by the organization to develop staff, legal mechanisms, start-up funds, prospects, and investment policies and procedures. Commitments and some monetary proceeds from planned giving programs begin to appear after three to five years of operation, but Lindahl (1990) points out that, at least in university fundraising, ten to twenty years of soliciting planned giving commitments may be necessary before a reliable flow of funds is assured. Volunteers play a key role in suggesting prospects and opening doors for staff solicitations, and staff knowledgeable in the field are also essential. When properly executed, planned giving programs have great potential for stabilizing organizational income, even during recessions and particularly if the constituent group has a large percentage of older persons.

Conclusion

The coordination of the fourteen fundraising methods described in this chapter requires skillful use of strategic planning concepts and techniques. Fundraising participants need to be trained and knowledgeable about the planning process. Market research to identify prospects and funding potential must undergird effective decision making. The culture and leadership styles within the organization exert considerable influence on the process and the place that fundraising planning occupies in the total effort. Maximum participation by volunteers and staff is essential, as the theory of participatory management attests.

Strategic planning instills an awareness of an organization's situation and potential in volunteers and staff. It creates common ground and understanding, cohesiveness, heightened morale, and solid teamwork. The time taken to plan is worthwhile beyond the actions decided, because the planning process itself creates a will to accomplish and the climate to succeed.

Five

---◼---

Shaping
Individual Roles
and
Organizational
Structures

The financial requirements of almost all charitable nonprofit organizations demand a sustained, organized effort to secure contributions and grants. Agencies without such well-organized development programs soon find themselves facing cash shortages and threats to services. This chapter explores the varieties of organizational form that are necessary for effective production of income from the private sector. Particular attention is given to structural attributes and to the explanatory concepts in organizational theory that will enable development officers to create and operate effective fundraising departments. The strategic organization of fundraising activities requires the competent selection of a complex array of organizational forms, a selection based on the factors that influence organizations.

Fundraising is always conducted in an organizational setting. Even face-to-face solicitations occur in an organizational context that gives legitimacy to the asking process. The scope and complexity of an organization's fundraising activities is determined by the nature of that organization, its mission and ser-

123

vices, and environmental variables. These elements define the potential sources of funds and the best methods to securing them. For maximum effectiveness, the structure within which fundraising occurs should follow identified principles of organization. Structure is not limited to the obvious consideration of reporting relationships or chain of command. It also includes other defining elements such as communication patterns, reward systems, and norms—all of which are discussed in the remainder of this chapter. Additional structural elements, the accountability system and decision-making procedures, directly involve management practices. These latter elements and the various operational processes of directing, controlling, and evaluating the performance of various organizational forms are discussed in Chapter Six.

Reporting Relationships for Fundraising

Years of experience and research of organizations in general and more recently of nonprofit agencies indicate that a sound chain of command alleviates many operational problems. Reporting relationships can be viewed from several perspectives including span of control, tall versus flat, unity of command, unity of direction, and centralized versus decentralized.

Span of Control

This classic management principle describes the feasible number of persons that should report to a single supervisor. The capital campaign, which was developed in the early 1900s and was one of the first methods of fundraising to be formalized, incorporates the hierarchical principle of grouping people into manageable units. Experience has shown that volunteer solicitors' reporting in units of five to a supervisor or "captain" who, in turn, reports with four other captains to the next highest level produces the best results. This practice dates back many centuries. According to the Bible, Moses found he alone could not lead all the Israelites, so he created groups of tens with leaders who were bunched with other leaders to report to leaders of tens of tens. Thus, the capital campaign has an honorable hierarchical tradition that proves effective to this day.

When volunteers are organized to solicit, the span of control needs to be short. Factors of restricted time to work, scant training, a limited understanding of the case, lack of continuity of service, and low enthusiasm for asking combine to make supervision by a volunteer leader of more than five volunteers a difficult, if not failure prone task.

A professional fundraiser can have more reporting relationships with paid staff because there are fewer of the problems typical of volunteers. Selection, training, experience, motivation, and team cohesion all work to integrate staff efforts toward goal achievement. Obviously, in small organizations with only one or two professional staff, span of control is not an issue. In larger organizations with different functions and units spread over regions and states, the number of persons to be supervised becomes critical to managerial success. On one hand, the nonroutine nature of fundraising and relations with prospects suggests the value of narrow spans of staff control, emulating volunteer spans. On the other hand, the increasing professionalization of fundraising personnel means managers can allow staff more independence and less supervision, extending the span to eight to ten professionals. Beyond these numbers, the solution is to develop tiers of supervisors.

Tall Versus Flat Structures

Decisions on span of control are reflected immediately in the number of management levels found in the development department. Many levels indicate a "tall" organization; one or two levels indicate a "flat" one. Frequently, both structures exist in the same development office with a flat structure comprising the professional staff and a tall structure comprising functions that use numerous volunteers, such as personal solicitations, membership campaigns, capital campaigns, and special events. The practicality of combining the two forms in one organization is supported by contingency theory, which states that management decisions must accommodate the particular factors found in each situation (Gannon, 1982).

Tall structures tend to exercise tighter control over personnel, with rules and procedures to govern the various layers of command such as careful assignment of prospects to solicitors, deadlines for action, and restrictions on independent approaches to foundations, corporations, and major donors. However, communication problems arise when information is filtered by successive managerial layers in traveling up or down the hierarchy. For example, tentative pledges of gifts-in-kind for special events may be reported as more certain pledges as the news goes up the chain of command, when in reality, the commitment is still quite problematic. The news that a major prospect is considering a gift proposal often is interpreted as a commitment by staff under pressure for increased production.

Flat structures rely less on rules and procedures and more on policies that offer general guidelines for action and on the adopted goals and objectives. Further, the professional competence of the staff justifies their greater independence. Planned giving professional staff know the types of gifts that are acceptable and the extent to which a commitment of terms can be given to a donor. They use their judgment to sense when a donor is ready to make a decision, and they do not let the pressing need to achieve a financial goal dictate a time line.

Unity of Command

Another classical management principle asserts that a person, whether staff member or volunteer, should report to only one superior. Staff and volunteer frustration, anxiety, mistrust, and confusion result from individuals' having two masters who demand conflicting performance. All too often a volunteer suffers from these problems when he or she is asked by a committee chairperson to provide an entrée to a prospect but then hears a staff person implying strongly that the volunteer should make a solicitation, not just a referral. Also, volunteer leaders resent being undercut by staff interventions, yet this action is required when the volunteers fail in their duties. Clarity of policies, procedures, and job descriptions tends to prevent these dilemmas. Sensitive observation of volunteer leaders by agency personnel and frequent, open communication with them also mitigate many awkward situations.

Unity of Direction

Strategic planning exemplifies yet another time-honored principle of effective organization, unity of direction. A plan with clearly stated goals and objectives for a group of activities having the same purpose develops organizational cohesion, energy, and commitment. Volunteers and staff then know where the organization is headed and can apply their efforts toward reaching those goals. For most volunteers and indeed some staff also, the most frequent and perplexing question about unity of direction arises over expectations for annual giving during a capital campaign. Funds raised by each campaign support the same organization, but for different purposes and programs. Volunteers sense that they and their prospects will be asked for two gifts at the same time, which they feel violates the unity of direction. The answer to this predicament is to establish an explicit case for both campaigns, based on the needs and services of the agency. In the process, leaders must convince volunteers and prospects of three differences between the two gifts. First, their annual gifts are expected to come from current income and their capital gifts from their assets or capital. Second, the timing of the request for each gift will be staggered during the year. Third, capital gifts can be made by pledges spread over three to five years, thus lessening the amount requested in any one year. While these points are made to convince prospects of the need for both gifts, donors' financial circumstances may cause smaller commitments to capital campaigns also to be paid from income. However, experience has shown that organizations that abandon their annual giving in favor of capital campaigns face great difficulty in regaining the all-important annual support from their donors, so it is important to maintain interest in both campaigns.

Centralization versus Decentralization

A major organizational design question for development officers is the extent to which authority is to be concentrated at the top of the department or delegated throughout the department. This issue applies primarily to large nonprofit organizations (discussed in greater detail in Chapter Nine). Small development departments with limited programs and staff do not face this design question. Centralized authority calls for all major and many minor decisions to be made by the chief development officer with the approval of the chief executive officer. It also gives the top volunteer officer and committee decision-making authority over the volunteer functions. Decentralized authority allows critical decisions to be made at lower levels, by department heads, regional officials, and volunteer leaders of subunit committees.

Again, a distinction must be made between staff and volunteer organizations. Tall volunteer structures tend naturally toward centralized authority to maintain more effective control over their volunteer relationships, which are looser than staff relationships. At the same time, considerable authority can be delegated to professional staff.

A major decentralization issue for larger organizations, especially those with major government funding, such as hospitals and public universities, centers on the advisability of establishing a foundation as an entirely separate charitable nonprofit corporation to fundraise for the host institution. Since this option rests principally with large institutions, it is discussed in Chapter Nine.

Governance Structure

The governance structure is the premier reporting relationship in nonprofit organizations and is crucial to successful fundraising. The board of directors should provide leadership, power, mission statements, goals, policies, and fundraising energy. Not all boards are well endowed with the ability to provide these elements, which leaves development departments the chore of shoring up the gaps.

Board structure and responsibilities are receiving continuing attention from scholars and students of the nonprofit sector; however, the extent of these authorities' concern for board fundraising tasks varies. Some writers acknowledge board responsibility for fundraising; others dismiss it as an operational activity that is not in the purview of a policy board. The discussion here is intended to show an ideal model of an effective board discharging its fundraising obligations.

A well-constituted board gives direction to the agency, provides outreach to the community, and renders careful judgment in determining agency policies. The board is concerned with internal agency operations only when it performs the tasks of hiring and firing the chief executive officer, when it reviews performance evaluations, and when it undertakes fundraising. The latter board role is legitimized by the fact that the board is responsible for the survival of the agency and is also the agency's liaison with the larger community. The corporate charters of nonprofit organizations designate the board members as the public stewards of these agencies that take on social responsibilities in return for their tax-exempt privileges.

The internal structure of the model board corresponds with the primary functions of the agency. The board members' various concerns about agency programs (service delivery), finance, and development are logically departmentalized into board committees. Other committees are formed to handle special organizational characteristics such as buildings and grounds. Internal board functions regarding nominations and personnel policies (including the selection process for the chief executive officer) also evolve into committees. These committees facilitate deliberation and recommendations to the full board about plans, policies, and issues that arise from the committees' functional areas. The chair or chief lay leader serves as the conduit to the chief executive officer (who may also be called the president, or executive director), relaying board decisions for managerial action.

The issue of soliciting income from private sources belongs in the board's development or fundraising committee. This committee functions most effectively if it consists of board members who are powerful community leaders and nonboard members who can serve as leaders of volunteer fundraising activities. These nonboard members become invaluable vertical communication channels within the organization's fundraising structure. The development committee recommends to the board policies, goals, and functions of fundraising that will ensure adequate gift income. In turn, committee members provide operational leadership to fundraising activities outside board deliberations.

As the delegatee of the chief executive officer, the chief development or fundraising officer serves as staff to the board development committee. Complete, open communication between the chief development officer and the chief executive officer builds trust and facilitates harmonious and effective operations. With leadership, structure, and staffing, the board has the organization to fulfill its mandate.

Basic Structural Elements of the Organization

The reporting relationships discussed earlier are more obvious to an observer than the other structures that give dimension and shape to the organizational environment in which development personnel operate. These other basic structures are communication patterns, reward systems, norms (or the culture of the organization), accountability systems, and decision-making procedures (Jones, 1981). (As indicated earlier, accountability systems and decision-making procedures are discussed in Chapter Six in view of their close relationship with strategic management principles.)

Communication Patterns

Information and data are vital to an organization. In fact, Galbraith (1977) declares that an organization is an information processing system. This concept of the organization is particularly appropriate for fundraising departments, which analyze prospect research findings, develop the fundraising case and promotional images, convey information to volunteers, and report results of solicitations in terms of commitment and funds. Communication is a structural element because the patterns according to which it flows within an organization shape and control that organization's decisions and actions and the ways in which the participants learn about expectations regarding their performance and relationships. The communication patterns in all organizations divide into formal and informal systems (Jones, 1981).

Formal communication systems include meetings, reports, management information systems, memoranda, publications, and one-to-one encounters between superiors and subordinates. All these systems can be found in nonprofit organizations and their development departments. Miscommunication in these formal systems typically arises from top-down, one-way messages, which are frequently perceived as authoritarian and unclear and are subject to competing interpretations. Further difficulties arise from poor or bureaucratic communication styles such as vague policies, wordy rules, and cumbersome regulations about gift processing, donor relations, and special events.

Informal systems spring up quickly from the failure of formal ones. No organization is totally exempt from informal information systems, simply because different people have so many different communication needs and preferences that formal systems cannot hope to accommodate all of them. However, attempts should be made to reduce the need for these informal systems and to prevent people from relying upon rumors, speculation, and networking in their effort to cope with a lack of quality information because these activities adversely affect organizations. Remedies for poor communication should focus on perfecting messages and their reception for clearer meaning, opening channels of communication throughout the organization, and helping managers become more open, visible, and receptive to everyone's comments and concerns. More formal solutions occur when managers and executives design coordinating committees and liaison roles, systematically "walk around" in operational areas, and obtain understanding from the opinion leaders in the organization (being aware that the true opinion leaders in volunteer committees and staff groups are not necessarily the formally designated leaders). Research in communication problems shows that a combination of oral and written methods produces the greatest accuracy (Dahle, 1954). Dahle's findings emphasize that interpersonal communication becomes more effective when those involved view it as a matter of encoding and decoding what is transmitted. Each communicator needs to understand how others interpret messages.

Reward Systems

Nonprofit organizations face the necessity of featuring dual reward systems, one for volunteers and another for staff. In most situations, these systems are the most powerful determinant of individual and group behavior. Since this behavior shapes the organization, the organization itself is ultimately structured by the reward system.

Development officers' salary schedules are frequently more lucrative than those of service and support personnel. This disparity ties directly to the agency's dependency on private funds, and on the methods or functions that produce the most revenues. Staff responsible for major gifts command higher compensation than persons involved with routine annual giving. Even so, all nonprofit salaries are below those paid for comparable responsibilities in private industry.

Intangible rewards have a paramount importance in fundraising because they are the basis for compensating volunteers and also because they are additional incentives for staff members. The external influences discussed in Chapter One operate forcefully in any nonprofit's reward structure. Among them, recognition, increased responsibility, participation in decision making, meaningful tasks, and increased variety of work are equally effective for volunteers and staff. In the application of these benefits, volunteer rewards should be differentiated from those awarded to staff. A meaningful task for a volunteer may well be routine for a staff member.

The effectiveness of reward systems comes in great measure from the *concept of expectancy*. This theory, elaborated by Nash and Carroll (1975), states that people will behave in ways that they expect will produce results that they value. The vision of success drives the individual, and recognition of that success reinforces the act producing it. Victory celebrations, awards ban-

quets, plaques and certificates, and special titles all provide necessary recognition and reinforcement for volunteers and staff.

Norms

Every organization quickly develops sets of expectations regarding members' behavior. These expectations come from formally
created policies, rules, and procedures, and more importantly,
they also arise out of the behavior and assumptions of the members themselves. The latter phenomena shape the norms or
culture of an organization (Ott, 1989), which can be defined
more prosaically as "the way we do things here." According to
Homans (1961), norms regulate members' interactions, activities, and sentiments in both the external and internal systems of
the organization. The external system acts on organizational
members when volunteers bring into fundraising activities values acquired from other relationships: for example, negative
feelings about divulging private financial information about
prospects—feelings that may hamper prospect identification
and research. The internal system rests on the power of relationships that are developed within each group or organization. For
example, when consensus evolves that each solicitor must make
a personal gift before asking other persons, an internal norm is
controlling solicitors' behavior.

Norms change over time. Scott (1987) observes that behavior shapes norms just as norms shape behavior. This phenomenon is noticeable in boards of directors when they are
confronted for the first time with the idea that directors have to
solicit funds if they expect others in the organization to do so.
The behavior of the members who accept this responsibility
works on the reluctant ones, so that in time the practice becomes accepted.

Influences on Development Departments

Beyond the basic structural principles, a number of explicit factors have been found to affect organizational performance.

These factors are directly pertinent to development departments, and they include environmental uncertainty, size, technology, and strategic plans.

Environmental Uncertainty

In the 1960s, the federal government's Great Society projects spawned a host of nonprofit agencies whose sole funding source was the government. Consequently, the fundraising function in these agencies entailed only grantsmanship, typically performed by a proposal writer and the executive director. When government policies and funds shifted, these organizations were forced to expand their fundraising effort to other sources, principally foundations and corporations at first and ultimately individuals. New divisions within their development functions sprang into being. Hazenfeld (1983) explained this phenomenon with the principle that the greater the variations and uncertainties in the environment, the greater the internal differentiation needed to accommodate them. Established nonprofit agencies also display this phenomenon. When demand for services and competition for funds increases, agencies' typical solution is to diversify methods of fundraising.

Organizational Size

Research in the field of organizational studies has produced evidence that, in addition to environmental uncertainty, organizational size and operational technology affect structure. As the number of employees increases, so does the number of organizational levels, divisions, sections within divisions, job titles, and specialized activities (Blau, Falbe, McKinley, and Tracy, 1976). Large educational institutions, health organizations, and youth agencies have multiple levels of staff members involved in fundraising activities: chief development officers (usually designated as vice presidents of their respective organizations), associate development officers, and specialists in annual giving, direct mail, planned giving, and other methods. Volunteers in these large agencies are organized into multilevel committees and subcommittees. Small agencies do not have such expanded structures, but rely on their chief executive officers and perhaps a development staff person to do all the fundraising from grantsmanship to direct mail. Even the numbers of volunteers available for service in small organizations are limited, and volunteer fundraising is structured through only one or two committees.

Technological Impact

The different technologies or methods employed in fundraising stimulate divisions in an organization. Face-to-face solicitations require different talents and personnel than direct mail or videocassette solicitations. Whole new structures are created for capital campaigns, with new levels of volunteer leaders, committee persons, and paid staff. Planned giving programs enlist the services of specially trained staff who are knowledgeable about financial and estate planning as well as certain aspects of law. Each of these specialized functions evolves into a subunit of the development department as assistants and clerical staff are added to accommodate the increased volume of gifts. Obviously, size (in terms of employees) and technology interact to affect structure more than technology would alone, simply because larger institutions have the funds, staff, and prospects to engage in a number of different fundraising technologies. Research by Child and Mansfield (1972) appears to confirm these observations about size and technology.

The technology used by nonprofit agencies in the delivery of their primary services has little influence on an agency's fundraising structure. Art and cultural organizations use displays and performances to provide their services, yet their prospects and means of solicitation are not much different than the prospects and means of solicitation of educational institutions, which use classrooms and laboratories to deliver their services. The only difference between the two is the delay that exists for educational institutions as they wait for students to become more affluent prospects as alumni. Health-care organizations and human service agencies employ treatment and counseling technologies that benefit individuals who, as prospects, are later approached for gifts in the same ways that other agencies use. An exception to this principle of similarity in structure despite differences in services can be found in public television stations, which exploit their medium through direct appeals to viewers; however, these stations also use direct mail, phonathons, and major gift solicitations.

Strategic Plans

A nonprofit organization's strategic plans play a significant role in its organizational design. In fact, Chandler (1962) believes that such plans are more influential than the organization's environment, size, and technology. For example, if the demand for services exceeds the capacity of the physical plant, strategic planners can elect to maintain current service levels or expand capacity. If the latter decision prevails, the plan will likely contain a provision to raise sufficient funds to build an addition or a new facility. This goal thrusts the development department into planning and structuring for a capital campaign. Similarly, changing needs of clientele may require new types of services and personnel that may or may not result in a strategic plan to seek project funding from corporations and foundations for a pilot program to meet the new need. Similarly, strategic goals to diversify revenue sources to protect against declining funding from government grants or other income losses stimulate redesign of organizational structures to meet the challenge.

Mechanistic versus Organic Systems

In the scenarios cited above, a dynamic mix of environmental volatility, strategic planning, organizational size, and technology plays a significant role in creating and maintaining the structure of an organization. The critical question is the ability of the organization to respond successfully to these influences. Burns and Stalker (1961) distinguish two principal types of organizations: mechanistic and organic. *Mechanistic organizations*, typically found in relatively stable environments, are more rigid in structure and have a more precise, specialized division of labor, a hierarchy of clearly defined and centralized authority, and formal, standardized jobs and procedures. *Organic organizations*, typically located in rapidly changing environments, exhibit more flexibility. They display job enlargement and enrichment, greater decentralization of authority, increased participation in decision making, and greater adaptability in policies and procedures. Nonprofit organizations cover a gamut between these two types, but the successful ones tend to be more organic, with an ability to adjust readily to changing conditions. Certainly in the development department, a flexible, organic form of organization can respond more readily to an uncertain, turbulent environment of variable funding sources, quixotic public attitudes, and unanticipated governmental regulations. Because this department is exposed to great external volatility, it is justifiable for it to be less rigid and more flexible than its host organization. Thus, the process of selecting and applying methods of fundraising can take problematic conditions into account in order to choose the best method for the task at hand.

Reasons for Departmentalization

Development officers continually face the issue of departmentalization: that is, they must decide whether to set up subunits to accommodate various fundraising methods. Departmentalization allows the development officer to divide up fundraising work according to the kinds of tasks to be accomplished. In large development offices, individual staff members find it easier to identify with a small group that remains concerned with the same methods and similar problems. The larger organization appears more impersonal and less cohesive (Cartwright and Zander, 1968). In fact, the creation of a development office in the first instance is an act of departmentalization that separates gift income production from service delivery and financial management. Four criteria influence the segmentation of fundraising activities: the purpose of the desired funds, the clientele or prospects from whom the funds will be obtained, the function or method by which prospect will be solicited, and finally, the prospects' location.

Purpose of Funds

Funds can be grouped into four categories based on their intended application: annual operating funds, special project financing, capital expenditures (buildings and renovations), and endowments. (This classification should not be confused with standard nonprofit accounting practices, which have a different function.) Each of these applications requires a particular method of raising funds. From the organizational viewpoint, this means a distinct structure is needed for each method.

Annual operating funds require an annual flow of income that corresponds to operating expenses and includes increases to meet expanded demand for services, inflation, and improvements in quality. The annual giving campaign organizes staff and volunteers into subunits to carry out the most productive fundraising methods for this campaign. Special project financing covers one-time expenditures for expensive equipment, pilot programs, technical assistance, or similar needs that fall outside regular budgets. Grants and major gifts from foundations and corporations are a typical source and require proposal development, writing, and formal submission.

Capital expenditures for buildings and major renovations are normally of such dollar size that they require highly specialized campaigns that command the largest possible gifts from all types of prospects. Endowment funds, which will be invested to provide regular income, also require major gifts totaling millions of dollars and are obtained through specialized efforts. Planned giving programs seeking bequests and deferred gifts are the usual source of these funds. Capital and endowment funds can be raised through the structures of either capital campaigns or planned giving programs.

Clientele and Prospects

The next major rationale for organizational division or departmentalization is the different sources of funds (sometimes called markets). As discussed in Part One, funding sources are individuals and small businesses, foundations and corporations, and various associations. For many agencies, government is also a source. Even though these varied sources are frequently solicited for the same purposes, the approach to them will be organized differently according principally to the total dollars expected and the rationale for giving. The larger the dollar amount, the more formal and extensive the presentation must be.

Method

Another criterion used for drawing departmental lines is the method of solicitation. Annual and capital campaigns use separate units, usually committees of volunteers and staff, to carry out personal appeals, major gift solicitations, phonathons, and special events. Direct mail and grantsmanship usually have no specialized volunteer committees, but are handled by departmentalized staff members.

Prospect Location

The location of prospects, especially for large regional and national organizations, can result in the need to departmentalize efforts for logically defined geographical areas. These geographical units may be further subdivided by type of prospect and method of solicitation. Thus, a Midwest division of a national health organization or a large university might have subunits for soliciting the different types of prospects, and those subunits would parallel the subunits at the East Coast headquarters location. Even a locally based nonprofit organization, such as a YMCA or a Girl Scout Council, that functions in a major metropolitan area with a large membership or clientele faces the need to establish geographical divisions to reach prospects efficiently.

Integration of Fundraising Subunits

Once development officers have improved organizational structure by designing departments that are logical in terms of purpose, prospects, method, and place, these officers are immediately faced with the problems of coordination, communication, and conflict among the different subunits. These problems arise primarily from questions of control and jurisdiction over prospects, timing, solicitation methods, and use of volunteers. The challenge is to create an effective integration among the separate units. Integration has been defined by Lawrence and Lorsch (1967) as the process of linking together the various components of an organization to accomplish its goals. Specialized integrating structures that experience and research have tested for their effectiveness are available. They include linking pins, task forces, project management, matrix organization, and liaison roles.

Linking Pins

Likert (1961) proposes that certain individuals be designated as linking pins. They will be members of both their own subunit and another one whose activities parallel or overlap in some fashion. Located throughout an organization, these linking pins would bear the responsibility to understand the special problems of both their units and work at integrating the units' efforts. The linking activity would extend both horizontally and vertically, so that effective communication would flow throughout the organization. In fundraising organizations, for example, a member of a corporate solicitation team would also serve on the major gift committee to inform each group of the other's activities and concerns and help the groups avoid conflict when a corporate prospect was designated as a major gift prospect. A chairperson in the personal solicitation hierarchy would sit on the foundation solicitation committee to serve a similar function when a foundation trustee is thought to be a personal solicitation prospect. Such integration lessens the staff burdens and provides more cohesion among volunteers.

Task Forces

A task force forms around a specific issue or problem to be resolved. Task force members are drawn from other units to serve in this additional capacity until the particular concern is resolved. Such a group might be set up to study the most effective use of special events during a forthcoming campaign. Once the matter is studied and recommendations made, the task force disbands. Another problem-solving task force might be convened when the performance of a service unit is causing an unanticipated public relations problem and adversely affecting fundraising. In this case, the task force would include members from the service unit, administration, and the fundraising department.

One difficulty with task force structure is its temporary violation of the principle of unity of command. The team members report to the task force chairperson in addition to their regular leaders. The latter must be willing to share team members' time and attention with the task force and not pressure or penalize them as a consequence.

Project Management

Capital campaigns illustrate project management in its most important fundraising role. In essence, project management is a means of accomplishing a specific objective. The project manager hires staff and enlists volunteers for the project and disbands them when it's completed (Gannon, 1982). Project management's large dollar goal and extensive organization with new personnel distinguish it from project funding, which is a recurring activity that solicits primarily foundations and corporations.

Project management has both positive and negative aspects. For example, capital campaigns require substantial commitments of time, energy, and funds from the host organization as well as considerable expansion of the development department. The necessary strategic planning and strengthening the case of the agency in anticipation of a capital campaign builds leadership and donor commitment. The acceptance of the case and goodwill generated by the promotional efforts of the campaign contribute long-term benefits.

However, at its terminus an intensive big campaign leaves

administrative and volunteer leadership exhausted and desirous of returning to neglected, ongoing duties. Often, this abandonment of fundraising interest leads to serious disorganization in the development department. Moreover, the cessation of campaigning inevitably leads to reduction of personnel and consolidation and reassignment of duties, causing morale problems and declining gift production. Even large fundraising staffs located in major private and public universities face these conditions, despite efforts by top development officers to create high-level ongoing campaigning. Thus, the instigation of a project management structure (in this case, a capital campaign) requires careful assessment and preparation for its effect on the host organization and its long-term funding efforts. Smaller agencies undertaking limited capital campaigns as projects enjoy the advantages of not creating the ongoing expense of extra permanent staff.

Matrix Organization

The reporting problems associated with project management can be resolved to a great extent by the creation of a matrix organization, a structure designed to combine at least two different types of departments to accomplish an organizational purpose (Gannon, 1982). In the fundraising arena, goal-oriented departments (such as capital or annual campaigns) are combined with functional departments (such as public information, special events, or major gifts) to produce an organization to accomplish a given objective. In a capital campaign, for instance, some personnel from the public affairs office could serve in the capital campaign structure to handle public relations, publicity, and publications requirements as needed while still reporting to the manager of the public affairs office. This arrangement eliminates the necessity of hiring specialized, short-term experts.

The matrix organization displays functional departments (participants' "home bases") as vertical lines of authority and goal or service departments as lateral lines where managers combine and coordinate the services of the functional specialists around particular projects or areas (Scott, 1987). This dual-reporting relationship sets aside the fundamental principle of unity of command and allows competing bases of authority to govern the work flow. Any latent departmental conflicts are now in the open and can be addressed on the basis of the disputed issue's value to the overall organization. Compromises and trade-offs are more evident. Resolution of conflicting departmental demands on personnel is handled by sequential arrangements of priorities. For example, writers and producers of the case materials, publications, and events for a small campaign will not be in continuous demand, but can serve intermittently and then resume their regular duties in public information departments in what is called the *matrix swing* (Davis and Lawrence, 1977).

Liaison Roles

In an effort to balance the independence of departments with the need of accomplishing overall organizational goals, organizations create liaison or integrator roles (Gannon, 1982; Scott, 1987). These roles seek to effect better coordination of independent departments or activities through the transfer of information and through facilitated decision-making and problem-solving processes to resolve conflicts. Examples of such liaison roles include professionals from service delivery departments working in development offices, and fundraisers assigned to program departments. In smaller agencies, the liaison role is usually filled by an associate executive director or the chief development officer. In larger organizations, a competent high-level professional from any department may be chosen. The personal qualifications of these individuals are all important. Basically, they must have technical and organizational competencies to command the respect of the departments involved; interpersonal skills to deal with conflict, ambiguity, and personality traits are also imperative.

In nonprofit organizations, committees are often given these liaison and coordinating responsibilities. These committees work well in resolving conflicting interests between service departments and the development department over the gift needs to be financed by an annual or capital campaign.

Conclusion

Development officers and their chief executives face innumerable choices of organizational design for their fundraising activities. The strategic question they must answer asks which designs will be most effective in achieving the organization's mission and goals. Scott (1987) acknowledges the difficulty of management's task to organize effectively. While he favors the open system concept, which stresses consideration of environmental factors, he cautions that "adaptation can be achieved in numerous ways, many of which contribute to the survival of the organization but fail to serve the interests of external constituencies" (p. 337). Management's role in dealing with that hazard while guiding the chosen organizational design falls within the purview of the next chapter.

Six

Strategic
Management
and
Leadership

Management as defined by traditional practices covers planning, organizing, staffing, directing, monitoring, and assessment. A well-run development office uses these managerial functions systematically in its operation. Strategic management also employs these functions while it emphasizes the ongoing, interactive process of both implementing the organization's strategy and adapting it to fit the circumstances found in an ever-changing environment (Mintzberg, 1989). Strategic management processes call for leadership skills. Indeed, Koteen (1989) sees strategic management as embracing "the entire set of managerial decisions and actions that determine the long-run performance of an organization" (p. 18).

The strategic aspect implies the choices to be made about the direction of an organization that is embedded in an uncertain, turbulent environment (Unterman and Davis, 1984). As discussed in the previous two chapters, strategic planning and organizing form the core factors influencing operating decisions. The management aspect concerns itself with leadership: How well do both managers and leaders execute their responsibilities and adapt to new conditions? For instance, is the chief development officer able to marshall volunteers and staff members into an energetic team dedicated to achieving the new, enlarged financial goals in an uncertain economy? A strategic plan is "incomplete until it is carried out and evaluated" (Koteen, 1989, p. 21). These aspects of strategic management affect the traditional functions of decision making, directing, monitoring, and assessment.

　　To achieve the purpose of long-term organizational survival, strategic management strives to perfect the adaptability of organization personnel by building capacity to solve problems, developing organizational skills, and accommodating planned change. This chapter discusses these concepts in the context of the fundraising organization.

Strategic Management and Fundraising

Fundraising benefits from such elements of strategic management as organizational vision, environmental awareness, flexibility and change, program and resource strategies, and orchestration and execution of strategic activities to achieve success. The vision of the nonprofit organization based on human needs to be served provides the fundraising case, which in turn motivates asking and giving. Prospects want to know what their funds will accomplish; hence, fundraising requires a picture of the future. Experience demonstrates that raising funds to "burn the mortgage" creates little enthusiasm because that action looks to the past. Museums and historical societies encounter more success when they direct attention to the past as a means of understanding the present and projecting future activity in their fields. Plans for a new museum wing can elicit a vision about exciting new exhibits or new subjects to be displayed, thus allowing the design of a challenging fundraising plan.

　　Because fundraising has an external focus for its financial sources and serves in a boundary role between its organization and environment, it readily detects changes in prospect attitudes and capacity for giving. Economic swings of recession and growth, fluctuations in public perceptions of such issues as homelessness, hunger, ecology, education, population explosion, compassion fatigue, and such equivocal images of nonprofit organizations as televangelism scandals—all these and more translate into an immediate impact on fundraising capabilities.

Chief development officers quickly sense the effects of more immediate problems. A news story on alleged poor service to some clients prompts an urgent call to public relations experts to provide damage control for any negative perceptions by prospects. Solicitation scripts undergo revisions to accommodate the changing environment. Capital campaigns frequently encounter unanticipated donor concerns that require change in program strategies. Student disturbances cause many colleges and universities to shift from broad-based alumni campaigning to narrow special gift efforts where "the real story" can be told convincingly.

The diversification by many nonprofit agencies of their funding sources to cause-related marketing, product sales, cold-list direct mail, and planned giving illustrates flexibility in resource strategy. Preparation for annual and capital campaigns stimulates the formation of advisory groups of existing and potential stakeholders. These groups become advocates for their sponsoring agencies, and they aid the agencies' long-term survival. Perceiving such new opportunities and acting on them requires leadership abilities.

Characteristics of Strategic Managers

The distinctive characteristics of strategic managers consist of sensitivity to new forces and developments affecting their organizations and the ability to create and direct change to meet the challenge of these new conditions. Of prime importance is a manager's constant attention to variations in the organizational task environment. For example, a competing organization quietly prepares a multimillion-dollar capital campaign. Or the United Way begins encouraging its agencies to expand their donor bases. Further, state legislators consider enacting stricter solicitation regulations. Community demographics begin to shift. These and other factors, however minor, portend a change in the fundraising market, signaling a need to the strategic manager to review and adjust goals and objectives.

Changes in strategies do not have to be dramatic to be effective. Small incremental changes can also serve organizations well. The timetable for a feasibility study can be advanced. Additional effort can be put into prospect research. A new advisory group representing ethnic diversity can be formed. Many of these adjustments are managerial decisions. Governing boards and development committees are advised of them but not required to participate in the decision making. Of course, the cumulative effect of many small changes, particularly in a short time span, requires that the governing board and its development committee consider a new round of major strategic planning processes.

New strategies arise not only from the pressure of outside events, but also from internal operations. Mintzberg (1989) calls these new plans *emergent strategies* (as opposed to deliberate strategies which result from the formal planning process). The hallmark of emergent strategies is the learning that takes place as fundraising activities proceed. For instance, when a capital campaign solicitor encounters a prospect who refuses to give because of need for current income, the idea of a deferred giving approach occurs. The resulting gift leads to the idea of a formal program to solicit planned gifts. Thus, a new strategy emerges. The key for Mintzberg is "the intimate connection between thought and action" (p. 29). As staff and volunteers work with their development programs, ideas about improvements or alternatives evolve. His research demonstrates that "strategies can *form* as well as be *formulated*" (p. 30).

The person principally responsible for strategic management is the chief executive officer. This individual has the overall leadership obligation, reports to the board on agency performance, and in the ideal model, obtains guidance on policy and high-level direction from the board (Koteen, 1989). The flow of information on programs, projects, finances, and fundraising culminates in this person. Also, this person's position as the operating head of the organization provides superior access to outside events and transactions that inform the person's strategic management function. If conditions warrant, the authority to initiate change is present, assuming that the willingness is also there. Many chief executives feel so comfortable with continuing past directions and practices that they are reluctant to enter into new and perhaps uncharted activities. However, the attitude of the nominal leader toward change permeates the whole organization. Without top-level interest and enthusiasm, emergent strategies die aborning.

The chief development officer has the opportunity to manage strategically under certain conditions. The most favorable situation calls for a strategically minded chief executive officer. Failing that, the degree of independence of the development department from other organizational functions determines how far the development chief can go in responding strategically to new situations. Such independence ranges from none because the chief executive assumes an active role in fundraising or is very authoritarian, to great freedom because the chief executive officer has effectively delegated authority or lacks interest or knowledge of fundraising.

The more dependent the agency is on private funding, the more opportunity and power the chief development officer has to implement change (Hazenfeld, 1983). By wise and discreet actions, this person can use the fact of this resource dependency to influence the chief executive to address needed improvements. Failing this redirection, the development officer can alter the style of management within the development department, adjusting gift need priorities, fundraising methods, and types of prospects to achieve financial goals. However, a note of caution is useful here: no department is completely free in its operation. The norms, culture, and other structures of the organization exert a controlling influence.

For strategic management to work effectively, the ideal model requires systemwide acceptance. A successful chief executive officer actively espouses and exhibits the strategic management concept. Department heads then follow suit. Volunteers are encouraged to contribute their vision and expertise. Staff members feel that their ideas will be welcome. Emergent strategies flow and thrive. Deliberate strategies resulting from this cumulative process are readily accepted by the members of the organization.

Despite the necessity for change, Mintzberg (1989) points out that changes are also disruptive and that stability should be the norm if maximum proficiency is to develop. Once volunteers accept proposed gift needs and the case to support them, they become more effective as they present these needs to different prospects. A change in priorities means retraining them and reinfusing their spirit. Changes in membership dues, fees, and gift club categories prove to be difficult for volunteers to promote even though the sound reasons such as increasing costs that prompt these changes are generally recognized as facts of life.

The issue for Mintzberg is the strategic manager's "need to reconcile the forces for stability and for change to focus efforts and gain operating efficiencies on the one hand, yet adapt and maintain currency with a changing external environment on the other" (p. 35). He proposes observing distinct periods of stability and of change. The duration of these intervals and the activities that take place in each of them will depend upon the nature of the organization and its service. For example, performing arts groups generate audiences geared to certain forms of entertainment. A sudden shift in the fare to forestall a slight decline in attendance or to attract a larger clientele can lead to disaster if traditional patrons, both viewers and donors, are unwilling to shift along with the organization. Management has to know the nature of its "business," present and potential clientele, and emerging patterns of interest to accommodate change successfully.

Strategy and Leadership

Strategic management is the process of instigating change effectively (Unterman and Davis, 1984). Plans, policies, and strategies do not cause change by themselves. People cause change (and oppose it, too). The way in which changes occur determines their success or failure, and the style of leadership is all important. Change is perceived by many individuals as a threat to their status and security. Sensitive, knowledgeable leadership diminishes these fears. The appropriate leadership style is especially critical for motivating volunteers who serve as leaders and followers without financial incentive in the challenging role of raising money. Yet most leaders, including volunteer chairs, chief executive officers, and development officers, are not conscious of their style, its effect on others, or alternate more productive styles.

The concept of leadership in organizations receives constant attention, but as yet there is no clear-cut agreement on the meaning of leadership for all circumstances (Bennis and Nanus, 1985). In fundraising, the style of a chairperson running a capital campaign differs markedly from that of a development officer attempting to reach consensus with service department heads on funding priorities. More variables enter the leadership question in view of the many different types of organizations the nonprofit sector comprises, from grass-roots community groups to multinational relief agencies.

Even though no single definition of leadership is universally applicable, Lassey and Sashkin (1983) believe that "leadership is clearly a role that leads to goal achievement, involves interaction and influence, and usually results in some form of changed structure, or behavior of groups, organizations, or communities" (p. 12). The leadership exemplified in a major capital campaign fits this description. Success in meeting financial goals, a high degree of staff and volunteer involvement, new programs funded, and if necessary, a changed perspective on the role of fundraising for board, volunteers, and staff all depend on effective campaign leadership.

One way to uncover a number of the important aspects of leadership is to compare the differences between what is commonly expected of managers and what is expected of leaders. Zaleznik (1989) asserts that managers and leaders differ fundamentally regarding "their goals, their work, their human relations, and their selves" (p. 300). Managers have a more impersonal, somewhat passive attitude toward goals, which arise for them out of necessity rather than desires. Leaders present a personal, active view of goals that evoke expectations and desires in volunteers and staff; fundraising campaigns become exciting events that meet human needs. Managers see their work as an enabling process for making decisions, resolving problems, and limiting extraneous choices, while leaders search for fresh approaches and new options, different ways to involve prospects, develop team work, and energize lagging solicitations.

In relationships with others, managers seek to reconcile differences, forge compromises, and establish balances of power. Leaders concern themselves less with order than with the forward movement of the task at hand, seeking to attract commitment and zeal regardless of the consequences. A phonathon with a competent leader generates excitement and passion that stimulate solicitors to higher levels of effort. With regard to their sense of self, managers view themselves as conservators and regulators of an existing order of which they are an essential part. Leaders exhibit a certain aloofness and separateness from their environment, a quality which allows them to seek out change. Case statements rarely remain static as leaders explore new ways to communicate needs of their agencies. From this perspective, leaders appear to have more of the qualities that fundraising strategies require.

Throughout the research on leadership two aspects of behavior remain paramount: a task orientation and a human relationship perspective. These dimensions, first identified by Benne and Sheats (1948), include such task functions as initiating activity, giving information and opinions, seeking data and clarifications, elaborating on goals, coordinating, summarizing, diagnosing, and evaluating. Relationship functions, necessary for maintenance of the group or organization, consist of encouraging members, setting standards of behavior, expressing group feelings, taking consensus, harmonizing, allowing opportunities for expression, and reducing tensions. The exercise of these functions is not confined to the designated leader; any member performing them fulfills a leadership role. Increasingly, volunteers drawn from the business community bring with them an understanding of these functions and facilitate the progress of fundraising committee work.

Executives of nonprofit organizations and fundraising departments often find themselves playing both roles, manager and leader at different times. The job at hand may require managerial performance such as supervising budget preparation, coordinating schedules of different activities, or hiring personnel. At other times, the task may demand leadership qualities of inspiring volunteers to make extra efforts in a lagging campaign, generating staff and volunteer commitment to achieve a new fundraising goal, or demonstrating the agency's value to a new constituency.

Leadership Styles

The degree and manner to which the leadership task and relationship functions are or are not employed determines leadership style. Four distinct personalities or styles can be observed in nonprofit organizations: the authoritative executive, the coach director, the collegial facilitator, and the laissez-faire official. These types are illustrated in Figure 6.1 in terms of two major attributes of the styles: first, the tendency toward executive dominance over volunteers and staff, and second, the tendency toward executive encouragement of volunteers and staff participation in important agency activities.

Figure 6.1. Leadership Styles in Nonprofit Organizations.

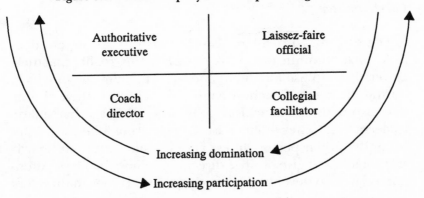

Authoritative Executive

Leaders of this type are strong-willed individuals who are often the founders of their agencies and know how to get funds from one or two key sources. They have single-minded views of their organizations' purposes, roles, and programs, with little or no tolerance for other views. They tend to dictate to board members and staff, avoiding consultation and participation with others. They appear as agency spokespersons and give little opportunity to others (board or staff) to be seen or heard. Their success depends on their vision, dominant will power, and relations with funding sources (typically governments or foundations).

When in the role of chief development officer, these individuals exhibit similar characteristics, often working to become more independent of their chief executives and establishing power bases with board members and volunteer leaders. Subordinates are closely directed, with little opportunity for personal growth and public roles. Morale is likely to be low. These individuals are successful as chief development officers when the agency depends significantly on donated funds and the chief executive dislikes or shuns fundraising. The underlying justification for the authoritative executive is the view that leadership is a function of position and role in a hierarchical organization and that it thus possesses the power to give commands that must be accepted (Weber, 1947).

Coach Director

Coach directors as leaders also demonstrate strong-mindedness, but to continue the sports metaphor, they realize that their players have to use judgment and need to be in the limelight during the game. Coach directors have clear, positive visions that inspire others to achieve goals. Like Weber's charismatic leaders (1947), they often enlist the support of followers by the strength of their personalities. They consult with their boards and leaders, but give positive direction, calling the plays. Attention is given to developing participants' skills. Coach directors look to staff for ideas but give instructions to act; they run tight organizations. Board members, other leaders, and staff appear as players and stars on the field. High morale is evident, and team spirit focused on achievement emerges.

Development executives in the coach role present similar qualities in relation to board members, leaders, and staff. In their relationships with the chief executive, they take an advisory stance, providing information and expertise from past successes and gradually molding their superiors in directions that will achieve fundraising goals.

The coach model for leadership reflects research findings on the application of the *human relations theory of organizations*: namely, that people produce more when their psychosocial needs are acknowledged. Participants' feelings of involvement and alignment of personal and organizational goals and the leader's recognition of participants' status and ability contribute to the effectiveness of this leadership style. Team building is an essential feature of this model.

Collegial Facilitator

While these executives know an agency's direction and how to reach it, they seek to empower others, encouraging leadership and participation by them. Collegial facilitators seek to direct through persuasion and development of individuals. Personally, they are positive, well-integrated, receptive, and open in their relationships. They integrate and coalesce external and internal demands made on their organizations. They also consult extensively, asking for input from board members, volunteers, and staff, while synthesizing and suggesting direction and trends. All their staff are fully involved in preparing and executing agency plans; staff development is highly valued; and morale is usually very high. Collegial facilitators' boards are actively involved in setting policy, plans, and goals; committee chairs are active and responsible; board power is strong. The agencies of these leaders appear dynamic and open, with board members and volunteers visible as leaders.

Development officers who are collegial facilitators operate in similar fashion. Their active engagement of board members, volunteers, and staff in the dynamics of fundraising produces greater results than passive or limited participation. The high level of enthusiasm and commitment in the agency carries over to prospects. Because learning and development are valued, professionalism increases, problems are resolved more easily, and individual psychosocial needs are met.

The rationale for this style is found in the social science research that emphasizes the importance of involvement and participation of volunteers and staff in decision making (Tannenbaum and Schmidt, 1973). Participants' feelings and views are as crucial to performance as leaders' direction. Leadership in this mode requires a high degree of perception and sophistication about human motivation.

Laissez-faire Official

This person gives little or no overall direction, letting volunteer leaders and departmental staff run the organization. Lewin, Lippitt, and White (1939) found this style in group experiments that also revealed the autocratic and democratic forms of leadership. These three theoretical dimensions of behavior were also found to correspond with real-life tests. Often, dispersion of power, confusion, or even anarchy exists in the agency headed by a laissez-faire official. Such leadership is commonly found when authoritarian leaders retire, lose their interest and zeal, or are terminated, and interim executives find themselves in charge. Risk avoidance, lack of clear direction, and only nominal effort characterize the performance of these interim executives, and other strong-willed individuals fill the power vacuum. Multiple power centers develop among board members, staff, and volunteers. The executive seems to be the board's secretary rather than its leader, and receives strong direction from staff who complain about everything. The organization appears diffused, weak, and ineffectual. Many voices speak without apparent coordination. Crises and collapse loom close at hand.

Development directors who are laissez-faire officials find

it difficult to marshall effective fundraising programs. Volunteer leaders soon move on to more promising organizations; donors lose confidence that their funds will be used effectively. Failed fundraising campaigns also create this type of deficient leadership in development departments. Recriminations about blame, dispirited volunteers, and frustrated department heads cause depression and inaction in development executives. Change in leadership becomes imminent.

Leadership Adaptation

Taken together, the four styles of leadership can be viewed as a continuum of behavior that ranges from highly structured to benign. At one end, the authoritative leader allows little deviation from orders. At the opposite end, the laissez-faire person provides almost no direction except for obvious routine and legal requirements. In between, the remaining two styles allow participants flexibility in line with goals and objectives. Each of these styles represents an adaptation to the history and circumstances of particular agencies. Blake and Mouton (1978) developed a leadership grid similarly based on two aspects of behavior: concern for production (task orientation) and concern for people. Leaders exhibiting high concern for production and low concern for people correspond to the authoritative leader. Leaders demonstrating low concern in both categories fit the laissez-faire model. The remaining two quadrants in Blake and Mouton's grid approximate the two other leadership types discussed here.

In most instances, the authoritative model arises within new organizations. Agency founders have clear visions of what services need to be provided and how the founders intend to provide them. Enactment of the vision requires positive convictions, courage, and resolute effort. Funding new organizations rarely comes easily, and disappointments from proposal rejections abound. Weak personalities do not survive, and it is no wonder that authoritarian individuals populate start-up agencies. Their tenure lasts until the growth of the organization requires new leadership that will involve participants adequately and achieve goals with less frustration. At this point, the authoritative personality has difficulty in adapting to the new methods of agency leadership that are required.

The laissez-faire manager also finds it difficult to change style to meet the demands for positive direction. The conditions that lead to weak leadership do not offer the designated leader opportunities to assume authority. The space vacated by a strong leader quickly fills with others seeking to enact their will on the organization. Thus, adaptation by two of the four types of leaders becomes problematic and a change of leader is inevitable. However, the other two types of leaders are often adaptable.

Executives who use the style of coach director or collegial facilitator find adapting to other people and situations much easier. The common ingredient is the executives' concern for involving and empowering their participants. The coach does it by inspiring and developing the individuals; the facilitator provides an arena in which the participants can develop themselves. The development officer as coach trains and directs volunteers to be solicitors; the facilitator allows the volunteers to understand and use their talents in effective ways of asking for donations.

The situational factors of the environmental conditions and organizational status directly influence leadership styles. Depending on circumstances, chief executives and development officers have to be able to adjust their leadership styles to be effective. A coach becomes more successful by shifting to the facilitator's role when a preponderance of volunteers experienced in resource development activities are participating. Conversely, a facilitator has to adjust to a coaching role when a sudden turnover of volunteers results in many who need training and direction, particularly in fundraising skills and methods. Shifts between these two styles can occur fairly easily because both styles honor the contributions of participants. However, unsettled conditions that cause internal confusion and loss of direction, especially sudden economic slumps or societal flare ups that trigger precipitous drops in donations, call upon participative leaders to become more authoritative.

The situational aspect of leadership receives support

from Hersey and Blanchard (1982) who declare that "leaders may still not be effective unless they can *adapt* their leadership style to meet the demands of their environment" (p. 149). Hersey and Blanchard formulate a four-quadrant grid, similar to Blake and Mouton's, with "relationship behavior" by leaders on one axis and "task behavior" on the other to reveal four leadership styles. In addition, they introduce the concept of the maturity of followers, meaning "the ability and willingness of people to take responsibility for direction of their own behavior" (p. 151). Their approach assumes that maturity varies among individuals and groups. Therefore, maturity is one of the factors a leader must carefully assess in selecting a leadership style. Further, Hersey and Blanchard point out that the degree of a person's maturity will vary over time and in relation to the specific task to be performed. As tasks are learned, individuals can take more responsibility for their performance. For example, volunteers selected to campaign for funds vary considerably in their competence and willingness to raise money. The more experienced persons gravitate to leadership positions, and others undertake less skilled tasks. A development director cannot hope to succeed if his or her style of leadership demeans experienced volunteers or overlooks training needs of newer members. Thus, the style of leadership must change to meet different situations.

The leadership grid developed by Hersey and Blanchard identifies four distinct modes that leaders can use, based on the maturity of participants: *delegating*, which calls for low task and relationship behaviors; *participating*, which has high relationship and low task behaviors; *selling*, which demands high task and relationship behaviors; and *telling*, which requires high task and low relationship behaviors (p. 152). Volunteers who are willing and able to solicit funds and therefore can assume responsibility without much need for direction and support will respond to a delegating leadership style. The participating role allows the leader and the follower who needs little direction but considerable support to share in decision making with the leader's main roles being facilitating and communicating. This style closely approaches the collegial facilitator model, in which fundraisers and volunteers collaborate on solicitation methods. The selling role follows the coach model with most of the direction and support provided by the leader to help followers buy into desired behaviors about how fundraising campaigns should operate. The telling leadership role defines what, when, and how participants perform tasks, corresponding to the authoritative model.

Ingredients of Leadership

Leadership does not come by birthright, nor is it an exclusive trait vested in some and not other persons. John Gardner (1990), a noted authority on the subject and co-founder of the INDEPENDENT SECTOR, claims emphatically that leadership can be taught. However, he cautions that obstacles exist that prevent human talents from being developed into leadership skills. According to Gardner, these blockages are the size and complexity of our social institutions and organizations, the specialization of professional education and training, the rigors of public life, and anti-leadership biases in our educational systems. Despite these obstacles, the pressing need is to focus on what can be taught about leadership.

Gardner echoes the themes of other investigators of leadership when he emphasizes leaders' relationships to the persons led. This essential connection shows up in the nine tasks of leadership he has identified. Leaders define goals, affirm shared values, motivate, manage, achieve a workable level of unity, explain, serve as symbols, represent the group externally, and renew the complex systems over which they preside. Although all of these tasks relate closely to the persons led, Gardner feels that leaders can delegate virtually every one of the tasks except the envisioning of goals. In delegating, the leader assumes the obligation to teach and to encourage the principles of leading regarding the tasks given to others. However, the key leader retains the responsibility of unlocking the talents and energies of those who are led by offering them a vision that incorporates basic human values and the group purpose. A chairperson's enthusiastic articulation of a campaign case statement illustrates this function. By dramatically portraying the benefits of a homeless persons' shelter, for example, the chairperson can enthuse major gift solicitors to carry a strong appeal to prospects.

Another approach to the essential elements of leadership comes from a study of ninety leading executives by Bennis and Nanus (1985), who found four major areas of competency or human handling skills. These areas or strategies consist of handling attention through vision, meaning through communication, trust through positioning, and the deployment of self through positive self-regard and focusing on success (p. 26). In developing the first strategy, handling attention through vision, Bennis and Nanus found that all ninety executives had an agenda and focused on outcomes with an intensity and commitment that built confidence in subordinates that they could succeed. The visions these leaders espouse animate, inspire, and transform purpose into action. The philanthropic purpose of fundraising lends itself easily to this strategy. No organized solicitation succeeds without an agenda of gift needs that leaders use to inspire solicitors and engage the attention of donors.

The second strategy calls for sharing the meaning of tasks performed and for interpreting the validity of the organization in order to impart a sense of significance and reality. Members of an agency need to know why they are engaged in asking for money before they learn how to ask. Organizing fundraising activities involves quantities of detailed data collection, prospect research, literature preparation and distribution, and committee work. Without a sense of meaning for this work, people lose their energy for meeting goals.

Trust through positioning, the third strategy, implies accountability, predictability and reliability. Followers know where leaders stand by their relentless dedication and tireless pursuit of the direction chosen. A preponderance of grant proposal rejections does not deter dedicated fundraising leaders; a campaign feasibility study projecting fewer gifts than required only energizes a development officer to expand prospect research, intensify cultivation of prospects, and enlist additional key volunteers. Leaders stay the course until the project is funded. Resolute action builds trust.

The deployment of self, the fourth strategy, hinges on recognizing one's strengths and compensating for weaknesses, nurturing one's skills with discipline, and then having the capacity to determine the fit between those skills and the job requirements. These leadership qualities foster positive self-regard, which, in turn, promotes self-regard in others; followers feel good about being guided by a positive personality. Development officers experience many periods of both joy and gloom since the job is not easy and the hurdles are many. Hiring able associates with complementary abilities reduces the burden, but success in leading under these circumstances depends on a reservoir of self-esteem. The value of these four leadership strategies, according to Bennis and Nanus, rests in their universal availability. Bennis and Nanus join Gardner (1990) in asserting that leadership can be taught to and learned by anyone.

The challenge facing development officers when they are hired is to apply these four strategies to achieve fundraising success. Typically, new jobs become available due to the former occupants' burnout or exhaustion, the number of program and organizational needs lacking necessary resources, or an organizational environment fraught with leadership problems.

One of the most difficult and sensitive problems facing development officers occurs when their leaders get derailed or out of alignment with the organizations' mission, goals, or culture. Tensions become severe, and confusion and conflict quickly ensue throughout the organization. The situation arises most frequently when the personal ambitions and values of these leaders dominate organizations and skew them away from accepted directions and patterns of operation. Desires for power and ideological control appear most often as problem behaviors, although other personality deviations are encountered as well.

Symptoms of derailment include unwarranted building expansion plans as testimonies of power; exclusive groups of wealthy donors allowed to dictate types of services; particular clienteles favored over others; excessive salaries and perquisites for select officials; small, elite cliques assuming governance; and many other similar actions embodying power, greed, and ideological preferences. Fundraising soon suffers as prospects and constituencies hear of these deviations. Other leaders lose interest. Enthusiasm over the case for support pales. Mission statements that value human needs appear to be contradicted.

Development officers sensing these situations have to move cautiously but without delay to address the problems. Their effectiveness will be imperiled if they allow difficulties to fester. The first step toward reestablishing appropriate leadership includes careful analysis of the situation to locate power centers and see how firmly and extensively attitudes and positions are held by both the persons involved in the problem and peripheral individuals. The examination should reveal who supports the undesirable actions and who is willing to help make a change. An avenue for progress can be outlined. At that point the question is, How can other leaders including staff officers bring about change?

Planned Change

Planned change or change management seeks to make adjustments in individual, group, and organizational behavior for more effective performance and the achievement of the organizational mission, goals, and objectives. Attention to process, how things are done, is the guiding concern of planned change. The underlying values of planned change include a positive belief in the worth of individuals and their desires for meaning, self-esteem, and achievement. More specific aims are to resolve conflicts, reduce disruptive tensions, and create more satisfaction for participants. Planned change also looks to improving organizational technology, structure, and power relationships. As previously mentioned, many authorities call such change organization development, and for the past twenty years, their output of books and articles on the subject has been voluminous. The discussion here describes the role of planned change in strategic management and leadership as it applies to fundraising.

The first principle in undertaking planned change is to understand the personal and organizational environment in which it is to take place. Leavitt and Bahrami (1988) caution that change is uncomfortable and emotionally charged. Logic and reason gain little acceptance. People facing the "unknown" experience anxiety, frustration, and inadequacy. The result is often aggression, particularly against the proposed change. When an established gift program that traditionally solicits one hundred dollar contributions for its "Century Club" tries to raise the amount by ten or twenty-five dollars, the outcry will be enormous. Changing the traditional date of the prime fundraising benefit is another example of a change that will incite resistance.

Leaders must also analyze the external environment. Bennis and Nanus (1985) and Gardner (1990) decry the complexity of society and its systems, people's lack of commitment to values and institutions, the absence of a sense of community, and the pervasive credibility gap surrounding organizations and government. These conditions exacerbate the insecurities and distrust that individuals continually experience, making change more difficult. However, agencies with programs addressing these problems find ready support when their case statements provide reasonable solutions.

In the organizational arena, Bennis and Nanus (1985) find four types of organizational "subpersonalities" that change agents must recognize and understand. The *manifest* organization is the one shown on organization charts, the *assumed* organization is the one participants perceive to exist, the *extant* organization is the objective organization seen by an outside consultant, and the *requisite* organization is the one that accords with the reality of a situation (pp. 50–51). One aim of planned change is to reduce the divergence of these subpersonalities so the organization can operate in a cohesive and concerted fashion. This objective faces particular difficulty in nonprofit agencies where volunteers occupy powerful positions as board members, key leaders, and participants in fundraising activities. Volunteers bring varied values and behaviors developed in other facets of their lives. Thus, welding these individuals into a common endeavor is not easy.

Within an organization, change needs to occur on three

levels. Piecemeal solutions do not survive the resistance raised by altering the way people do things. Goodstein and Burke (1991) identify the three critical levels as individual, structural and systems, and climate/interpersonal style (p. 10). At the individual level of planned change, skills, values, attitudes, and emotional behavior require attention. At the structural and systems level, reward systems, reporting relationships, and work design come under scrutiny. At the climate/interpersonal style level, leaders must be sure the change encompasses how people relate to each other, how conflict is managed, and how decisions are made. For example, new or small agencies typically find board members are reluctant to do fundraising. The difficulty arises from and is supported by emotionally held attitudes and values, the climate of the agency and its board, and the structures controlling activities. To change reluctance to cooperation, changes will have to occur in all these affected areas, not just one or two of them.

The chief executive officer bears the primary responsibility for detecting the need for change and for setting it in motion by designating who will guide it. At the board level, the responsibility can remain with the chief executive or be delegated to a knowledgeable board leader, an associate executive who has good rapport with the board, or the chief development officer. The difficulty with the last option rests in the obvious self-serving position of the development officer who seeks to raise board members' level of giving or to increase their fundraising obligations.

For most charitable agencies, once the need for change is identified, the problem becomes finding persons who are knowledgeable in change management to assist the leader. The process of change demands a sensitive, informed facilitator, yet only a few of the larger nonprofit organizations have human relations experts or organization development specialists on staff to manage the work of change. However, great numbers of these experts can be found in large business corporations. Some of these experts can be enlisted as volunteers, and of course, independent consultants are available.

The change process can use one or more of the intervention techniques that will be discussed here. The classic model for change grew out of Lewin's work in group dynamics (1948). As previously described in Chapter Two, Lewin found that individuals and groups go through three major steps in making real, lasting change: unfreezing the situation or attitude, moving toward new ideas, and refreezing or acceptance of the new mode. Unfreezing occurs when individuals sense conflict, dissatisfaction, isolation, failure, or other discomfort in their current situation, and think there may be a better way to function. In other words, a looming crisis overshadows the group. The more entrenched their current inadequate behavior, the harder it is for individuals to unfreeze and the more severe the crisis will become.

Lewin's view is a helpful guide in most situations where change is necessary. For instance, in the example of the board that is loathe to do personal fundraising, the unfreezing begins when revenue shortfalls, rising costs, competition from other agencies, demands from other volunteers for the board to take leadership in fundraising, or other similarly severe factors stimulate a sense of inadequacy among board members. The tension rises, the debate gets more emotional, and the hope for a solution emerges. Movement begins as the board explores new ideas, options, examples and helpful information. The leader's task is to communicate and educate regarding desirable solutions, perhaps examining a new plan for board participation. The leader and others who are willing to change must empathize with resistors and acknowledge their concerns. Involving the resistors in the search for solutions assists their movement; they become instrumentalities for change.

Refreezing takes place gradually through board acceptance of minor steps suggested in the movement phase of change. Incremental commitment comes through small decision steps, preferably occurring in small group settings before large group action is necessary. The informality of small groups facilitates adjustment and decision making. Group pressure stimulates a new conformity (refreezing); rewards and symbols assist the process; new language or terms encourage acceptance. For those who continue to resist, a give-or-get assessment may ease the perceived threat of having to ask for funds. A new image or identity develops. What was once the "board fundraising plan" becomes the "participation plan." The end result increases group solidarity, justifies actions taken, and discourages counterarguments.

Planned Change Interventions

Problems arising in fundraising lend themselves easily to methods of resolution, or interventions, that have been developed through group dynamics and organizational behavior research. These interventions are described here through selected examples of their application to fundraising. Leaders who thoughtfully consider these examples will discover numerous other situations in which the interventions can be used to improve fundraising participants' functioning.

Interpersonal Communication Interventions

Barriers between people melt away more easily when communication becomes open, often, and optimal. Fears over prospect control and exclusion subside with frank discussion and honest expression that establishes the basis for the equitable assignment of prospects to certain divisions or committees. This type of communication is especially important to staff who are responsible for dollar targets.

Consensus Building Interventions

Differences over fundraising methods and plans—for example, how to run a special event—can be resolved by group decision-making procedures. The process requires carefully defining the problem, clarifying each member's views on the situation, identifying group members similarities and differences, and defining a course of action that everyone finds acceptable. Consensus does not require that all participants agree with the decision, just that all participants can abide by it. Using stand-aside questions such as, "Is there anybody who cannot live with this?" reduces tension and brings about consensus.

Team Building Interventions

Fundraising depends largely on group effort, from governing boards deciding the direction of the agency to small committees planning a cultivation event for prospects. These groups become teams when members function harmoniously with a common understanding of four essential factors: the goals of the group, the role of the group and each of its members, the procedures by which the group will operate, and the relationships necessary for completing tasks. Teams' effectiveness grows through the establishment of mutual trust and support, recognition of people's differences, use of their distinct talents and skills, and employment of leadership and conflict resolution techniques. Development officers skilled in these factors enhance their own effectiveness by helping staff and volunteers learn and apply them.

Self-Managed Teams Interventions

Following team-building activities, leaders have an opportunity to achieve more productivity by creating a climate and process in which participants take on greater management responsibility for the success of their projects or programs. Similar strategies go by names such as *quality circles, semiautonomous work groups,* and *natural work groups.* As preparation for developing self-managed teams, leaders must adopt a facilitative leadership style, one that encourages team members to set personal goals and reinforcements aligned with the tasks at hand (Manz, Muto, and Sims, 1990). Self-managed teams acquire power from managers to control team activities within organizational guidelines for values, standards, and goals for successful performance. Volunteer groups respond well to working in self-managed teams, particularly in small agencies where few staff are available. Special events are also an opportunity for this type of intervention.

Problem-Solving Processes Interventions

While problem solving is one of the tasks typically required of managers (Drucker, 1990), involving those affected by the difficulty in the problem-solving process makes the solution more effective and permanent (Fox, 1987). Again, the situation calls for facilitative behavior by the person leading the discussion. Starting with a careful group review of all aspects of the problem, the facilitator tries for an acceptable problem definition. This essential step in group consensus making prevents runaway debates on unrelated issues. Next, the group brainstorms solutions. Finally, it achieves consensus on the best solution, which is then applied. The group also arranges for periodic assessments of the solution's effectiveness. Problems at all levels of fundraising and other organizational operations including board controversies, morale difficulties in campaigns, personnel and leadership concerns, and interdepartmental squabbles respond well to this process.

Conflict Resolution Interventions

Conflict in organizations can be creative; the tension causes awareness of problems and gives participants opportunities to express their concerns, frustrations, and values. Without resolution, however, conflict disrupts activities and entire organizations. Emotional attitudes and perceptions about interpersonal relationships form the basis of most conflicts. To bring about resolution, a leader defines the relationships of the parties involved, works to remove blockages in the relationships, defines the parties' interdependencies, identifies the problem and the resources available for help, then begins a problem-solving process similar to that cited above but involving only the parties to the conflict. This intervention works well with conflicts among any persons involved in nonprofit agencies—board members, volunteer leaders, staff, and volunteers.

Role Negotiation, Job Enlargement, and Job Enrichment Interventions

These interventions deal with individuals' tasks, opportunities, and responsibilities in an effort to remove job dissatisfaction and align individuals' personal goals with the larger entity. Role negotiation elicits what individuals feel that they can do best, like to do, and want to do. While these desires may not be realizable in the specific task environment, airing the grievances reduces tension and opens up related solutions, such as reassignment, transfer, or job alteration. Job enlargement grants more scope or assigns more content to a position. Job enrichment provides greater decision-making authority and responsibility in an occupation. These interventions make incremental alterations that can add up to major planned change when conducted throughout an organization. The climate generated by these actions tells participants that leaders feel concerned about their welfare, and thus their morale increases.

Productivity Improvement Interventions

A central challenge for strategic managers lies in increasing the productivity of fundraising programs and other organizational operations. Drucker (1992) insists that productivity comes about only through an intervention that develops a partnership between the responsible worker and the organization. Nothing else will work. He advocates that leaders analyze work in the knowledge and service sectors by seeking answers to three questions. The first asks, What is the task to be accomplished? Redefining each task and eliminating unnecessary steps easily increases output. Many fundraising jobs contain activities quite peripheral to the central task of requesting funds from prospects. The second question asks, What do we pay for in terms of the value the job is supposed to add? Answers to this question lead to restructuring jobs to focus on the payoff for the development department. The third question asks, What works? The answer requires organizational processes to be analyzed step by step and operation by operation. Inefficiencies such as cumbersome funding reports with inadequate control data that arise from unquestioned habit or tradition give way to productive practices. Drucker advocates that leaders undertake this intervention every three to five years or whenever significant organizational changes occur in an organization.

Conclusion

Strategic management principles apply to fundraising as much as to any other organizational activity. The fundamental activity of fundraising provides resources to improve the quality of human life. The fact that human needs change is the rationale for organizational change. The dynamic environment of fundraising requires prompt reactions to meet new challenges. No single change strategy applies in all situations; therefore, leadership judgment must be used in making alterations. Fundraising demands skilled leaders who recognize the different leadership styles appropriate to varied situations. Quality leadership's underlying rationale, respect for the value of human beings, aligns with the ultimate purpose for which all nonprofit funds are raised. However, nonprofit organizations do not always model good human relations in their structure and management, thus reducing organizational effectiveness and making planned change necessary. When managers become leaders and leaders institute effective operating principles, organizations become ready to face their many external challenges. The nature and demands of these new circumstances are examined in Part Three.

Part Three

---◼---

CRITICAL
CHALLENGES
AND
OPPORTUNITIES

Changes in organizational environment and size have profound effects on fundraising practices. The first three chapters in this section take a conceptual and pragmatic view of organizational responses to shifting financial opportunities, ongoing evolution (in smaller agencies), and increasing complexity (in large organizations). The final chapter (Chapter Ten) offers an integrative perspective on the topics discussed in this book and outlines expectations for the future of fundraising.

Variations in economic and demographic conditions and changes in an organization's stakeholders and values require nonprofit leaders to consider new fundraising means and sources. Organizational responses to change have implications for both internal strategies and external relationships.

Small and middle-sized agencies depend proportionately more on fundraising and government grants than larger organizations, yet they have more limited personnel and financial resources. Therefore, the leadership styles, ambitions, and abilities of smaller agencies' chief executives have a greater influence on agency survival and growth. The requirements and hazards of expansion to achieve stability affect smaller organizations and demand that they be adaptable to changing conditions.

Large organizations face the complexities of managing multiple functions and varied operational sites. This complexity raises issues of centralization, decentralization, coordination, and control. The impact of location, technology, professionalism, culture, and leadership affects the structure and outcomes of large organizations' fundraising.

Seven

◼

Responding
to Change
and
Increased
Competition

An understanding of a nonprofit's ever-changing environment becomes even more critical when the organization seeks financial resources. The challenge for charitable agencies lies in correctly assessing which factors will be essential to organizational maintenance and growth and which strategies can be employed to cope with changes. Agencies must also learn how to recognize and accommodate the effects of these new factors and strategies on their organizations. To illustrate ways to meet this challenge, this chapter examines typical changes in market resources, responses to these changes, and the organizational effects these responses produce when they are used.

Changes in Market Resources

Nonprofit agencies are quite vulnerable to, but not necessarily aware of, transitions in their environments in terms of market resources. These changes can appear overnight if funders suddenly shift their attention to other needs, or can materialize slowly if the public develops a greater interest in different human needs. Economic conditions affect donor decisions, population shifts upset constituency bases, actions of other organizations disrupt anticipated market resources, and catastrophic events direct attention away from local concerns. Many of these changes also lead to increased human needs, calling for further service delivery by the nonprofit sector.

Economic Shifts

The recession of the early 1990s brought immediate problems of declining revenues and staff layoffs to nonprofit organizations (Moore, 1991). Large national agencies such as the American Red Cross and the Muscular Dystrophy Association reduced personnel costs by dismissing employees and not filling vacancies. Lower revenues decreased governmental support for charitable and educational institutions. Smaller agencies with less latitude for personnel cuts responded by diminishing services. The national economic condition revealed other problems affecting nonprofit resources. The debt burden of individuals with overloaded credit cards and the bonded indebtedness of corporations reduced the funds available for gifts and grants. The economic policies of the 1980s left many middle-income families with less disposable income and increased the importance of major donors. The paucity of U.S. citizens' personal savings gave them little help in meeting the recessionary difficulties of the 1990s, and constricted many individuals' spending and giving decisions, even though total giving increased.

The recession increased the social problems demanding attention and resources. Homeless families and individuals, acute low-income housing shortage, and rising crime rates have become center-stage issues. Lower tax revenues from reduced business activity compound these difficulties, putting more pressure on charitable donations to supply essential services. During economic downturns, reduced corporate earnings limit both direct contributions and additions to company foundations; the foundation shortfall has a long-term effect on available funds. Additionally, the wave of corporate mergers and acquisitions in the 1980s eliminated numerous corporate contribution programs, with no corresponding increase in giving by the acquiring firms. Some firms' home offices moved, leaving their former communities with little call on corporate largess. These economic shifts demonstrate the wide scope of recent changes in market and governmental resources and the subsequent impact on nonprofit organizations.

Population Variations

The composition of the nation's population varies much more slowly than national or regional economies. Yet the slow cumulative effects take on sudden meanings at the moment when agencies realize what has taken place. For example, some thirty to forty years after their birth during the baby boom of the 1950s and 1960s, those now aging baby boomers are entering their most productive income period and spending less on household expenditures. They can open a vast new market for fundraising, particularly after the return of economic good times. Counterbalancing this opportunity is the pessimistic outlook for the postboomers, who are not expected to better or even match their parents' income levels. This prediction arises out of the loss of middle-income jobs due to business restructuring and the postindustrial swing to a service-dominated economy. Middle-manager positions and high-wage occupations face severe reductions caused by technological innovations, overseas employment trends, new managerial practices, and global competition. The effects of these changes will increase and cause reduced fundraising markets.

The increase in women and minorities in the work force presents both problems and opportunities. Typically, they occupy service and other low-skilled jobs, which pay less than manufacturing and professional occupations. National wage surveys show women earning only seventy cents for every dollar men get. Increased costs of clothing, child care, and transportation associated with working outside the home eat into take-home pay. The time and energy consumed by working and commuting detracts people's attention from the client needs of nonprofit organizations and restricts volunteer involvement, particularly in households where both adults work.

Despite their lower wages, women gave a remarkable $28.3 billion in 1991 (Hodgkinson, Weitzman, Noga, and Gorski, 1992). This sum represented a 2.4 percent increase over their 1989 gifts, even during a recessionary economy. At the same time, men decreased their giving 21.7 percent, to $33.5 billion. These data do not include gifts from families with incomes over $200,000, who are the prime source for major gifts. Women own 60 percent of U.S. wealth and are giving an increasing number of large gifts. They are also exercising greater independence in their giving decisions, moving away from male advisors, and funding needs of direct interest to themselves.

Minorities have lower average incomes than whites, but as growing percentages of the population, they are becoming a more significant market. Black households making contributions increased from 61 percent in 1989 to 64 percent in 1991 (Hodgkinson, Weitzman, Noga, and Gorski, 1992). While fewer minority households overall give to charity, blacks gave the highest percentage of household income (2.7 percent), compared with whites (2.2 percent) and Hispanics (2.1 percent).

The large influx of immigrants during the late 1980s and early 1990s exacerbated the demand for services, especially on the East and West Coasts adjacent to ports of entry. New agencies sprang up to meet these needs. Foundations and corporations responded with coordinated giving programs encompassing both new and existing agencies. The drain this kind of giving activity may put on private funding sources was noted by Law and Hazenfeld (1989) in their study of earlier refugee resettlement services. Additionally, immigrant populations often have little understanding of philanthropy and the importance of giving when they are financially able. However, many immigrant organizations recognize the value of fundraising and encourage their constituents to participate.

Organizational Changes

Nonprofit charitable organizations occupy a crowded fundraising and fund giving environment with other organizations:

governments, businesses, other nonprofits, and funders. The total nonprofit sector contained 1,100,000 organizations in 1991 (Internal Revenue Service, 1992, p. 35). Just in the charitable sector (counting organizations listed on the Internal Revenue Service Master File), the net growth from 1990 to 1991 was 5.4 percent, bringing the number of nonprofit institutions, excluding churches, to 516,564.

The most dramatic market resource change affecting many nonreligious nonprofit organizations is the steep decline in federal funding along with the modification of federal policies to encourage private initiative. As a result of these changes, the many nonprofit agencies spawned during the Great Society programs of the 1960s have had to move into the private giving arena to survive. State governments received additional burdens of federally mandated programs and passed portions of them on to county and city governments. Diminished tax revenues at all levels are currently compounding the financial shortfall for nonprofit agencies.

Changes in tax laws have a profound effect on charitable giving. Scala (1990b) reports that studies show a loss of $4 billion a year in donations that would have been given if the 1986 Tax Reform Act had not been passed. The act eliminated charitable deductions for nonitemizers and severely reduced the volume of gifts of appreciated property.

Competition from for-profit organizations presents a serious problem to nonprofit agencies. Pifer (1987) notes that the trend toward privatization of human service delivery systems weakens the bond between private donors and charities. This for-profit trend is being stimulated through governmental regulation and financial incentives. Private firms competing with charitable counterparts include art galleries, clinics, fitness centers, rest homes, retirement homes, schools, and training services. Because for-profit firms seek to maximize their income, they search for clients who are most able to pay and for whom successful treatment is more likely. This practice usurps affluent clients, leaving only the poor and low-income clients to the nonprofit agencies (Lewis, 1989), and further weakens nonprofit organizations' fee and donation base.

Another source of competition for market resources is

the growing number of nonprofit organizations that are not charitable and fall into Internal Revenue Service classification 501(c)(4). Trade associations and similar groups recognize the advantages of establishing charitable foundations to enhance their public images, reduce operating costs, and create new programs for their members without increasing dues (Bullock, 1988). Even the National Society of Fund Raising Executives conducts fundraising campaigns for its foundation. Other groups, such as advocacy, fraternal, civic, and social organizations, find this an attractive (and deductible) means for their members to help financially. Membership status and privileges become an important incentive for contributions.

In addition, the availability of market resources to charitable nonprofit agencies comes under pressure because of some organizations' unacceptable practices. Publicity about exorbitant fees charged by commercial fundraising firms and low percentages of revenues turned over to client organizations undermines public confidence in legitimate fundraising programs. A report on charitable contributions by the California attorney general's office shows that in 1990 only one-third of the $94 million collected by 165 commercial fundraisers registered in California actually went to charities ("Institute, Firms Accused of Fund-Raising Fraud," 1992, p. A22). The United Way of America suffered serious loss of credibility and diminished dues from local members after the disclosure of excessive salary payments to top executives and the funneling of purchases to for-profit organizations controlled by management (Bailey and Millar, 1992). Such scandals reverberate throughout charitable constituencies, creating doubts and resistance to giving.

Value and Attitude Shifts

Market resources succumb to the beliefs and feelings of constituent groups. Dunn (1988) asserts that donors have a "show me" syndrome; they want specific benefits and demonstrated results from their gifts. Harvey and McCrohan (1990) echo this view, declaring that donors increasingly base their giving on enlightened self-interest rather than "blind altruism," and further, that donors have both a high degree of skepticism and a

lack of understanding about the methods and purposes of philanthropy and fundraising. These views show up, for example,
in widespread public reluctance to support government payments to the welfare system. These public views then encourage
political candidates and leaders to propose restrictions and
funding reductions. Media attention to welfare problems also
makes fundraising difficult for human service programs.

Changing life-styles that arise from variations in values
and attitudes influence market resources. The widely acknowledged complexity of modern life in the last decades of the twentieth century limits the time people have for volunteering, a
primary method for securing new donors. In households with
two working adults, the problems of child care, commuting, and
high housing costs drain time, energy, and funds that could otherwise be available for support of charitable agencies (Wolpert,
1988). In 1991, the number of volunteers declined by 4 percent
compared to 1989 figures, but the average hours volunteered
per week increased slightly (Hodgkinson, Weitzman, Noga, and
Gorski, 1992).

The time pressures associated with complexity create a
short-term perspective that drives individuals to view tasks as
short term also. On the one hand, this view simply causes people
to acquire household labor-saving devices. On the other hand,
it distorts people's perceptions about the need to save money
(reservoirs for future donations), the effectiveness of gifts
devoted to long-term needs, and the slow progress on social
problems.

Other current life-style pressures breed new trends that
affect market resources. A popular observer of this flux, Faith
Popcorn (1991), cites several trends that are worthy of note by
nonprofit organization managers. Many working women and
men are questioning their personal and career goals and opting
for satisfaction from simpler living. This alteration in views suggests that more time will be available for volunteering but that
less income will limit giving. Individuals' desire to protect themselves from the harsh, unpredictable realities of the outside
world creates a "cocooning" mentality that causes individuals to
insulate themselves from the very problems that nonprofits are
trying to bring to their attention. However, Popcorn also be-

lieves that computers have created a sterile era and that people desire to make personal statements to react against this sterility, thus giving nonprofit agencies an opportunity to involve these individuals. Analyzing the baby boomers, she finds them nostalgic for their carefree childhood, seeking comfort in familiar pursuits and products of their youth. Agencies concerned with youth, education, outdoor environments, and recreation can take advantage of this trend.

The effects of market resources changes do not apply uniformly to all nonprofit organizations. Each agency must make its own analysis of the factors encountered or likely to occur. Disastrous futures attend those that do not actively scan the environment on a regular basis. Moreover, no single or collective group of responses to these changes can be prescribed; Follett's *law of the situation* applies wherein all the facts are observed objectively to arrive at decisions (Metcalf and Urwick, [1941] 1960).

Organizational Strategies for Change

Nonprofit organizations use a variety of strategies to respond to market resources challenges. Their efforts fall into two classes: strategies that the organizations can initiate themselves and strategies that require significant relationships with other organizations. This section deals with self-initiated strategies; the next section describes interorganizational approaches.

The basic processes for considering the viability of both new and old strategies involve the strategic planning, organizing, and managing concepts presented in earlier chapters. Therefore, the discussion in this section assumes that the proven principles and practices of fundraising examined earlier are available to an organization at the time a shortfall occurs in available financial resources. The questions then become, What are the different options available to the strategically managed and structured organization? What are the positive and negative aspects of each of those options? What is their specific impact on the instigating agency?

The starting place for change is knowledge of the organization's current status. Weisbord (1987) emphasizes the importance of an organization's taking a "snapshot" of its existing conditions, assembling reliable data, and allowing the affected members of the workforce to be partners in developing solutions. Without this partnership, proposed changes will not find the acceptance necessary for enduring results. A helpful process for getting the necessary snapshot is a management audit. This audit resembles the SWOT analysis (strengths, weaknesses, opportunities, and threats) that takes place in an intensive strategic planning process, but it concentrates on managerial competencies and readiness that will be called into play by new circumstances (Brinkerhoff, 1984). The audit can range from a full-scale detailed review of these competencies down to a limited analysis of the managerial functions that will affect the new activities.

The array of strategies cited in this section gives nonprofit organizations multiple solutions to their resource needs. Most of these solutions will require the charitable agencies to make philosophical adjustments in their values and operations and to instigate different activities, shift financial burdens, and accommodate outside influences.

Milofsky and Romo (1988) stress the importance of conducting diverse activities and gaining support from many sources to facilitate the organization's survival in uncertain times. Their research demonstrates a remarkable flexibility on the part of neighborhood-based organizations to shift to new resources when government funding dwindles. Kramer (1990) also supports diversification, suggesting that nonprofit agencies seek supplemental funds by instituting one or more of the strategies reviewed below. (Options related specifically to fundraising are discussed in Chapter Four.)

Business Ventures

The pressures and incentives on nonprofit agencies to start business ventures come from many sources. Corporate executives serving on nonprofit boards see such activities as extending their personal economic philosophy, producing needed income, and reducing demands on themselves for contributions. Foundation administrators follow a similar line of thinking because many creators and trustees of foundations have strong business orientations. The Foundation Center advocates this direction (Skloot, 1988).

When staff leaders facing tight budgets and increased service demands turn to profit-making ventures, they encounter such issues as tax problems and acquiring the necessary experience, financing, and marketing. Barsook (1987) asserts that serious commitment to venturing by the highest administrative level is an absolute must, otherwise the effort, funds, personnel, and facilities will not be available in the quantity and times needed.

Small business operators have complained that nonprofit organizations that do not pay taxes on their business enterprises have an unfair advantage. With the support of the Small Business Administration of the federal government, these firms beseech Congress to rectify this perceived disadvantage. Fortunately, continual lobbying by the INDEPENDENT SECTOR offsets this threat, which could seriously affect the net income that nonprofit organizations strive to produce.

The data fueling this debate are incomplete to the extent that foundations are funding research studies to shed more light on the controversy (Landy, 1992). Preliminary investigations of Internal Revenue Service (IRS) data derived from the financial reports (IRS Form 990) that nonprofit organizations are required to file show that, between 1982 and 1987, the percentage of revenues derived from business activities increased for the vast majority of nonprofit categories. Income from business ventures increased 20 percent for health services agencies and more than 14 percent for religious and educational institutions, yet declined 2.5 percent for scientific and technical research entities.

The weapon that small businesses hope to inflict on nonprofit agencies consists of stricter enforcement of the unrelated business income tax. The definition of unrelated business income receives continual interpretation, but in general, it means income from products or services sold that have no relation to the mission and purpose for which the organization's tax exemption was granted. For example, libraries can sell unwanted purchased or donated books without incurring unrelated business income taxation, because the books are educational in value and are irrefutably related to library purposes and holdings. Girl Scout cookies have been sold for over sixty years without a business challenge. Girl Scouts of America has consistently promoted the importance of the sales as a means for girls to learn goal setting, money handling, marketing, public relations, and leadership. Business appears quite reluctant to attack this well-recognized enterprise.

Despite these examples, it is customarily very difficult to establish a charitable purpose for an obvious for-profit enterprise. However, the difficulty can be resolved simply, according to Skloot (1988), by operating the activity as a profit-making venture and paying taxes. In this way, problems of administrative confusion, misalignment of mission, and personnel diversions are forestalled, not to mention an IRS audit.

Cause-Related Marketing

Cause-related marketing has many allures for nonprofit organizations, who use this device to tap new sources and obtain wider visibility for espoused causes. Cause-related marketing is particularly attractive when agencies have insufficient donor bases. According to its proponents, it provides a mutually beneficial relationship between a corporation and a nonprofit organization in which the former pursues marketing and promotional objectives while the latter seeks fundraising and public relations objectives (Sheridan Associates and Zimmerman Associates, 1988). Typical examples include programs involving donations for credit card use, coupon redemption for retail consumer products, and concurrent sponsorship of special events such as walkathons, cultural performances, or restoration projects. A notable example of such a concurrently sponsored special event was the Statue of Liberty restoration, one of the first of these ventures featuring a credit card tie in.

A small percentage of the revenues generated by product

sales or service fees go to the participating nonprofit organizations. Sponsoring nonprofits generally feel that such programs are indeed beneficial but not as major sources of promotion or income. Income generated for nonprofit organizations typically represents less than 10 percent of total revenues. Corporate marketers have no doubt about the efficacy of these promotions to move products and demonstrate corporate interest in the public sector, resulting in good advertising and image enhancement (Levine, 1986).

Gurin (1991) has sounded a strong note of caution about the wisdom of making a "philanthropic cause dependent in a substantial way on consumer acceptance of a product or service which could trivialize and demean the cause" (p. 76). He felt that businesses get enough value from nonprofit organizations' creating a better social environment without having to use the nonprofits' causes for profits. Moreover, these ventures tend to relieve volunteer leadership from engaging in traditional fundraising methods. They also invite scrutiny by the IRS, seeking to tax unrelated business income.

Pop Concerts

In another form of cause-related marketing, entertainment entrepreneurs have found concerts and special events a fertile field for raising money for charity. While benefit performances such as BandAid, Hands Across America, and USA for Africa have often taken in large sums of money, their greatest success appears to lie in raising public consciousness of areas in which help is needed (Galant, 1987). Additionally, they broaden the philanthropic base by reaching new, younger donors who have not previously been givers. Unfortunately, as organizations, these promotions do not have the durability of the more staid relief organizations.

Corporate Sponsorships

Corporate sponsorships of public events conducted by nonprofit organizations are showing a remarkable increase in their numbers and the media coverage they can command. University and college championship football contests are a prime example. The large sums paid to charities and the blatant publicity of corporate products and sponsorship concerns the Internal Revenue Service ("Bored by the Bowl Games?" 1992), which contends that many corporate payments have little to do with the tax-exempt functions of the nonprofit organizations, are not charitable contributions, and constitute pay for advertising privileges. Recent IRS rulings would allow nonprofit organizations to acknowledge corporate sponsorships without paying taxes on fees received, provided such acknowledgments are not so profuse as to appear to be paid advertisements for products and services (Williams, 1993). However, the exact interpretation of these rulings will continue for several years.

Contracting for Services

Direct contracting for provision of human services by governments has now become standard practice, and nonprofit organizations need to watch the direction the practice will take. Will it become a cooperative partnership model, or a competitive market model? When competitive bidding severely reduces costs, the quality of service faces diminishing standards. Also in the past decade, nonprofit organizations themselves, particularly human service agencies, have increased their contracting with other agencies to perform the direct services that the original agency would ordinarily provide (Kettner and Martin, 1990). This trend gives organizations the flexibility to meet changes in demand, determine precise costs, and retain continuity of existing structures and personnel. However, the practice raises serious questions about stable relations with donors, who tend to expect donee organizations to render services directly to deserving clients.

Increasing Fees

Agency attempts to increase revenues by increasing fees receive mixed support. Modest increases show the best result because clients and patrons can more readily absorb small costs. Sharp increases typically lead to declining patronage of the nonprofit organization during the first year of the increase, but subsequent years produce reasonable recovery. Meanwhile, total revenues remain steady or show an increase. Higher education institutions, especially private schools, can raise tuition precipitously each year but maintain enrollments due to the strong demand for their services from parents and students and the availability of scholarship funds.

Imposing Fees

Setting fees for previously free services produces sudden but usually temporary drops in numbers of clients and patrons. Charges for admission to or use of nature preserves, botanical gardens, parks, public medical clinics, meals for homeless persons, meeting rooms in churches and other nonprofit facilities cause usage declines. British museums went through this trauma, but regained admission levels gradually ("Making Money out of Museums," 1991).

Reward Strategies

As more research on donor behavior becomes available through scholarly publications and news reports, development staff are adjusting their appeals to fit donor interests. Dunn (1988) recommends using "tangible rewards" to meet widespread donor desires for specific benefits (p. 10). These tangible items range from the thank-you gifts so extensively marketed by public television stations to donor recognition plaques, honors, and recognition events. An interesting aspect of the trend toward appropriate rewards is the intangible reward that donors get when they know their donations have been used effectively. Harvey and McCrohan (1990) report that donors give significantly more funds when informed that efficiency, defined in terms of amounts going directly to clients, rises above 60 percent.

Constituency Shift Strategies

Emerging social problems challenge nonprofit organizations to shift program emphases to meet developing needs. Girl Scouts of America accommodates the changing diversity of the nation's population by recruiting girls from disadvantaged neighborhoods with programs addressing these girls' needs to cope with teenage pregnancy, drug dealing, and high crime rates (Espinosa, 1992). The agency's new directions attract interest and additional support from United Ways and foundations across the nation, thus increasing its total income.

The joining of Big Brothers with Big Sisters and Boys Clubs with Girls Clubs reflects a constituency shift and accommodates changing patterns of youthful relationships and needs. YMCAs across the country now include women in their programs in response to women's needs for physical fitness programs and facilities. Seniors' cardiac rehabilitation programs, some undertaken jointly with local private hospitals, are on the increase at YMCAs, despite the "Young" in the agency name. The seniors benefit from the programs, and the agency benefits because the seniors are promising candidates for major and planned gifts. Museums in urban centers are altering their exhibits and collections to attract and serve a potential clientele of increasing ethnic diversity.

An interesting effect of these agency shifts and mergers is that the composition of board, staff, and volunteer groups are changing to reflect the new constituents. Personnel adjustments do not come easily unless leaders recognize and intervene in the difficulties that are inherent when some individuals must give up power and position to accommodate others. Experience has shown, however, that agencies making these adaptations emerge stronger and better able to survive ensuing environmental problems. Several community foundations have gone successfully through this transition by rotating off older white male board members and recruiting younger individuals of means who reflect the ethnic and gender characteristics of their local areas. The resulting diversity has provided greater rapport with community needs and potential donors.

Commercial Services to Aid Fundraising

The increase in for-profit firms that sell fundraising services to nonprofit agencies is demonstrated by the large number of these vendors who exhibit their wares at conferences held by the

Association for Healthcare Philanthropy, the Council for Advancement and Support of Education, and the National Society of Fund Raising Executives. These firms offer computerized data management services to nonprofits and also undertake such tasks as telemarketing and studying prospects and demographics. The nonpayment of pledges continues to plague nonprofit organizations. Addressing this problem, commercial organizations offer collection services that emphasize soft-sell direct marketing techniques to redeem pledges and maintain links between donors and agencies ("Services Take Aim at Uncollected Pledge Money," 1991).

Advertising for Donations

The need to broaden their base of support has led to nonprofit organizations' renewed interest in advertising to secure donors outside traditional constituencies. Over several decades, Pomona College featured, with apparent success, its planned giving programs in financial journals and newspapers. Now, other colleges and nonprofit organizations are finding this a cost-effective strategy for major gifts as well as planned giving (Paustian, 1985). The advertisements describe the charitable institution, its purpose, and generalized needs, along with a brief description of the advantages of giving. Institutional image and name recognition play a crucial role in convincing readers about the safety of funds to be entrusted. This activity may invite questions about an institution's tax-exempt status if the thrust of the advertisements abandons charitable intent in favor of an investment strategy which features financial returns to the donor from planned gifts.

Fundraising advertisements can take many different forms. Free-standing newspaper inserts produce remarkable results for a Chicago charity taking care of homeless children (Hall, 1993a). The inserts pay for themselves, and the donors they attract continue levels of giving that surpass direct mail donors. Program-length television advertisements, or *infomercials*, are being broadcast by large national organizations such as World Vision, Childreach, and Save the Children (Hall, 1993b).

While the cost seems prohibitive at $100 per donor for most charities, the larger ones find that well-done programs bring in about four times the cost to produce and broadcast them. Future production and air time costs, competitors' responses, and results from less expensive commercials will determine the long-term viability of this method of fundraising.

Mailing List Sales

Organizations with sizeable membership and donor lists often receive additional income by renting their mailing lists to other nonprofit agencies. The revenues support list maintenance and additional mailings. The March of Dimes enjoys substantial income from its national list of four million names segmented by donor characteristics obtained from periodic surveys (Grande, 1992). A recent court case determined that selling or renting mailing lists complies with tax-exemption regulations and that the income is not taxable as unrelated business income (Hart, 1990).

Electronic Data Processing

The advent of computers and electronic data processing allows both small and large nonprofit agencies great flexibility to meet rapidly changing environmental demands. Computers give agencies extraordinary ability to research and store information on donors, and then to solicit them, acknowledge their gifts, and track relationships with them. National data bases available from Dialogue and other firms furnish extensive information on organizational donors that can be added to prospect profiles. Statistical models for evaluating prospect and donor potentials through computer analysis are emerging (Lindahl and Winship, 1992; Blanchette, 1993). Constituency lists can be correlated with geodemographic data, household income, past giving habits, and agency involvement to provide estimates of the most likely individual prospects. Several large fundraising consulting firms provide these services; however, their cost can limit their use to larger charities. Through programs to prepare complicated planned gift proposals quickly and accurately, computers have opened this form of fundraising to smaller agencies, without the need for specialized, highly trained staff.

Electronic fund transfers allow donors to make gifts directly from their checking accounts to the donee agency routinely every month or at other regular periods, thus tapping donors' desire for convenient and "painless" giving. Amnesty International reports that almost 20 percent of its twenty thousand monthly "Partners of Conscience" have agreed to automatic transfers from their bank accounts, resulting in nearly 100 percent fulfillment of pledges for this subgroup. Arranging to accept credit cards is another means by which agencies can provide ease of payment and reduce donation processing costs. Knudsen (1985) estimates that more than half of the philanthropic dollars move to nonprofit organizations during the last twenty-five and the first seven days of the calendar year. Agencies should be aware that increases in forms of regular giving throughout the year will decrease this extraordinary flow of year-end gifts. Furthermore, Knudsen sees efficient, computerized fundraising as enabling smaller agencies with less affluent constituencies to survive by asking for five- and ten-dollar gifts.

Interorganizational Strategies

In recognition of the crowded organizational environment with its limited financial resources, nonprofit agencies engage in myriad interorganizational strategies. Their purposes are, first, to ensure their survival, and second, to stabilize and control their dependency on external resources. Financial resources, especially donated funds, are the primary targets of these arrangements among agencies, but acquiring power, sustaining growth, and enhancing autonomy are also important objectives (Scott, 1987). The fundamental arrangement exchanges valued assets such as time, authority, personnel, funds, and information. These transfers take place through the following interorganizational forms (Mars, 1972).

Cooperation

Cooperation involves efforts between voluntary agencies to achieve some mutual goal or mission. AIDS organizations work together to conduct special events such as walkathons to reach the broadest range of participants, gain the most publicity, and secure the most funds possible. Church-related organizations in Washington, D.C., meet regularly to share ideas, promotions, solicitation proposals, and training. Scala (1990a) reports that the development directors of these organizations have discovered the benefits of pooling their skills and resources. Their cooperation results in better relations with funders, more effectiveness in appeals, and more contributions.

Coalitions and Networks

Coalitions and networks are specific forms of cooperation that provide valuable avenues for exchange of information, useful combinations of power and influence, and early warnings of threatening regulations and legislative proposals. The informal nature of the cooperation allows flexibility while achieving additional outreach. New organizations that lack such cooperative arrangements find it difficult to survive adversity. For example, InterAid, a private-sector agency formed to raise funds for Ethiopian famine relief, did not establish cooperative relationships with other relief groups. When faced with a media crisis over alleged misappropriation of funds, InterAid had no reservoir of trust and goodwill among other groups to draw on to sustain its image and fundraising ability (Chapel, 1988).

Alliances and Partnerships

Drucker (1992) suggests that nonprofit organizations such as universities and health-care institutions form alliances and partnerships with businesses that have similar service, research, and product interests. Potential activities in common range from engineering design and product development to biomedical research and pharmaceutical innovations. Profitable royalties can result from patents obtained by these charitable institutions while interchanges of personnel enrich all alliance members. Certainly, the competitive challenge at home and abroad drives corporations to search for innovations and to support research at universities and nonprofit institutes. A potential hazard is that the nonprofit organization may lose autonomy and impartiality with respect to research subjects and findings. Also, governments' emerging interest in actively fostering economic growth and international competitiveness will influence the future scope of these arrangements.

Coordination

Coordination requires voluntary agencies to relate to each other through some other party for the purposes of sharing information, setting standards of behavior, or promoting their common interests. The rise of statewide trade associations for nonprofits illustrates one method of coordination. Trade associations can present members' common views to legislatures, establish codes of ethical conduct, and provide group health benefits, discounts on services, credit unions, and similar group services. Trade associations for nonprofit organizations are differentiated by the geographic areas they cover and by such fields of interest as health, education, social services, and youth. When agencies coordinate their efforts through these associations, they reduce costs, coalesce political power and influence, and advance the image of the assembled agencies.

Integration

Integration includes the formal transfer of administrative, funding, or programmatic functions from one agency to another. The long-time example in fundraising is the United Way's local workplace campaigns on behalf of member agencies. Other examples are the geographically based associations independent colleges and universities have formed to solicit corporations and foundations. The United Negro College Fund, for example, works on behalf of black colleges located principally in the Southeast.

Newer and nontraditional nonprofit organizations fought to gain acceptance in integrated structures such as United Way with little effect until they formed their own group, the Independent Charities of America Federation, to push for the inclusion of group members in workplace campaigns in federal and state governmental offices. A recent change of workplace solicitation programs permits donors to designate recipient agencies, whether or not the agencies are formally included in the allocation of funds. Agencies encourage their members to use these donor option policies to augment the agencies' receipt of funds.

In recent years, the proliferation of environmental organizations led to the establishment of the Environmental Federation of America, now known as Earth Share. It raises funds through Combined Federal Campaigns and other governmental office campaigns for distribution to its participating agencies. Earth Share grew out of pioneering efforts led by the Environmental Federation of California in 1982, and other statewide associations continue to come into existence (Blauner, 1992).

Even governmental agencies use their offices to raise funds for charitable organizations. California income tax returns provide space for taxpayers to make contributions to a variety of charitable causes. The property tax bills for Alameda County, California, have forms for the public to send voluntary contributions to the County Art Commission, which makes grants to arts organizations.

Shared facilities appeal to many new agencies. For example, the Oakland, California, organization A Central Place provides space, office equipment, answering service, and a receptionist to agencies who can then share administrative functions at a fraction of the cost of providing the same services in separate locations. The savings permit over twenty struggling small agencies to concentrate on service delivery and fundraising.

The National Association for the Exchange of Industrial

Resources (1992) solicits corporations for donations of new and excess inventories, which are then redistributed to the nonprofit agencies and public schools that are association members. These organizations pay only annual membership dues and costs of shipping and handling for the goods they receive.

Mergers and acquisitions force a complete integration of functions and services in their newly joined agencies. While some of these unions are voluntary, they occur principally as a result of pressure from large organizational funding sources. Foundation and corporate giving programs administrators see many duplications by agencies in grants proposals. With finite amounts of money to disperse, these program officers suggest cost savings through mergers or acquisitions in order to eliminate duplicate services, administrative functions, and fundraising efforts.

Change Strategies' Effects

When nonprofit organizations address market resources changes by instigating new strategies such as those cited in this chapter, the strategies themselves affect the organizations in two crucial areas. First, the organizations shift toward more commercial and businesslike conduct. Second, they experience diminished agency autonomy as a result of relating to other organizations. Both effects have far-reaching implications for organizational image, culture, values, governance, management, and clients.

Commercial Conduct

When charitable organizations choose commercial ventures to raise funds, that choice raises serious questions about organizational image, philosophy, and mission. Will these business activities diminish charitable images and affect fundraising? Will the skills and values necessary for successful profit ventures "corrupt" volunteers and staff members? Will clients suffer from these commercial practices? Steckel (1989), a strong advocate of for-profit activities for nonprofits, readily admits change will not come easily. He points out that people are being asked "to accept some fundamental changes in the way their organizations run, and change is frightening. The greatest fear in organizations that turn to enterprise is that quality will be sacrificed for money" (pp. 177–78).

Venturing still needs to prove that it is compatible with the public image of charitable organizations. Different values about profits, different methods of operation, and bottom-line thinking can conflict with a human service perspective. Perlmutter and Adams (1990) state that "profit-making ventures by voluntary agencies pose new questions and have unclear short- and long-term consequences for the 'voluntary' status" of social welfare agencies. Such ventures, they say, affect "the unique character and mission of the social welfare enterprise itself" (p. 1). Due to their long history of providing nonprofit services, charitable agencies in other fields, such as education, health, environmental protection, arts and culture, and international affairs, have similar transitional problems.

The composition of an agency's governing body requires adjustment to provide the experience and judgment that for-profit enterprises demand. Acceptance of persons with the appropriate qualities and values proves difficult for traditional boards. Political infighting occurs and may hamstring initial undertakings. However, the increasing reliance on recruiting employed adults for leadership and professional services in these ventures is opening agencies to an infusion of business thinking. These individuals seek to use their knowledge and talents developed in for-profit organizations to satisfy their personal motives for volunteering. They gravitate naturally to areas where they can excel. Their leadership interests propel them into board memberships where their values impact governance through policy and managerial decisions. The successful integration of these volunteers requires top volunteer and staff leadership to exercise considerable interpersonal skill.

Board members with traditional nonprofit values find themselves exhorted to alter their thinking and accept the new strategies. In view of the current reduced availability of funds, Lant (1988) urges boards to change the way they do business, and he laments that some board members have not changed with the times and that their attitudes are undermining organizations. However, internal conflicts over the new business orientation also keep alive healthy organizational debate on the philosophy behind philanthropy and on the values of charitable organizations.

Management also has to adjust. To plan and launch new ventures, top management requires entrepreneurial attitudes and abilities. The chief executive officer does not have to be an entrepreneurial type, but commitment by top leadership to undertake the new enterprises is absolutely essential. Steckel (1989) recommends Fayol's principle ([1916], 1949) of *separation of functions*. Organizational leadership can set up a "department of enterprise" to staff and conduct the new for-profit activities. Such an enclave provides the for-profit staff with freedom of action and protection from uncommitted leaders. It also allows the acquisition of staff with the requisite motivations and skills. The department of enterprise usually exists alongside the fundraising department, except in small organizations where the chief executive officer can handle the two areas together.

Not all nonprofit managers are devoid of entrepreneurial motivations. Young (1986) in his landmark studies of nonprofit staff executives clearly identifies numerous entrepreneurs spread throughout the nonprofit sector. In analyzing their activities, he finds a wide spectrum of motivations, such as the pursuit of income, power, autonomy, security, professional accomplishment, creative achievement, strong beliefs, or simply self-identity. Thus, he conjectures that nonprofit organizations can be validly described with a behavioral theory of conduct rather than a conventional maximizing theory. The latter describes enhancing routine, day-to-day activities within accepted rules, technical constraints, and traditional goals, while the former depicts entrepreneurial actions.

Donor reactions to changed organizational strategies vary widely. When donor-supported programs receive additional funds from other sources, these funds can validate the programs and justify committed persons' continued giving. However, some donors with strong convictions about the value of philanthropy can resent or only reluctantly accept the intrusion of profit-making activities to support agency programs. Also, individuals with low commitment often feel that their contributions are of diminishing importance and see other forms of agency income as an excuse to stop giving. Fundraising executives face the challenge of reenforcing the case for their organizations' use of for-profit activities, and communicating this case effectively. Another tactic to encourage donor approval is volunteer leaders' endorsement of or participation in the new activities.

When agencies become more businesslike, clients feel the effects directly. Fee increases and reduction or elimination of free services force individuals and families with marginal resources to reduce their use of or even abandon the needed services. As a result, the client base shifts to a more affluent constituency. This shift puts original organizational purposes and goals in question, engendering confusion and conflict among leaders and donors. Dedicated staff may also take exception to new practices which undermine staff devotion to serving client needs regardless of clients' economic circumstances.

Interorganizational Demands

In view of the complexity of the nonprofit sector, individual charitable organizations rarely find themselves devoid of relationships with other organizations. The challenge for nonprofit leaders and staff lies in managing those relationships to maximize resource acquisition and reduce dependency while constraining the costs and time expended.

The most obvious effect of the interorganizational strategies described earlier in this chapter is that collaborating organizations must accept some restrictions and obligations. For example, when organizations participate in United Way allocations, they surrender their freedom to solicit corporations and corporate employees and to conduct general fundraising campaigns during United Way solicitations. Other integrated efforts impose similar restrictions. Conforming to the administrative rules and regulations of the overarching agency or group requires adjustments in member organizations' accounting and reporting, along with an adherence to prescribed accountability measures.

In addition, logical prospects for a given organization can cite their donations to the collective group to refuse further gifts to the individual agency. Even a board member who has "social credits" with a prospect faces weakened leverage. Agencies' reduced fundraising potential must be carefully weighed against the benefits to be gained from the integrated approach before committing to this path.

Their organizations' dependency on a group solicitation has given numerous boards an excuse to avoid fundraising. This condition became painfully obvious when United Ways were unable to meet rising financial needs from existing agency members while admitting new organizations to membership. For existing member agencies, the lack of volunteer and staff experience with fundraising forced retrenchment, reassessment of board responsibilities, and subsequent recruitment of new board members willing and able to raise funds. These changes put pressure on board members who claimed they were not enlisted to fundraise; they had to reevaluate their positions or resign.

The restraints imposed by other joint efforts also affect participating organizations' missions and goals. One agency's plans to initiate new services with attendant costs run into scrutiny by other agencies if funds are expected from the joint effort. The other organizations feel justified in reviewing the need as well as judging the requesting agency's appropriateness and capability as the service provider. This review may even question a fellow agency's requests for funds for accepted purposes if those funds are perceived to permit unwarranted expansion.

The time required of staff and volunteer leaders to engage in various interorganizational relations constitutes a major cost to agencies. Chief executives and board leaders may be diverted from fundraising tasks, not to mention oversight and governance responsibilities in general. However, the presence of these leaders in broader endeavors promotes good public images, adding to the credibility of the participating agencies.

The linkages established with community and regional power structures enhance organizational effectiveness.

Interorganizational relationships make demands on management styles. Authoritarian executives find it hard to cope with shared responsibility, consensus decision making, and other leaders' values. Conflict occurs constantly; therefore, interpersonal and conflict resolution skills are a valuable asset. Executives with facilitative or collegial styles win more benefits for their agencies from interorganizational efforts than authoritarian or laissez-faire executives.

Although interorganizational relationships have their costs, the benefits outweigh these costs. Larger markets emerge. Public images are strengthened. Early warnings of environmental changes occur. Sources of key information open up. Adroit leaders manage their interorganizational dependencies to reduce negative effects and take advantage of the ways in which these relationships ensure survival and growth in competitive and complex environments.

Conclusion

Environmental changes force nonprofit organizations to live in a quixotic landscape, especially where their market resources are involved. The large percentage of failures, especially among new small agencies, demonstrates how perilous the environmental conditions are. Strategies to meet these conditions come in a variety of forms and dimensions. When the principles and practices of effective fundraising are employed and still more resources are needed, nonprofit organizations turn to strategies that they can initiate themselves, principally commercial activities, and to interorganizational strategies that build group strength. Problems and issues that flow primarily from the size and range of a nonprofit organization are examined in the next two chapters.

Eight

---◼---

Fundraising
in
Smaller
Organizations

Small organizations with assets under $500,000 make up the largest segment of the charitable nonprofit field but enjoy only a small percentage of its total revenues, including gifts. Small nonprofit organizations' turnover rate rivals that of small for-profit enterprises, and their average life span is only a fraction of that for large organizations. They either grow or fade away, confirming systems theory, which says organizations are unable to remain static. When small nonprofit organizations' evolution propels them into the ranks of the middle-sized agencies with assets up to $10 million, they acquire considerably more stability. These phenomena give rise to questions of how and why these small agencies evolve.

Small agencies' importance cannot be questioned. They provide many avenues for practical action to address social interests and needs. They allow their constituents to express concerns, debate and develop solutions to pressing problems, and undertake advocacy for issues and ideals. Small organizations are an immediate expression of democratic and community values. This chapter explores the fundraising opportunities and hazards encountered by small agencies as they grow. Factors that affect small agencies' existence and funding include societal needs, leaders' personal ambitions, public awareness and interest, governance issues, and management capacities. An examination of middle-sized organizations concludes the chapter.

Dimensions of the Small Nonprofit Organization Sector

Small charitable organizations' typical condition is revealed by comparing their absolute numbers and their revenues and total assets. Two studies of charitable organizations on record with the Internal Revenue Service that were carried out in 1987 (Hilgert and Mahler, 1991) and 1989 (Hodgkinson, Weitzman, Toppe, and Noga, 1992) demonstrate that small agencies dominate the nonprofit field in sheer numbers, but are woefully lacking in financial resources in relation to larger agencies. Later statistics from the IRS (1991) show that all charitable 501(c)(3) organizations amounted to slightly over 460,000 in 1989 and 516,000 in 1991. Small organizations were estimated to make up 92 percent of these totals.

Precise financial data on these small organizations remain elusive. Federal requirements exempt charitable organizations with annual revenues of less than $25,000 from filing IRS Form 990. Furthermore, of those that did file a Form 990, less than 30 percent supplied financial data. Hodgkinson, Weitzman, Toppe, and Noga (1992) conclude that "other than names and addresses, little is known about 70 percent of charitable, nonprofit organizations" (p. 185). Obviously, the 327,000 organizations without enough revenue to report in 1989 fall into the small organization category. Of the 133,600 organizations that did file in 1989, approximately 72 percent can be classified as small: that is, they have annual expenses below $500,000; their total expenses represent less than 4 percent of the filing agencies' total expenses; their assets, taken together, are less than 6 percent of the filing agencies' total assets, and they receive about 11 percent of the total public support (both private gifts and government grants) given to the filing agencies.

Using 1987 data, Hilgert and Mahler (1991) show that small charitable organizations had only 2 percent of the total assets held by the 122,000 organizations filing financial information for that year. The small organizations' income from contributions, both direct and indirect and not including government grants, totaled 12.2 percent of the amount going to all charitable organizations. These different figures demonstrate the difficulties of obtaining a precise view of the small organization sector; nevertheless, a general picture of small agencies' place in fundraising emerges.

The 1987 data demonstrate that smaller agencies depend significantly on private donations, which amount to more than one-fourth of their total revenues compared to one-tenth of larger organizations' total revenues. When government grants are added to the private contributions, smaller organizations are shown to rely on these combined sources for nearly half of their revenues compared to one-fifth of other nonprofit organizations' revenues. Thus, fundraising and grant seeking are crucial activities for small charitable organizations.

The turnover in small organizations can be seen in the changes in the IRS master file of charitable organizations. More than 110,000 organizations were added between 1987 and 1989, and 41,000 were removed during the same period (Hodgkinson, Weitzman, Toppe, and Noga, 1992). The Hilgert and Mahler study (1991) shows the number of charitable organizations increasing at rates of 8 to 15 percent per year. However, once again, the lack of reporting requirements for 70 percent of the charitable organizational population leaves the final dimensions and financial resources of the sector in question.

Additionally, no comprehensive data are currently available on small organizations' structures, modes of operation, and environmental conditions, all of which affect fundraising. Detailed research is still needed before we can fully understand small agencies' evolution. Yet, the sector's general characteristics have become apparent to funders, consultants, and trainers.

These typical experiential aspects are described in the rest of this chapter.

Small Nonprofit Organizations' Beginnings

Nonprofit organizations begin their activities in response to observed needs that demand attention. These needs range from remedies for poor social conditions and vulnerability to disease to opportunities for artistic expression and recreation. The needs may be recent in origin, such as those springing from the AIDS crisis, or ongoing such as the demands caused by poverty and mental health problems. The typical scenario shows an enterprising individual who determines that some action can and must be taken to respond to a pressing situation. With a tentative plan, this person gathers a few other individuals, usually friends and former co-workers, to discuss the matter and arouse their enthusiasm and commitment to help. Next, the emerging executive director recruits staff for delivery programs and searches for volunteers to serve as board members and to help with programs. The structure of the new organization develops from its functions, illustrating an aspect of *structural functionalism theory,* which states that form follows function. A new AIDS agency may devote its energies to public information and education, which will require publicity, training, and advocacy on the part of the agency, or it may specialize in aid to the stricken individuals themselves, who need the services of professional and volunteer caretakers.

The extent of public awareness of the problems or needs facing these organizations conditions the response of individuals and funding sources. Immediate support of time, money, and gifts-in-kind comes from individuals known to the founder, but after the initial period of operation and the securing of tax-exempt status, the founder looks beyond the initial limited circle of friends for other easily acquired financial resources. Foundations and corporations in search of new frontiers become likely prospects. In addition to the perception of need mentioned above, it is the availability of grants from government agencies that frequently inspires enterprising founders to create their own agencies. In determining what agencies to support, these government granting organizations respond to public perceptions of the seriousness of the conditions to be addressed, the views of political office holders, and the impact of relevant legislative initiatives.

During the formative months of intense organizing and a subsequent year or two of gaining experience in delivering services, new nonprofit organizations pay very limited or no attention to developing informed constituencies of prospects. The funding available from foundations and government agencies, and perhaps a few affluent members, often gives new agencies unrealistic positive expectations of their environment. Fundraising, if undertaken at all, rests with the executive director, who usually writes proposals for grants, or with a volunteer who creates an ad hoc fundraising event. Thus, the brand-new agency enters the next phase of its existence with little fundraising experience and a limited base of donors. This condition has concerned foundation executives, many of whom have instituted technical assistance and challenge grants to develop fundraising capacities in smaller agencies (Lane, Levis, and New, 1989).

Small Organization Characteristics

Small agencies tend to have lean administrations; staff is concentrated in service delivery. As a consequence, overwork and burnout are potential liabilities for the management staff. The chief executive, usually titled executive director, faces the overwhelming task of training and supervising service delivery personnel, as well as a bookkeeper and a maintenance person, with only the help of an administrative assistant. Despite these burdens, many small agencies survive due to the belief, commitment, and skills of the founder.

The founder typically functions like the authoritative executive described in Chapter Six. This behavior appears to be prompted by the founder's entrepreneurial tendencies as a visionary organizer. Decision making is usually centralized in this individual. Board members exercise little direction, defer to the founder's judgment, and sometimes are not even consulted on key decisions.

Adequate income is always problematic, with financial growth's hinging on government and private grants, fees for services, and a small group of private donors. The pressure for increased revenues quickly forces responsibility for fundraising to be imposed by the executive director on a staff person who also has other responsibilities. Usually, the first function assigned is proposal writing for grants followed by planning for special events and experimenting with limited direct mail efforts or neighborhood canvasses. Gradually, the increased workload and growing returns from fundraising justify full-time effort, and fundraising or development becomes a differentiated function with a staff fundraiser, or development officer.

Development officers in these situations stretch their attention and time from grant writing and special events to publicity and annual giving programs. Support staff for prospect research and donor record keeping and acknowledgments often do not exist or are embodied in a sole administrative assistant/secretary. Evidence of this phenomenon is provided by the 1992 Profile Study of the National Society of Fund Raising Executives, which reports that 34.6 percent of its 12,600 members work without other professional colleagues, and 36.9 percent of members work with only one or two other professionals (Mongon, 1992).

Small agencies' budgetary limitations preclude the use of specialized services and techniques available to larger organizations. For example, the important work of identifying and evaluating prospects, if done at all, is left to casual investigations and analysis. A survey by the American Prospect Research Association (1992) discloses that only 4.2 percent of their 1,300 members work in organizations with budgets of $500,000 or less, and most of these small organization staff people devote only a portion of their time to this prospecting function. Planned giving programs are completely beyond individual small organizations' capacities. Direct mail campaigns and telemarketing programs of sufficient size to produce a viable donor base cost more than these groups can afford.

Impetus for Growth

The conditions that stimulated the formation of a small agency will continue to exist despite agency services. The human needs served by nonprofit organizations lie beyond the capacity of any one agency or group of agencies to solve. Hunger, homelessness, insufficient recreation, disease, desires for artistic expression, and other pressing situations constantly resurface, demanding renewed attention. These needs arouse the entrepreneurial characteristics of executive directors, whose desires for achievement are seldom satiated (Young, 1983). As their organizations stabilize, these individuals seek new challenges; their restlessness increases, to be satisfied only by expansion of existing services or creation of new ones. Although, public concern for problems waxes and wanes, posing uncertainty about continued public support, volunteer and staff leaders often envision that the enlargement of services will fulfill the motivations that created their organizations.

Current successes justify taking on additional workloads or even new activities. Organizational funders' initial favorable responses are misinterpreted as long-term commitments to programs or the agency. Although each small agency faces a precarious funding future, the impetus for growth and evolution gathers strength. The founders' vision, energy, and determination engage the commitment of volunteers, staff, and funders, who continue supporting the agency. But problems and hazards increase also and cause many of the newer agencies to fail.

Evolutionary Problems

The problems facing evolving small organizations fall into two clusters: first, concerns about organizational readiness to operate effectively in the areas of management, governance, personnel, facilities, and funding; and second, concerns about the organizational environment changing in the areas of competition, funding climate, funders' priorities, regulatory agencies' demands, coordination arrangements with other agents, and public policies.

Management and Governance

All too frequently, chief executives' ambitions outstrip organizational members' capacity to accommodate the necessary changes. Confusion about mission and goals occurs when new programs and projects are introduced without adequate consultation with affected parties. Goal displacement results from the interjection of unrelenting personal aims that skew organizational direction. For example, an executive director attempting to build a notable reputation for himself may constantly pursue the latest grant opportunities regardless of the changes in services that the new funds demand and the effects on client needs. However, Zander (1985) reports this welcome finding: "When participants [in small groups] differ in the purpose each wants the group to have, they try to reduce these differences and to develop a common point of view" (p. 12).

Creators and builders of new organizations have a leadership style that differs from the style adopted by managers of ongoing organizations (Bennis and Nanus, 1985). The creators and builders have less patience with administrative procedures and policies, yet delegation of authority appears difficult for them. Rather than manage their existing organizational successes, they seek new programmatic areas to establish. Advice from their development officers, if they even have such officers, fails to make an impression. They become impatient with the lead times necessary to build community acceptance, donor constituencies, and annual funding.

Governing boards become obstacles to expansion-minded executives. The limited linkages that small organizations have with the larger community result in a narrow field of board candidates who have experience with governance and especially with fundraising. In addition to their possible inexperience, board members come to organizations with preconceptions of the projected size and scope of proposed operations. They resist change and often lack the capacity to govern larger and different functions. Also, as described earlier, when board members are enlisted without any mention of fundraising obligations, they resent the imposition of responsibilities for which they are neither prepared nor temperamentally suited.

Personnel, Funding Abilities, and Facilities

Disputes over issues of expansion and fundraising disturb group cohesion and commitment in the evolving agency's board. The psychological adjustments to proposed new activities and enlarged oversight duties are often difficult for board members to make. Subsequent resignations, either voluntary or forced, may change the character and direction of the board. Valuable time and energy is lost while new and old members adjust to each other and establish effective working relationships (Zander, 1985). Further, the new members may bring with them some of the old values and prejudices, such as distaste for fundraising, doubts about expansion of services, penchants for intervening in operations, or demands for higher client fees regardless of economic circumstances.

When initial funding comes relatively easily due to government mandates and foundation grants, small agency staff are lulled into complacency about future support. They see no need to exert themselves to cultivate volunteers as prospects nor to concern themselves with donors. Their orientation leans toward serving the clients. Inexperience with fundraising activities leads staff to view them as alien to the delivery of services and the organization in general. The development officer has to struggle to build a supportive internal environment for fundraising. The important ingredients of a fundraising case based on successful services to clients are hard to assemble because the necessary documentation, supported by careful record keeping and evaluation reports, is often lacking. Because fundraising is seen as peripheral, office quarters for development staff are usually inadequate; staff are stuck in makeshift accommodations as an afterthought. The need for expanded space to serve increased fundraising activities comes as a surprise.

Competition

Organizational environments change constantly and new agencies are no more immune to these changes than established ones. The same conditions that prompt the creation of one nonprofit organization serve to spawn others. Larger agencies see opportunities for new services to expand and revitalize their operations. Competition for clients, volunteers, and funds becomes a way of life for new and old, small and large organizations.

Funding Climate

The funding climate varies also. Economic recessions slow the volume of contributions even though the need for services to disadvantaged people appears more clearly. Scandals about fundraising excesses, diversion of funds, and outright fraud cause donors to be more cautious in giving and selection of agencies. Oversaturation of donors with direct mail and telemarketing fundraising reduces response rates from the less-committed constituencies. Press and television coverage of natural disasters and exceptional social conditions divert the public's concerns and funds from ongoing needs. In all of these circumstances, smaller organizations face greater difficulties than larger organizations in getting their funding needs recognized. Compounding these adversities are the changing interests of foundations and corporations that seek new areas to fund to satisfy their entrepreneurial impulses.

Funder's Priorities and Regulatory and Coordination Effects

Regulating and coordinating agencies, public and private, add to the uncertain funding environment of small organizations. State governments are enlarging surveillance for excessive fundraising costs that diminish services to clients. Federated fundraising organizations, such as United Ways and the Combined Federal Campaigns, give many small agencies access to workplace giving, but federated groups also add to the competition by accepting ever-increasing numbers of member agencies. In 1992, United Way of the Bay Area (San Francisco) quadrupled the charities on its approved list, increasing agencies from 325 to 1400, by signing contracts with six other federations of nonprofit organizations (Smith, 1992). Despite this unprecedented expansion, only 7 percent of the nation's nonreligious charities receive support from United Ways, according to National/United Services Agencies (1992), one of the six workplace federations that joined with United Way of the Bay Area. This group found survey respondents overestimated the number of agencies receiving United Way support by up to 36 percent. Increasingly, federations are imposing reporting requirements and minimum levels of funding from other private sources on their members, thus limiting the amount smaller agencies can receive from them (Brilliant, 1990). Additionally, these federations encourage and even enforce consolidation of operations and agencies to conserve costs and reduce funding.

Small organizations form bridges with other organizations to increase stability, influence, legitimacy, acceptance, and resources (Scott, 1987). Small agencies' linking up with others creates an exchange of support that enhances all parties (Spread, 1984). The same kinds of benefits described in Chapter 7 for arrangements among nonprofit organizations apply equally to arrangements among small agencies, and other programs are also available. For example, San Diego Community Foundation offers small agencies assistance in planned giving programs and a pooled fund for investments (Stehle, 1990). Technical assistance organizations such as the Support Center furnish fundraising training programs and counseling services for small charities.

Public Policy

Public policy changes influence small agencies' funding opportunities. Weisbrod (1988) notes the dynamic impact governmental actions have on nonprofit funding. Political debate over definitions of unrelated business income, tax deductibility of gifts, and government support programs adds to the uncertainty of the funding climate. Changes such as the Tax Reform Act of 1986, that affect donors' ability to deduct gifts from income taxes, slow the growth of total donations. The increase in the amount allowed for standard deductions on federal and state income taxes reduces donors' incentive for making the modest gifts on which small organizations depend. The declining role of government funds in nonprofit organizations in the 1980s has been widely reported. All these changes make it particularly difficult for smaller organizations to thrive and attract donations.

Overcoming Funding Difficulties

The evolution of each small organization either proceeds or subsides. The key to proceeding rather than subsiding lies in applying principles of organizational development and growth to fundraising. Weisbord asserts that "organizations and people have to become learning systems if they wish to prosper" (1987, p. 23). Through continual learning of effective and efficient management and leadership, executives of small agencies can turn aside or redirect the many forces that impede progress. Most of the strategies that follow have been discussed in earlier chapters; they are reintroduced here with emphasis on their relevance for small organizations. These strategies center around creating new settings, clarifying values, developing appropriate images, building capacity, using appropriate management styles, and revitalizing governance. Additional statistics that apply to small agencies but do not need further elaboration include adapting to the environment, linking with similar organizations in coalitions and federations, building a constituency, reinforcing the organizational mission, and reassessing fundraising practices.

Creating New Settings

After their founding and a short period of gestation, small organizations become ready for the next steps in their evolution. At this stage, they have created a setting that can be defined as people who "have come together in new relationships over a sustained period of time in order to achieve certain goals" (Sarason, 1972, p. 1). The most basic principle they must heed at this point is the one that calls for developing consensus on the underlying values that guide the organization. Without this consensus, individuals will attempt to move the organization in different directions, according to their own criteria.

Clarifying Values

The areas in which key values must be determined are the extent to which funders will influence the organization through grants and contributions, board members' commitment to personal fundraising, scope of profit-making activities, revenue burdens to be placed on clients, donating criteria for board members, degree of community representation, future size of the organization, range of services to be offered, roles of volunteers and staff in agency operations, style of management, and many others. Agreement on these kinds of major issues builds cohesion and enables the organization to set goals, objectives, and procedures for operational activities and services.

Developing Appropriate Images

The enthusiasm and creativity of organizational founders soon flags or becomes clouded if it is not instilled in new staff and volunteers. A vision of what the agency can do to help people generates commitment in newcomers as does asking them to participate in reassessing the organizational purpose. Revisiting the mission in concert with others can be a dynamic experience. Small organizations have a great advantage in undertaking this process because of natural small-group dynamics that develop commitment and foster cohesion (Zander, 1985).

The solid core of values and commitment that ensues when staff and volunteers participate in building a vision and setting goals helps organizations project positive images to people and other organizations in their operating environments. Funders quickly sense staff solidarity of purpose, donors are attracted by obvious dedication, and other stakeholders are also impressed. An agency's constituencies grow more readily when word gets around that the agency is "doing a great job" or is "a solid operation." Donors like to know that they are contributing to a successful organization. But positive steps must be taken to assure that the image flows to the most promising prospects.

Building Capacity

The competencies small organizations can demonstrate will grow when the activities that create shared values are orchestrated by effective management and governance practices. The principles of strategic planning, organizing, and management discussed in Part Two provide the platform for quality performance. Unfortunately, small organizations' need for rational planning is often obscured by their straightforward purpose and limited number of personnel. Their situations appear simple; therefore, their founders see planning as unimportant or not worth the cost in time and energy (Gorczyra, 1987).

Using Appropriate Management Styles

A chief executive in a small nonprofit organization has the obligation to become a generalist manager who stresses team or participative management. This means sharing responsibilities, information, authority, and decision making. The necessary skills include being a broker, facilitator, mediator, integrator, coordinator, educator, and evaluator. Managing a small nonprofit organization is not an easy task. Advice and counsel can be found among experienced board members, if the chief executive shows an interest.

Revitalizing Governance

The role of governance and board members always remains problematic in evolving small organizations. Friends invited to serve in the formative period may not have the skills and sophistication to govern when the organization readies itself for growth. Policy development and review has to replace earlier hands-on operational activities, except in fundraising where active participation by board members provides leadership, personnel, and outreach to sources of funds. The board's guidance for the chief executive comes through regular reviews and evaluations of the chief executive's performance. These reviews should be based on previously established criteria because following the principle of clarified expectations reduces conflict (Zander, 1985). The style of management necessary for growth can be negotiated diplomatically with the chief executive by astute board members, but changing any person's behavior remains difficult. The basis for the change will be the values decided when the setting is created and when subsequent vision and mission discussions are held.

The chief executive's relationship with the board should remain a two-way avenue of discussion, advice, and agreement. While the board directs the chief executive through policy and performance expectations, the latter educates and reformulates the board in light of the organization's expected future. New organizational directions often mandate new talents and skills on the part of board members. Growth requires new funding and fundraising methods. The board needs members who have the skills and willingness to be operational in this area. A major issue for new boards centers around the type of individuals to be recruited, especially when these individuals must be people of wealth and influence in order to fulfill board fundraising expectations. Community-based activists see influential business persons and affluent individuals as a threat to their power and ideals. Less sophisticated members feel inadequate associating with experienced community leaders. The chief executive and top lay leader must exercise their leadership skills to resolve such fears and help the board arrive at a consensus on values, goals, and means.

Further Strategies

Small organizations require staff who can share knowledge about their roles and duties simply because the limited number of staff precludes highly differentiated functions and specialties. The chief executive has to comprehend all the functions of fundraising and integrate them into the planning, thinking, and understanding of all staff members. With a development department that consists only of a development officer, who may even be part-time, the agency needs backup personnel who can fill in when required. Periodically intensive activities such as annual campaigns or special events demand that such a resource be available. The fundraiser has a critical role in following up the chief executive's initiative about fundraising. The fundraiser must provide staff with information and training to demystify the various fundraising processes and the critical relationships with donors. Volunteers and prospects need ongoing attention. They do not readily understand or accept attention that is paid to them only when they are being asked for funds.

In view of all the demands, issues, and problems facing small nonprofit organizations, the annual growth in their numbers seems almost impossible, and their evolution into middle-sized, mature entities seems miraculous, yet hundreds arrive at that status. A ground swell of public interest and concern carries some beyond minimal existence; witness those agencies involved with the AIDS crisis, environmental issues, and housing. Beyond that external impetus, however, credit must be given to those remarkable leaders who know how to motivate others and adapt themselves and their organizations to a changing environment.

Middle-Sized Organizations

Nonprofit organizations at either end of the size range can be readily visualized and categorized. Large organizations dominate public attention by their scope and power. Small agencies are recognized by their limited resources in personnel and facilities and by their sheer prevalence. To be identified as middle-sized, however, organizations must first be defined in terms of their service or purpose classification. For example, private two-year colleges are viewed as small in the higher education field, yet almost all have expenditures and assets of over $500,000, qualifying on a strictly financial scale as medium or even large nonprofit organizations. In contrast, an arts organization with similar financial figures would be considered a large organization in the arts field. Thus, the organizational environment plays a part in the discussion of middle-sized organizations.

Financial data provide those dimensions of middle-sized charities as indicated by their expenses and assets listed on their 990 forms for the year 1989. Nonprofit organizations with expenses of $500,000 up to $10 million account for about 24 percent of the total filers. Smaller agencies, as mentioned earlier, make up 72 percent of the total and the largest institutions just 4 percent (Hodgkinson, Weitzman, Toppe, and Noga, 1992). Not included in this array are 327,000 small agencies not required to file. The middle-sized group, consisting of approximately 32,000 organizations, commands 37 percent of public support revenues, a percentage that includes total gifts, grants, and contributions from private and government sources. Both their assets and expenses amount to 19 percent of the assets and expenses of all Form 990 filers who included financial data. Hilgert and Mahler (1991) found similar ranges in their 1987 study of IRS data and show middle-sized organizations receiving an estimated total of $10.8 billion in gifts and $9.7 billion in government grants in 1987.

When middle-sized organizations move beyond the precarious status of small agencies, certain factors appear to explain and sustain their greater stability and experience. The leaders, both volunteer and staff, recognize the value of private gift support. The founders of City Year, Inc., a youth service corps in Boston, epitomized this virtue by raising $941,000 in their first year of operation, and projected that they would have an income 50 percent higher two years later (Richman, 1990). This success resulted from sound financial and program planning.

Middle-sized organizations also exhibit other characteristics. Their boards of directors take responsibility for ensuring adequate funding to meet expenditures. The organizations have a number of fundraising methods in place, such as unique special events, systematic annual giving, grant writing, and major gift solicitations. Their services fill a niche in community needs, and a constituency of clients, volunteers, and donors exists for these needs. Operating policies and procedures for funding have been developed and tested. Personnel know their work and observe standards for performance. Factors beyond fundraising, such as adaptable management styles, sound organization, strategic planning, and professional competence, ensure more than bare survival.

The data on total contributions tend to confirm the presence of these agencies' active fundraising programs. Regrettably, research information on the size of their development departments is not available. Experience suggests that middle-sized organizations at the lower end of the financial spectrum have a minimum of one full-time fundraiser plus clerical assistance for that person, and that the larger organizations have three to seven professional staff in the fundraising department.

Many examples of successful performance exist among the thousands of middle-sized organizations. A mental health clinic in a market area of one million persons provides one illustration. The clinic achieved its stature through the efforts of a very able executive director who later earned a master's degree in nonprofit administration, restructured and trained his board to undertake fundraising, and financed a new building with a capital campaign. Along with directing a successful fundraising program, the executive director managed a very competent counseling service that increased client loads and projected a quality image to the public.

Middle-sized nonprofit organizations, like their larger and smaller relatives, exist in changing, uncertain environments. Their environmental concerns are not only external but internal. One particular danger is that leaders may become complacent, losing the vision and energy that propelled the agency to its present size. A regional historical society reached such a plateau when its leaders became satisfied with its membership size, library, and location. However, the receipt of valuable records and donations began to dwindle while salaries, preservation costs, and building deterioration increased. A period of turmoil ensued, and new direction and increased funding occurred only after a change of leadership.

Increasing costs put differing pressures on programs, budgets, and resources. Leaders' entrepreneurial spirit may be aroused by these pressures, and these leaders may set the organization off in untried directions such as for-profit ventures to increase income. Burdensome bureaucratic, controlling practices can invade operations, stifling initiative. Communication up and down the organization tends to become one-way when leaders take defensive positions on budgetary problems. One residential center for developmentally disabled persons fell into the morass of these pressures, and the many governmental regulations surrounding this service compounded the agency's stultification. Fortunately, a recently retired corporate executive was recruited to the board to help with finances. This person quickly saw the underlying blockages and used the financial needs as a means to instigate planned change. The rallying point was the vision of new funds to be raised from an enlarged constituency that included the executive's personal friends in the corporate world who could be persuaded to support the agency.

Other internal difficulties are typical of middle-sized nonprofit organizations. Annual fundraising efforts often lose their challenge for volunteers. Donor and prospect lists become overworked, reducing donors' potential for new and increased giving. Turnover of development personnel requires new or expanded recruitment and training processes in addition to the time necessary to develop trust and working relationships with volunteers and donors.

The kinds of external influences and pressures discussed in earlier chapters cause repeated changes in fundraising practices for these organizations. New sources of funds such as cause-related marketing or mailing list sales are explored. Successful ventures attract attention and emulation. Competition from new and expanding agencies for clients and funds is ever present. New human needs emerge or existing social problems spring to new prominence. Granting organizations shift their interests to other fields or to other organizations not previously funded. These changing circumstances place increased demands on the organizations' fundraisers to provide the necessary financial support.

Conversely, several aspects of middle-sized agencies aid survival and growth. Operational and management skills acquired over the years provide stability. Financial resources are known, and potential funding opportunities are actively contemplated. Fundraising capabilities have been cultivated. The case for support is well articulated. This reservoir of experience enables these agencies to meet changing conditions, experiment with new solutions, and further solidify good existing practices. The critical mass necessary to undertake enlarged funding efforts is present. Despite their tendency to formalize structure and procedures, many middle-sized organizations are not too large to have the requisite flexibility and cohesion to meet new threats and opportunities. The overarching ingredient in their continued existence and growth is inspired leadership with the vision and ability to bring about change. With these ingredients, the middle-sized organizations not only maintain themselves, but some of them develop into large institutions.

Conclusion

The high volume of turnover in small nonprofit organizations indicates their extreme vulnerability to internal and external demands. Excessive work loads, limited staff, inadequate funding bases, and narrow constituencies—all combine to thwart the aims of founders. The tendency of executives to be authoritative and unyielding in their entrepreneurial ambitions is sometimes coupled with unrealistic expectations of continuing financial support from original funders. Competition from other charitable organizations, especially larger ones, steals vital revenues from fees, gifts, and grants. Smaller organizations are particularly exposed to shifts in public and private attitudes, interests, and support.

Survival and growth of small nonprofit agencies occur because of the determination, vision, and leadership of their founders and executives. These individuals pursue their goals with a willingness to learn and adapt to changing environmental conditions. They create appropriate settings for agency operations, clarify values of participants, develop viable images for their organization, build their individual capacity of their members, use effective management styles, and revitalize governance. Such actions often propel the agencies into the stable middle-sized category of organizations and even beyond.

Larger organizations are characterized by skillful leadership, broader support bases, and informed constituencies, along with competent staff, quality working conditions, and open communication practices. Agencies that are well managed are positioned to grow even larger. The issues they will encounter in this new status are discussed in the following chapter.

Nine

Fundraising in Larger Organizations

The largest charitable organizations comprise the smallest segment of the nonprofit sector but own the greatest share of the assets and receive over half of the private contributions. Because of their size, they face issues of structure, coordination, prospect control, communication, donor involvement, goal alignment, leadership, and environmental adaptation in their fundraising activities. These issues arise in the context of historical precedent, organizational culture, and changing information technology. Many of them are common to all nonprofit organizations, but in the larger organizations, they have a more critical impact on management control and organization effectiveness.

The fields of interest and service of the larger organizations include advocacy (in a number of areas), arts, disaster relief, education, health, housing, public affairs, research, social welfare, and youth development. Analysis of these organizations is valuable to all charitable agencies because size is closely associated with visibility. Therefore, these organizations are more likely than other nonprofit agencies to be targets of the media and state regulatory bodies, and also more likely to provide practices, such as major gift programs, that can be successfully adapted by smaller agencies (Scott, 1987).

Profile of Large Organizations

Larger charitable nonprofit organizations are those classified by the Internal Revenue Service as having assets of $10 million or more, held in the form of property, investments, and other financial resources. The combined assets of these organizations totaled $447.3 billion, or 85 percent of the dollar value of all charitable organizations, in 1987 (Hilgert and Mahler, 1991). Their total net worth, or fund balances, amount to more than half of their assets. This economic strength belongs to only 6,103 organizations out of the 1987 total of over 460,000. These large organizations received over $21 billion in private donations in 1987, more than all the other charitable organizations together. The next smaller sized organizations, those having assets of $1 million to $10 million, jump in number to over 21,000, but their total assets comprise only 12.3 percent of the assets of all the nonprofit organizations in the study, and their charitable donations amounted to $8.8 billion, or slightly less than one-fourth of all contributions.

Religious organizations are not included in the figures above because so few of them provide data on their financial resources. They are not mandated by law to report their financial condition, as is the case with charitable nonprofit organizations, but are given the opportunity to do so. About 1 percent of those that did provide data to the IRS in 1989 had expenses of $10 million or more and commanded 51 percent of total assets of all those reporting financial data. These few largest religious bodies had 60 percent of total reported annual expenses, and received a third of total public support of the reporting groups (Hodgkinson, Weitzman, Toppe, and Noga, 1992).

Financial size is only one measure of large organizations. Other important aspects are numbers of clients and participants, geographical scope, and numbers of employees. For example, the American Cancer Society, American Heart Association, and United Cerebral Palsy Association reportedly have over two million volunteers each, while the American Red Cross and Salvation Army claim one million or more volunteers each (Kinkead, 1987). Other organizations that qualify as large on their financial assets have limited numbers of volunteers (UNICEF, CARE, and Goodwill Industries of America) but hundreds of thousands of clients. The number of employees in these large agencies ranges from a few thousand to over twenty thousand. Agencies with the greatest number of local chapters or units spread throughout the nation naturally have the largest number of employees. These large nonprofit organizations have a considerable advantage in fundraising due to their name recognition and the public's general knowledge of their services to society.

However, for examining specific fundraising issues, financial resources coupled with structural forms remain the most pertinent factors since some of the wealthiest organizations, such as medical centers and private universities, still have only one principal location. Furthermore, large financial resources are closely related to the ability to raise funds. A fundraising axiom states that "it takes money to raise money." With ample funds, fundraisers can be hired, offices equipped, promotional materials developed and distributed, and prospects cultivated and solicited.

Fundraising Structures

The structural forms of fundraising in large organizations are as diverse as the purposes, clients, and histories of these entities. Some organizations, such as UNICEF, have highly centralized fundraising activities managed through their headquarters; others, like Girl Scouts of America, are almost completely decentralized, securing private support through local units; and still others use either a centralized or decentralized structure, depending on gift size, the structure and services of the host organization, and its evolutionary experience. These variations suggest that the underlying theme is a contingency approach: each organization employs the structure that adapts best to its variety of resource needs, environmental conditions, and historical influences (Scott, 1987).

The size of a large fundraising organization is an important determinant of its structure and appearance to prospects, but other factors are also critical, for example, reporting relationships, autonomy, accountability, information needs, and control of resources. Structure is the means by which an organization divides up its work or tasks and controls and coordinates its activities. As discussed earlier, the usual model of development activities separates annual giving programs from capital campaigns, and further divides each category into subunits based on anticipated dollar amounts of gifts. The various sources of funds, such as individuals, foundations, and corporations, also create divisions of labor within the asking organization. Compounding the question of structure for large organizations are issues of multiple gift needs, geographically widespread prospects and service units, and gift volume. Large-scale fundraising activities respond to these variables by creating both greater numbers of similar development units and more highly specialized forms to reach specific markets. For example, many large organizations have resource development offices both in New York City to facilitate solicitation of grants from foundations and in Washington, D.C., to pursue governmental grants.

Centralization and Decentralization

The principal structural question for large organizations is whether centralization or decentralization produces the best organizational form for their large-scale fundraising activities. Different stimuli spawn different solutions. One stimulus arises from the specific technologies or methods of fundraising; other stimuli include geographical dispersion, the degree of professionalization of host organization staff, their relationships with clients, and governmental support.

Fundraising Technology

Fundraising technologies or methods may inspire either centralization or decentralization. The March of Dimes uses a highly centralized direct mail process that it pioneered. Its nationally recognized name, coupled with its centralized decision making regarding its gift needs and case for support, provide the rationale for this type of management structure. Amnesty International, although more limited in size, employs this same means for its principal revenues. Many smaller, less well-known agencies, ranging from environmental groups and health agencies to civil rights organizations and religious movements, have grown to major proportions using sophisticated centralized direct mail and telemarketing programs (Warwick, 1990).

The use of special events by large national organizations usually occurs at the local level because of required participation levels of volunteers and patrons. Local units decide on and produce the type and size of events that will both fit their environments and meet national guidelines. Frequently, these special events are coordinated with national promotions to enhance a sense of unity, image, and cohesion even though the events are locally planned and staffed. Television offers a unique exception to the need for decentralized events: witness the success of concerts by Africa USA in collecting funds for famine relief thousands of miles overseas.

The fundraising method of planned giving requires highly specialized professionals to assist prospects with the necessary legal and investment procedures. As this form of giving becomes more prevalent within an agency, it moves from a centrally decided inception to decentralized prospect identification and cultivation, while the final negotiations and solicitations typically remain with centralized core staff, as is the case with Girl Scouts of America. Multicampus universities, however, tend to acquire decentralized planned giving staff because of the volume of prospects. Due to economies of scale, the investment of funds almost universally remains centralized in headquarters offices. Exceptions to this practice can be found in separate foundations related to host institutions. Board members of these foundations find satisfaction in the management of investments, often as a diversion from the perceived burdens of fundraising, and therefore, they keep the investment activities in-house.

The potential for large gifts causes the formation of special structures of major gift staffs and departments for several basic reasons. The method of the large-gift solicitation is different from other solicitations in that the prospect is more frequently involved in developing and negotiating the final uses of the gift, and routine procedures are less applicable. The amount of dollars involved makes major gift decisions more vital to the success of the institution than many other gift decisions, so staff who deal with major gifts require more professional experience and training in solicitation techniques and the sophisticated use of volunteers. At the high end of gift tables, where potential gifts range from $100,000 to $1 million or more, major gift staff stay centralized. In fact, the chief development officer and the chief executive officer may take over the solicitation. Trustees and volunteers appear to be somewhat less responsible for obtaining these top gifts to higher educational institutions according to Altizer (1992), who suggests that trustees and volunteers may be used more for identification and cultivation than for the actual solicitations.

Geographical Location

The geographical dispersion of prospects and service delivery programs plays a major role in tilting fundraising toward decentralization. University alumni quickly fan out to home towns or occupational opportunities. Therefore, effectiveness in cultivation and solicitation of alumni mandates placing alumni offices and activities in regions where former students are concentrated. Widespread service delivery programs such as nationally sponsored youth programs, social services, and health care follow the same pattern. In these instances, prospective donors evolve from prospects' participation in chapter and branch activities. Localized fundraising appeals tap this relationship more effectively than distant national solicitations.

Where efficient national computerized mailings are used,

the appearance of decentralized activity, the local angle, is exploited through the insertion of hometown references in the letter and the use of local return mail addresses known as mail drops. In centralized multimillion-dollar capital campaigns, the number of gift prospects and locations forces the creation of decentralized operations as well, based on geographical concentrations of prospects. The local offices focus on potential gifts one or two steps down the gift table, leaving the very top gift prospects to centralized staff who have more professional expertise and can exercise sound judgment on the many variables involved in large capital campaign solicitations. The federated, or integrated, form of fundraising has a strong geographical rationale. United Ways illustrate the technique designed on this rationale (Brilliant, 1990). The financial needs of local agencies combined with the desires of employers to control workplace solicitations spawned the combined campaign philosophy and practice. The larger goals of a federated effort command more attention, stronger leadership, and larger gifts. Nationwide concern for human needs is developed by staging simultaneous campaigns throughout the country.

Professional Staff

Large organizations whose principal delivery services require highly trained professionals, such as doctors or specialized teaching faculty, face unique forces that propel decentralization. The professionals the organizations require exercise considerable authority and independence from central administrative offices by virtue of their specialized disciplines, extensive education and training, and external standards. In this arena of freedom, they seek to enhance funding for their research and professional advancement by launching their own fundraising efforts.

These professional staff members also develop reputations and personal relationships with clients and other persons interested in their work. These linkages produce fundraising opportunities with foundations and corporations as well as wealthy individuals. Professionals view the resultant grants and gifts for their work in a proprietary light. They frequently view policies and procedures for coordination as interference with their prerogatives and relationships with donors.

A strong case for decentralized fundraising is made by Hall (1992) in her study of large research universities. She concludes that "decentralization substitutes coordination for control and produces a broader base of high-level academic involvement in development" and "thereby enhances the university's ability to obtain private support" (p. 581). However, she also acknowledges the issues of transfer of power that result from shifting resource acquisition to deans of colleges, and the difficulties of tracking the information flow on prospects and the results of solicitations.

While the trend toward decentralization in fundraising by universities' professional staff seems to be increasing, another study raises questions about the effectiveness of deans and faculty in obtaining major gifts. Altizer (1992) found that these two groups of persons were the least responsible for securing a major gift, falling behind the president, chief development officer, major gift officer, trustees, and volunteers. Halls' and Altizers' different results may be due to the number and nature of their respondents. Hall surveyed a larger sample of development officers in both decentralized and centralized higher education institutions (156 total), while Altizer queried the principal members of the Council for Support and Advancement of Education at 57 institutions including private colleges, public and private universities, and independent elementary and secondary schools.

In past years, when university deans and star professionals were blocked by administrative restrictions and tight budgets, they frequently set up separate foundations to administer funds for their own use. Most of these independent foundations arose before host institutions had established development offices and policies to control fundraising activities.

Governmental Support

A rationale similar to that used by professional staff when establishing independent foundations is used by central administrations to support the creation of legally separate entities. In these cases, the purpose is to thwart control by larger bureaucracies: namely, federal and state governments. Large hospitals and medical centers channel their gifts and grants through related foundations to prevent their federal funds from being reduced by the amount of the gifts the institutions have raised. Public universities and colleges also use these foundations to avoid funding reductions by state legislatures, which are prone to substitute gift dollars for state tax revenues in determining budgets.

Related Foundations

A related or "captive" organization is a legally incorporated public foundation with 501 (c) (3) charitable status conferred by the IRS. It has separate articles of incorporation, bylaws, and boards of directors from its host organizations. However, its statement of purpose usually refers to the host organization as the beneficiary of the related organization's funds, and the articles of incorporation or bylaws call for the selection of some or all of the board members from the host institution. These related organizations are useful to corral miscellaneous solicitations that spring up in entrepreneurial subunits of the host organization, such as specialized research projects, academic study centers, and service delivery programs.

In fact, some organizations encourage decentralized fundraising by these subunits in order to capitalize on the relationships that have been developed by professional staff, autonomously minded alumni, and other participants. Related foundations are also used to co-opt preexisting foundations, using the rationale of reduced administrative costs and effective separation from the host institution. Ironically, these related foundations also present problems of divided authority, external control, and inappropriate allocations with respect to the goals and objectives of their host organizations. Over time, their board members and executives develop a sense of power and independence that affects their decisions on use of funds. Such problems of control and standardization make the use of related foundations undesirable for many host organizations.

Coordination and Control

The division of labor arising from structural forms requires means of coordination and control. The main concerns are to sustain organizational identity, integrity, and cohesion. With prospects and donors widely dispersed, different perceptions can emerge about the organizational operation and needs. Additionally, prospects, donors, and granting organizations have varied linkages with the host organization and the local units through which they receive diverse messages. Resource dependency forces large organizations to exert considerable effort to maintain effective relationships with prospects and donors while securing from organizational members adherence to mission, policies, goals, and objectives. Large numbers of staff and volunteers compound the need for effective coordination and control.

Prospect Control

An issue of central importance to chief development officers is control over the cultivation and solicitation of prospects and donors, many of whom have multiple charitable interests. Competing solicitation efforts by different units within a large organization cause confusion and even disaffection among targeted persons and organizations. The problem becomes particularly acute in organizations such as hospitals and universities that have large numbers of professional service delivery personnel. At the heart of the matter is the host organization's need to determine which person or unit has the best linkage to the prospect, whose need for the gift takes priority, and what types and timing of cultivation and asking will be most effective. Underlying all these issues is need to ascertain the interest of the prospect. For example, visualize a wealthy prospect who graduated from an undergraduate school of engineering, earned a graduate degree in business administration, and who in later years has become a well-known administrator of a public regulatory body. Where does this prospect belong?

Policies or guidelines might stipulate that the earliest relationship governs, or that a period of active involvement as a business school alumnus is a key determinant, or that the prospect's active consulting arrangement with the university's public policy institute is more crucial. Meanwhile, the prospect has developed a keen interest in medieval history. Obviously, the wishes of the prospective donor are paramount, but the informal cultivation attempts by powerful deans and institute directors can both influence and undermine the outcome. Top-level, centralized intervention becomes imperative if the prospect is to be cultivated successfully.

Such situations become control and coordination issues. They can be resolved in part by policies, rules, and guidelines. Disputes over borderline cases of who can solicit whom for what purposes ultimately rise in the fundraising hierarchy to be decided by coordinating committees, as in the case of some universities, by chief development officers, or even by chief executives if the prospective gift is quite large.

The issue of prospect control is no less severe in national organizations with numerous local units. Despite early distinction and allocation by potential gift size, prospects and donors develop multiple linkages with leaders and staff members at local, regional, and national levels. These relationships also require sorting out by formalized procedures and dispute resolution.

Large organizations without viable local fundraising units strive to give prospects a sense of belonging to the central organization. The various methods of obtaining individual commitment discussed in earlier chapters become the tactics of cultivation and involvement. Membership enrollments, gift clubs, opinion polls, and leadership selection processes are commonly used.

Coordinating Processes

Local units may be loosely or tightly, formally or informally coupled to the headquarters office in terms of reporting relationships. Means for coordination and control of fundraising range from strict personnel hiring policies and regulations to looser guidelines, long interval (five- and six-year) organizational reviews, and uniform training methods.

Loosely coupled organizations, such as local YMCAs and 4-H Clubs, maintain control and coordination by several means. Extensive training and indoctrination tell staff and volunteers the organization's expectations about their performance and teach the paths to success in funding. Typically, these instructions also exist as formalized rules and procedures printed in large, bulky manuals or numerous handbooks that participants are expected to consult when fundraising questions arise.

Professional qualifications required of staff members provide a means of coordination and control. For fundraisers, these standards evolve through educational and certification programs instigated by national trade and professional associations. The National Society of Fund Raising Executives, the Council for the Advancement and Support of Education, and the Association for Healthcare Philanthropy conduct standardized courses and rigorous written examinations that, along with acceptable practical experience, form the basis for certification. The growing body of knowledge about fundraising concepts and practices informs practitioners and leads to acceptable behavior and successful outcomes. Local staff members may even be more proficient than national officers, and thus require less supervision and control.

In many cases where the local unit hires the chief executive and thereby maintains ostensible local control, the names of qualified candidates come principally from the national offices. Local executives having career aims quickly recognize the source of future opportunities; thus, effective control is accomplished. The same process applies to development officers who may be hired locally.

Red Cross chapters and Girl Scout councils, which function in a loosely coupled fashion, are reviewed by national staff at intervals of five and six years respectively. These reviews evaluate fundraising practices, and seek to confirm compliance with the general rules and regulations laid out by the national office. The national organization's control comes from its power to renew or deny local units' charters. Problems of performance or violations of standard practice may shorten the interval before the next review. Of course, sharp deviations from standard practice and performance during intervening years invite visits by national office representatives.

Regional structures are prevalent in large organizations to guide and maintain organizational performance and cohesion. In loosely coupled agencies, regional managers use persuasion and knowledge to assist local units in their fundraising activities. They fill a facilitative role in communicating up and down the hierarchical structure between national and local offices, often serving as advocates and interpreters regarding acceptable and effective practices. In this capacity, they deliver early warning signals about potential problems that need resolution.

Tightly coupled national organizations, such as March of Dimes, exercise control by the authority vested in headquarters offices. This power arises from formal bureaucratic structures and also from historical precedents, governance processes that foster old-boy networks, and authoritarian executives. It is sustained by the ability to hire, advance, or fire local staff executives. Policies and procedures for fundraising activities become binding under these conditions.

Postcampaign Reductions

The termination of major capital campaigns or the loss of significant amounts of annual funding also poses coordination and control problems. The subsequent downsizing of personnel and activity creates morale and communication difficulties among staff and volunteers. Uncertainty about future employment or volunteer roles wreaks havoc throughout fundraising organizations. When the terminus of a campaign approaches, staff without assurance of continued employment divert their attention to job hunting, with a consequent loss of effort on the remaining solicitations and continued donor cultivation. Development officials at Stanford University sought to avoid a similar anticipated problem following the institution's $1 billion campaign by getting prior agreement on a sustained high level of

development staffing. This agreement was based on careful assessment of projected needs and potential gifts, which ensured
profitable use of retained development staff. Unfortunately, the
commitments themselves become vulnerable to unforeseen internal and external changes. Stanford had to cut below agreed
levels, but the reductions were less than would have been the
case without prior agreement.

In volunteer ranks, campaign terminations cause disloca-
tion of leadership and productive relationships. Some volunteers welcome these changes as an excuse to reduce or terminate
their commitment; others feel a sense of rejection and a loss in
their altruistic commitment to serve. Valuable connections with
other volunteers and prospects tend to wither away or get lost.

Other large institutions, particularly health-care institutions, museums, colleges, and universities, have recognized the
cost of postcampaign letdown and are now resorting to long-
term or continuous capital campaigning. In these plans, staff
have the expectation of continuing employment in a continual
campaign rather than dismissal at the end of a limited campaign. Additionally, the start-up costs of a new campaign are cir-
cumvented, and staff are able to operate at continuing levels of
efficiency. Careful planning to establish identifiable mileposts
allows a rotation of volunteer leaders who become exhausted
from intense campaigning. Cultivation of donors and prospects
can continue, with demonstrated returns. Prospects who are
unable or unwilling to commit large capital sums at the initial
request frequently overcome their problems later and join with
others in making sizeable gifts.

Culture of Large Organizations

An accurate assessment of fundraising in large organizations
requires a close examination of their cultures, which have developed over many years. As stated earlier, an organizational culture consists of the values, attitudes, and precedents that bind
the entity together. This culture is sometimes expressed as the
"glue" that envelops everyone in an organization, or as the many

ways people are informed about the "way things are done." The culture of a particular organization arises out of its historical functions, leadership personalities, and proactive efforts at training and indoctrination and out of participants' coalesced feelings and values. The culture determines attitudes about fundraising and influences its acceptance and success.

Historical factors play an important role in individuals' attitudes. Agencies that developed sizeable local service programs without concomitant fundraising activities have great difficulty in adjusting to an operating environment that demands fundraising to survive. For many such organizations, participation in United Way campaigns had required them to abandon or curtail their own efforts. In this way, local YMCAs and Red Cross chapters lost much of the expertise developed in earlier years by staff and volunteer fundraisers. In another arena, public colleges and universities grew rapidly after World War II without the need to ask their alumni and friends for private support. Participants in these and many other organizations found great satisfaction in devoting their attention and interests to the organizations' programs. Turning such cultures around to new ways of doing things like asking for money always takes considerable time and persuasion.

Prominent sources of income other than donations encourage a culture without a fundraising emphasis. The widely recognized cookie sales by the Girl Scouts cause parents and friends to avoid fundraising, using the time and energy spent in product sales as justification. Even with a national policy to increase giving, local councils find it difficult for fundraising to replace the 40 percent of total revenue produced by cookie sales. Goodwill Industries, with its highly visible thrift stores, clothing donations, and workshops, has had problems in shifting interest and effort to increased fundraising.

Technological advances also affect the culture, and sometimes the mission, of organizations. In the case of the March of Dimes, two factors changed the way funds were raised. The widely heralded discovery of a polio vaccine eliminated the need for the agency's extensive network of local volunteers who had provided well-developed care services to polio victims. The programmatic strategy, developed from a new mission focusing on birth defects, required mainly educational activities at the local level, reducing dramatically the need for volunteers. At the same time, the success of the agency's direct mail program centralized fundraising activities as the volunteer base available for fundraising shrank rapidly.

Alignment of Goals

Large organizations often find that their national gift needs and appeals become differentiated from those of their local units. The Planned Parenthood Federation of America uncovered great donor interest in the agency's advocacy for issues surrounding women's reproductive health. The national fundraising appeals by direct mail and related publicity soon emphasized this approach. Meanwhile, the local units were seeking funds to support client services. The different messages tended to confuse prospects and hamper local efforts, causing strained relations with the national office and subsequent negotiations to find solutions.

The complexity of large-scale fundraising operations can also be seen in the American Red Cross, one of the largest nonprofit agencies in total revenues. For funds to support local service needs, individual chapters participate in United Way campaigns, send out membership enlistments during Red Cross month in February, and solicit for special projects at other times. Disaster funds are raised by national direct mail appeals, corporate donor campaigns, and by quotas assigned to local chapters, which, in turn, resort to local constituents. While the national organization holds the only 501(C)(3) classification, the local chapters exercise considerable authority in determining their gift needs, planning and conducting campaigns, and hiring their chief executives and development personnel. A heightened sense of competition as well as goal displacement results from these different approaches. For example, chapter solicitations for local operating costs may at times conflict with national appeals for disaster relief.

Volunteer Leadership

The volunteer leadership issues in large fundraising efforts are recruitment, continuity, and relevance. A national campaign's success depends on its recruitment of a widely known leader or celebrity, such as a former president, an entertainer, or a television personality, to publicize and endorse the need and services addressed by the agency. There is no lack of candidates for these major roles. However, recruitment problems exist for large-scale campaigns with local scope: the multimillion-dollar campaigns for hospitals, colleges and universities, libraries, museums, and other significant projects. Leaders are expected to give major sums and get others to give similar amounts. The proliferation of these campaigns taxes the leadership pool of persons who have the prestige, power, and capital in the amounts demanded.

Persons prominent enough to be considered leaders for fundraising have many demands on their time, talent, and treasure. Rarely can they afford to devote all their attention to one institution. After heading up a campaign for two or three years, they feel their initial obligation to serve has been met and that other tasks command their abilities. Against this short tenure come the increasingly prevalent five- to ten-year capital campaigns. Continuity of power and linkages becomes a major issue in these campaigns.

Public attitudes about power, status, and philanthropy in American society constantly change. Today, questions are being raised about legitimacy of wealthy individuals' and families' dominating tax-deductible charitable activities (Odendahl, 1990). The complaint centers on individuals who support such activities as operas, symphonies, private universities, and art museums that appear to benefit the donors more than they do disadvantaged persons or even society in general. Should these individuals have the power to allocate funds which otherwise would be taxes paid to government?

These challenges fly in the face of proven experience that large-scale campaigns must command the attention and funds of persons in the power structure to succeed. Support of capital needs for hospitals, public colleges and universities, and natural preserves benefits all citizens, not just the wealthy. Related to this issue is an assumption that philanthropy is the province only of the wealthy and that the millions of small donors, whose gifts total billions of dollars, are not important. The issue lies with adjusting negative attitudes toward prominent, wealthy leaders. Large charitable organizations need both sizable gifts and small donations to succeed. Large gifts make multimillion-dollar goals possible, and small donations in large volumes attest to broad public acceptance of the needs being met. The benefits of the projects and programs supported with private funds flow to all participants, not just to wealthy leaders.

Conclusion

Large fundraising organizations will continue to function and raise millions of gift dollars, but their effectiveness and growth will depend on how well they address the issues discussed here. In the fundraising process, size can be both helpful and difficult. Centralization of processes works well for some programs and organizations; decentralization is the best solution for other organizations and conditions. The basic challenge is to find the structures and processes that bring donors and donees together for optimal gift results. Factors to be considered include fundraising technologies, geographical locations, professional staff, governmental support, related foundations, prospect control, coordination techniques, staff retention, organizational culture, goal alignment, and voluntary leadership. Organizational leaders have the responsibility to face the known problems and apply sound principles of management informed by the knowledge of the fundraising principles discussed in this book.

Conclusion

◼

Future
Directions
in
Fundraising

For more than two hundred years, fundraising has been practiced in the United States to support charitable organizations and their causes. Yet, systematic, organized solicitations of funds came into being only during the last eighty years, and even then general knowledge of the methods was limited to a few large organizations and a handful of professional fundraising firms. Widespread information about the techniques of fundraising began to be disseminated after World War II, through the auspices of associations connected with colleges, universities, and community chests. In the last twenty years, an explosion of advice on how to conduct specific fundraising activities has taken place in the form of hundreds of publications, seminars, and workshops. However, only recently has an effort been made to understand the organizational workings and management of fundraising or to provide a conceptual framework that would guide the study and practice of this human activity.

In addition to their new interest in fundraising theory and management, researchers and practitioners have also been

241

examining fundraising's host environment, charitable non-profit organizations, more closely. As late as 1989, Simon complained that "nonprofit research is still in its early days" (p. 470). General concepts and theories of nonprofit organizational behavior were being derived principally from investigations of for-profit businesses and governmental agencies. Fortunately, significant impetus for thorough study is coming from the Independent Sector, the Association for Research on Nonprofit Organizations and Voluntary Action, and the more than twenty-six academic research centers dedicated to the nonprofit field. The sheer size of philanthropy in 1992, in terms of dollars raised ($124.3 billion) and numbers of contributors (69 million households), demands attention and understanding.

Preface to the Future

In an effort to establish the underlying principles of fundraising activity, this book has focused on individuals' and organizations' rationales for giving, the managerial and organizational strategies necessary to tap giving resources, and the internal and external dynamics of change that affect all charitable agencies. These three facets of fundraising are inexorably linked: nonprofit organizations cannot hope to secure adequate gift support without knowing what appeals will match donors' rationales, what kind of operational strategies will engender suitable responses, and what changes they will encounter as they and their environments evolve.

Rationales for Giving

In summary, people give because of their internal motivations and external influences. Internal motivations fall into three categories: personal concerns, social relationships, and negative feelings. External influences can be clustered into groups of proffered rewards and other stimuli such as experiences. The ultimate rationales for corporate and foundation giving are enhancing their operations, fulfilling their missions, and providing satisfactions for personnel.

The gift transactions between individuals and donating organizations are a social exchange process, not an economic or quid pro quo arrangement. Social exchange takes place between two parties that have some underlying relationship, be it participation in common activities, coexistence in a certain geographical area, or shared concerns about human conditions. The gift giver receives some return, or reward, for the gift. Most often the return is some form of personal satisfaction for the giver; however, no specification attaches to the return. The exchange is noncontractual, open, and voluntary with no time limits involved; nevertheless, without some return realized by the giver at some point, the relationship withers.

Individuals benefit from fulfilling such personal motivations as the desire for status, achievement, or affiliation and also from responding adequately to external influences such as human needs, community values, or peer pressure. Corporations' satisfactions derive from such returns as an improved public image, a better cultural environment for employees, or community recognition of executives, and so forth. Foundation officials find satisfaction in seeing grantees produce beneficial results that are aligned with the foundations' values and missions.

With knowledge of the values inherent in social exchange, leaders in nonprofit organizations can motivate volunteers and staff to overcome their anxieties about asking for gifts. Leaders can prepare strong appeals for funds and develop effective satisfactions for donors. Many objections and disinclinations to giving on the part of individuals and organizations can be anticipated and strategies can be developed to resolve the objections. The various forms of asking—face-to-face presentations, telephone calls, letters, group activities, or electronically generated requests—become more productive when the social exchange conveys appropriate giver satisfactions. However, fundraisers must also be cognizant of the particular psychological effects on donors that result from each form of communication. An unexpected telephone solicitation rarely pleases a major prospect, nor does the time taken up with a personal visit from a fundraiser seeking a minor sum of twenty or twenty-five dollars.

Organizational and Managerial Strategies
That Enhance Fundraising

The collective management and organizational activities that make up the second facet of fundraising position nonprofit organizations to create social exchange and obtain gifts. Existing theories and concepts of organizational behavior suggest the strategies that will be effective in planning, organizing, and directing fundraising efforts. Since the rationale for giving is based fundamentally on the existence of needs to be served and the satisfactions givers derive from serving these needs, fundraising is tightly woven into the overall organizational missions and strategies of nonprofit institutions. The questions of who will be served, in what manner, and at what cost, with what financial resources should directly influence the fundraising methods that are employed.

Planning in general causes organizations and their fundraising activities to look to the future. By selecting the optimum direction for the total organization, strategic planning proposes what should happen and how the organization can create that future rather than simply react to current trends. Strategic planning examines the strengths and weaknesses of the organization and the opportunities and threats it faces in its operating environment. The direction chosen in relation to the organization's mission, which may be redefined in the planning process, establishes fundraising goals and objectives. These intentions also influence the selection and application of the fourteen major fundraising methods that are available. Each of these means has strategic requirements that affect the subject organization and anticipated revenues. Selection of methods requires careful consideration of essential criteria drawn from the areas of needs, organization, and operation. A prudently drawn development plan is one attuned to internal and external probabilities and poised for accomplishment.

The organization of effective fundraising departments and activities follows theories and concepts derived from organizational behavior studies. These theories suggest effective methods for establishing reporting relationships, shaping the structural elements within organizations, carrying out departmentalization, and integrating and coordinating various functions. Departure from these well-documented concepts produces inefficiencies, lost production, and failures. It is of prime importance that a nonprofit agency's governing body take a central role in fundraising, with personal obligations for each member and overall responsibility for making fundraising successful.

Management skills and leadership are essential to effective fundraising. Leadership styles such as the coach or collegial models, which engage the active participation of volunteers and staff, tend to be more productive than authoritative or laissez-faire models. However, the "law of the situation" may require a leader to adopt more or less centralized authority to handle certain organizational and environmental conditions. Traditional patterns of organizational leadership were derived from bureaucratic structures. Today, staff leaders in fundraising need to understand and apply tested interventions to secure improved performance from all participants. These interventions can also be thought of as concepts of planned change, which include enhanced interpersonal communications, consensus-building, team development, self-management activities, problem-solving and conflict resolution processes, role negotiation, job enlargement, and job enrichment. All these actions, which have been developed by thorough research, lead to improved fundraising productivity.

Without a conceptual base fortified by research, fundraisers will not get the professional management standing they seek. Acceptance of their work will continue to be troubled by negative attitudes developed in the vacuum of ignorance.

Regrettably, chief executive officers and administrators tend to look mostly at the fundraising record of candidates for fundraising positions, caring little about certifications and degrees. Fundraisers aspiring to more professional status have the responsibility of advancing the concept that education based on research and scholarship is vital to good performance. They can demonstrate the value of this background by their productive results. Then perhaps those executives doing the hiring will

believe that certification, education, and a solid body of knowledge are equally as important as a candidate's fundraising track
record.

Internal and External Dynamics of Change

Nonprofit organizations function in a crowded, complex environment, which changes rapidly and cannot be ignored. Economic conditions, demographic shifts, value and attitudinal
changes, and variations instigated by other organizations affect
funding outcomes. Growth in small, middle-sized, and large
organizations forces adjustments to meet new revenue requirements. New strategies become the means for survival and
achievement of funding goals.

This third facet of fundraising requires that nonprofit
organizations examine a variety of internal and external responses to create new revenues. Internally, the many new
fundraising strategies undertaken by successful agencies demonstrate the vitality and flexibility of charitable organizations;
they also indicate that the character of nonprofit organizations
may change permanently. The pervasive swing is toward for-
profit enterprises and more relationships with commercial
firms, with consequent concerns among competing small business operators. Product and service sales coupled with cause-
related marketing and corporate sponsorships mark this shift.
New and restructured fees for services also affect the constituencies served.

Externally, charitable organizations seek to tame an un-
ruly environment by forming relationships with other agencies.
These arrangements take the form of cooperative agreements,
coalitions and networks, specific alliances, coordination of activities, and even integration of services. All these new relationships portend changes in public and governmental views of the
charitable sector. Although these opinions are not yet fully
formed, they promise to have dramatic effect on these new ventures and their host organizations.

Small nonprofit organizations, the overwhelming majority in the charitable field, face stiff odds for survival. Not only do

they encounter more difficulty than larger organizations in securing individual and organizational donations, but they have internal problems of governance, management styles, and personnel that affect their fundraising abilities. However, their ever-increasing numbers suggest that many make the necessary adjustments to their environments and grow, rendering vital services and providing an outlet for a variety of human concerns.

Larger nonprofit organizations confront similar internal problems, but compounded by the complexities of size, geographical dispersion, multiple interests, and needs. Their fundraising effectiveness lies in their solving questions about structure, centralization, decentralization, coordination, and control. They must also deal with questions concerning their nature and history. Contingency theory and other concepts of organizational behavior can provide guidance to leaders wrestling with these questions. Because most organizations are resource dependent, they all share the same main consideration: they must determine the organizational structure and posture that will best bring prospects and donors into a social exchange that benefits both givers and receivers.

Thus, the most pressing issue for large nonprofit organizations is the control and coordination of prospect cultivation and solicitation, especially at the major gift level. Structures must be chosen that will provide clear jurisdictions and policies. Mediation and conflict resolution devices are also needed, particularly when the pressures on staff to meet goals intensify.

Future Opportunities and Hazards in Fundraising

Complex forces are always at work in the charitable arena, and their directions will continue to shape the course of fundraising and the growth of philanthropy. Fluctuations in nationwide economic conditions influence giving. Attitudes about the government's role in providing human services affect the volume of grants to charitable agencies. Tax policies governing charitable deductions change the amounts given to charity. Concerns over accountability stimulate fundraising regulations, and the costs and effectiveness of such regulation are debated.

The effect of nonprofit organizations' visible business ventures on donors' giving practices is still being determined. For-profit enterprises that enter the human service field seem to attract the affluent clients, leaving charitable organizations with lower-income constituencies with less potential for giving. All these issues will continue to raise questions about the legitimate scope of charitable services and fundraising to support them.

Within the fundraising field itself, other critical issues are causing debate and will affect nonprofit organizations' futures. The influence exercised by wealthy contributors concerns some observers who feel these contributors' personal interests are being served at the expense of needy individuals. Women's groups protest that insufficient funds are allocated to their concerns. Blacks, Hispanics, and other minorities also raise this objection. However, the volume of charitable funds concentrated in foundations and corporations suggests that some private, privileged agendas regarding social policies will prevail.

The trend toward more for-profit ventures by charitable agencies offends traditionalists. Marketing ploys worry other observers. Voluminous direct mail appeals are overwhelming conscientious donors and raising a negative image of all such appeals as junk mail. The costs of fundraising are a topic of concern among donors, volunteers, and government officials, yet some tactics to reduce costs are being questioned too. Tying commercial products and services to charitable requests appears to denigrate the needs thus served. Workplace fundraising attracts questions about methods of choosing recipient agencies and allocating the funds, and questions about what kinds of corporate pressures affecting job security are put on individuals to give.

The competition of hundreds of thousands of nonprofit organizations for funds will continue to compound the difficulties of raising money. Small agencies are overshadowed by large institutions that meet similar needs. Donors become confused by the plethora of requests. Similar sounding organizational names frustrate unwary prospects, causing them to make uninformed choices or to abandon giving in the area of concern. Pressure for performance piles up on the small agency executives who have to do their agencies' fundraising and on large organization development officers charged with reaching million- and billion-dollar goals. Ethical questions have arisen about fundraising tactics that appear to force gifts or gift increases and support activities that do not accord to donor interests. Volunteer leaders are also feeling burdened and wonder when the pervasive demands for their service will abate.

People's negative feelings about asking and being solicited stem in part from the actions of some commercial fundraising firms. These companies hire salespersons to make high-pressure telephone solicitations from temporary banks of phones in boiler-room operations located in prospects' hometowns. Donations go into accounts controlled by the firms, expenses are deducted, and net proceeds paid to the charity. The extraordinarily high expenses and the soliciting tactics continue to give fundraising an exceedingly poor image. These operations need to be distinguished from those of ethical firms that also hire solicitors but turn over all funds to the charitable agencies; expenses are then paid on the basis of previously negotiated contracts. However, even ethical commercial firms' costs remain high in comparison with in-house phonathons using volunteer and client callers.

Legislation and regulations affecting fundraising increase with each passing year, almost in a direct ratio to charitable organizations' numerical growth and extension of methods to obtain new and increased revenues. The dilemma facing governmental authorities is the need to curb "illicit fundraising while protecting and unburdening legitimate behavior" (Greenfield, 1991, p. 220). Concerns by the general public and legislators over fraud, excessive costs, commercial ventures, tax avoidance, improper accounting practices, and further abuses of charitable purposes have stimulated this trend. More than two-thirds of states have laws regulating solicitations. Federal and state reporting requirements for nonprofit organizations have tightened, accompanied by federal and state data sharing to ensure compliance. Limits on the tax deductibility of gifts have emerged, and other restrictions have been enacted (Fremont-Smith, 1989; Hopkins, 1991).

Uniform accounting practices for nonprofit organizations are being continually promulgated by the Financial Accounting Standards Board, an independent policy-formulating organization with wide acceptance among accounting professionals, financial advisors, and government officials. While these standards will produce greater uniformity and comparable data, associations of nonprofit organizations and fundraisers are interjecting their own recommendations into the policy process to try to prevent unwanted paperwork and undue restrictions on their operations. The challenge for fundraisers and their host institutions is to manage their operations ethically and to promote voluntary standards of conduct that will reduce the need for more regulations while also enhancing philanthropy.

The allocation of resources among small and large nonprofit organizations parallels the concentration of wealth and power in the economy and society in general. The large organizations have more funds to finance fundraising efforts. Their case presentations and methods of soliciting dominate existing and potential constituencies. Small agencies tend to feel crowded out. To compete, they stress their more intimate and personalized affiliations for donors and greater care and attention to the clients being served. At the same time, in the face of competition from large organizations, many small organizations collect into federations and coalitions to accumulate and share resources.

Together, these ongoing forces, issues, and strategies are a volatile mix that has both present and potential impacts on the direction and future of fundraising. The debate within the field of fundraising and outside in the larger public arena requires more information and understanding about the role of fundraising among both donors and donees. A solid conceptual base that illuminates the place, function, and values of fundraising will help clarify many of the issues listed here. Without such knowledge, the returns to individuals for sharing their resources for a common good will become clouded, to the detriment of charitable agencies' abilities to meet human needs.

Leading experts in the nonprofit field also make the case for greater knowledge and wider dissemination of research findings. Lyman and Hodgkinson (1989) argue that "philanthropy, broadly defined, is seriously at risk because of the prevailing ignorance, even among its practitioners, of its history and defining characteristics" (p. 480). They urge that practitioners and scholars cooperate in sharing their findings from experience and research. The risk of not improving and not distributing knowledge lies in uninformed decisions by governments and lack of support from the public. Lyman and Hodgkinson cite the difficulties incurred by the confusion over noncharitable nonprofit organizations and charitable ones. When this distinction is not common knowledge, charitable agencies may be more severely regulated than they require, to the harm of their services.

The urgency of acquiring a more thorough understanding of fundraising efforts has resulted in part from the obscurity that fundraising has endured under the cloak of philanthropy. The processes and management of fundraising are not ready topics in discussions of philanthropy. Some scholars' skepticism about fundraising as a field of inquiry continues. Yet research and study in a variety of fundraising areas are needed. The National Society of Fund Raising Executives recognizes this problem and has issued a study entitled *Research Agenda and Policy* (1992) that calls for the development of greater understanding about donors and volunteers, the impact of fundraising on philanthropy, economic factors in fundraising, the fundraisers themselves, organizational aspects of fundraising, and the management and practice of fundraising. The association looks for opportunities to encourage scholars to delve into these subjects and offers its membership as a potential data base. Other professional associations, such as the Council for the Advancement and Support of Education and the Association for Healthcare Philanthropy, recognize the importance of this undertaking and are adding their strengths to the effort.

Lyman and Hodgkinson (1989) entreat practitioners to "make an effort to communicate with researchers, and scholars [to] give more attention to collecting information from practitioners. There is a need to test theory against practice and to develop better definitions and descriptions of the work"

(p. 479). On the one hand, Lyman and Hodgkinson view practitioners as a key resource because these individuals see the whole nonprofit sector and not a portion carved out by a specific academic discipline. On the other hand, scholars can provide a perspective from the data collected and give recognition to the key concepts and theories that inform fundraising practice.

These exhortations are being addressed. The fundraising listings in the *Philanthropic Studies Index* (Burlingame, 1993) increase with each issue. The growing number of fundraisers with advanced degrees based on research in the field indicates a promising environment for the development and acceptance of a body of fundraising principles that will lead to informed practice. The results of research are being presented at the national conferences of professional associations of fundraisers. Additionally, the breadth of knowledge about fundraising can be seen in the scope and variety of topics being presented at these conferences and the hundreds of workshops and training sessions held throughout the country. Academic centers and associations are giving greater attention to fundraising in their studies, courses, and journals. The professional goal of a solid body of knowledge about fundraising is becoming a reality.

The principles of professional fundraising being identified and developed will not only assist the practitioners in the field but will also enable charitable organizations to better serve their millions of clients and donors.

REFERENCES

Altizer, A. W. *Seeking Major Gifts: How 57 Institutions Do It.* Washington, D.C.: Council for the Advancement and Support of Education, 1992.

American Prospect Research Association. *Membership Survey.* Washington, D.C.: American Prospect Research Association, 1992.

Apodaca, R. A., and Mixer, J. R. *Fundraising Skills Training for Community Agencies.* San Francisco: Pacific Bell, 1987.

Auten, G., and Rudney, G. "The Variability of the Charitable Giving by the Wealthy." In R. Magat (ed.), *Charitable Giving: Studies in Varieties and Goals.* New York: Oxford University Press, 1989.

Bailey, A. L. "1989 Corporate Gifts to Charity Total $6.45 Billion." *Chronicle of Philanthropy,* Aug. 7, 1990a, p. 1.

Bailey, A. L. "Big Gains in Giving to Charity." *Chronicle of Philanthropy,* Oct. 16, 1990b, p. 1.

Bailey, A. L., and Millar, B. "United Way: The Fallout After the Fall." *Chronicle of Philanthropy,* Mar. 10, 1992, p. 1.

Barry, B. W. *Strategic Planning Workbook for Nonprofit Organizations.* St. Paul, Minn.: Amherst H. Wilder Foundation, 1986.

Barsook, B. "Is a Retail Business for You?" In S. F. Dolnick (ed.), *Fundraising for Nonprofit Institutions.* Greenwich, Conn.: JAI Press, 1987.

Benne, K. D., and Sheats, P. "Functional Roles of Group Members." *Journal of Social Issues,* 1948, *4*(2), 41–49.

Benner, R. V. "Strategic Planning." Paper presented at National Society of Fund Raising Executives, Golden Gate Chapter, San Francisco, June 15, 1984.

Bennis, W. G., Benne, K. D., and Chin, R. (eds.). *The Planning of Change.* (4th ed.) Troy, Mo.: Holt Rinehart, & Winston, 1985.

Bennis, W. G., and Nanus, B. *Leaders: The Strategies for Taking Charge.* New York: HarperCollins, 1985.

Blake, R. R., and Mouton, J. S. *The New Managerial Grid.* Houston, Tex.: Gulf Publishing, 1978.

Blanchette, R. *Predicting Giving Behavior.* Rochdale, Mass.: Rene Blanchette (self-published), 1993.

Blau, P. M. "Social Exchange." In D. L. Sills (ed.), *International Encyclopedia of the Social Sciences.* New York: Macmillan, 1968.

Blau, P. M. *Exchange and Power in Social Life.* (2nd ed.) New Brunswick, N.J.: Transaction, 1986.

Blau, P., Falbe, C., McKinley, W., and Tracy, P. "Technology and Organization in Manufacturing." *Administrative Science Quarterly,* 1976, *21*(1), 20–39.

Blauner, E. Personal interview by author, Apr. 2, 1992.

"Bored by the Bowl Games? The IRS Wasn't." *Business Week,* Feb. 10, 1992, p. 88.

Boris, E., and others. *1990 Foundation Management Report.* Washington, D.C.: Council on Foundations, 1990.

Boulding, K. E. *Towards a Pure Theory of Foundations.* Danbury, Conn.: Non-Profit Report, 1972.

Boulding, K. E. *The Economy of Love and Fear: A Preface to Grants Economics.* Belmont, Calif.: Wadsworth, 1973.

Brilliant, E. L. *The United Way: Dilemmas of Organized Charity.* New York: Columbia University Press, 1990.

Brinkerhoff, P. C. "The Management Audit: A Task Whose Time has Come." *Grantsmanship Center News,* Spring 1984, pp. 44–47.

Brittingham, D. E., and Pezzullo, T. R. *The Campus Green: Fund Raising in Higher Education.* ASHE-ERIC Higher Education Report No. 1. Washington, D.C.: School of Education and Human Development, George Washington University: 1990.

Broce, T. E. *Fund Raising: The Guide to Raising Money from Private Sources.* (2nd ed.) Norman, Okla.: University of Oklahoma Press, 1986.

Bryson, J. M. *Strategic Planning for Public and Nonprofit Organizations: A Guide to Strengthening and Sustaining Organizational Achievement.* San Francisco: Jossey-Bass, 1988.

Bullock, R. L. "Starting a Foundation." *Association Management,* 1988, *40*(6), 107–111.

Burchill, T. "Ethics." *NSFRE News,* 1990, *27*(8), 4.

Burlingame, D. F. *Philanthropic Studies Index.* Indianapolis: Indiana University Center on Philanthropy, *2*(2), 1993.

Burns, T., and Stalker, G. M. *The Management of Innovation.* London: Tavistock, 1961.

Callero, P. L. "Role-Identity." *Social Psychology Quarterly,* 1985, *48*(3), 203–215.

Carlisle, H. *Situational Management: A Contingency Approach to Leadership.* New York: AMACOM, 1973.

Cartwright, D., and Zander, A. (eds.). *Group Dynamics: Research and Theory.* (3rd ed.) New York: HarperCollins, 1968.

Chandler, A. D. *Strategy and Structure.* Cambridge, Mass.: M.I.T. Press, 1962.

Chapel, G. W. "Ethiopian Relief: A Case Study in Failed Relations." *Public Relations Review,* 1988, *14*(2), 22–32.

Child, J., and Mansfield, R. "Technology, Size, and Organization Structure." *Sociology,* 1972, *6*(3), 369–393.

Children's Home Society of California. *1992 Annual Report.* Los Angeles: Children's Home Society of California, 1992.

Christenson, J. A., Hougland, J. G., Jr., Ilvento, T. W., and Shepard, J. M. "The 'Organization Man' and the Community: The Impact of Organizational Norms and Personal Values on Community Participation and Transfers." *Social Forces,* 1988, *66*(3), 808–826.

Cialdini, R. B. Influence: *The New Psychology of Modern Persuasion.* New York: Quill, 1984.

Council on Foundations. *Corporate Philanthropy: Philosophy, Man-*

agement, Trends, Future, Background. Washington, D.C.: Council on Foundations, 1982.

Council on Foundations. *Managing Smaller Corporate Giving Programs.* Washington, D.C.: Council on Foundations, 1983.

Crowder, N. L., and Hodgkinson, V. A. *Compendium of Resources for Teaching about the Nonprofit Sector, Voluntarism and Philanthropy.* Washington, D.C.: INDEPENDENT SECTOR, 1991.

Dahle, T. L. "An Objective and Comparative Study of Five Methods of Transmitting Information to Business and Industrial Employees." *Speech Monographs,* 1954, *21*(1), 24–27.

Davidson, R., Timmer, D. A., and Eitzen, D. S. "Neo-Marxist Theory and Corporate Social Expenditures." *Contemporary Crises,* 1982, *6*(3), 207–225.

Davis, S. M., and Lawrence, P. R. *Matrix.* Reading, Mass.: Addison-Wesley, 1977.

Dienhart, J. W. "Charitable Investments: A Strategy for Improving the Business Environment." *Journal of Business Ethics,* 1988, *7*(1), 63–71.

Dorsey, E. C. "A Sense of the Sector." *Independent Sector Update,* Aug. 1990, p. 2.

Drucker, P. F. *Managing the Nonprofit Organization: Principles and Practices.* New York: HarperCollins, 1990.

Drucker, P. F. *Managing for the Future.* New York: Truman Talley Books/Dutton, 1992.

Dunn, T. G. *How to Shake the New Money Tree: Creative Fund-raising for Today's Nonprofit Organizations.* New York: Viking/Penguin, 1988.

Edie, J. E. *First Steps in Starting a Foundation.* Washington, D.C.: Council on Foundations, 1987.

Emery, F. E., and Trist, E. L. "The Causal Texture of Organizational Environments." *Human Relations,* 1965, *18*(1), 21–32.

Ermann, M. D. "The Operative Goals of Corporate Philanthropy: Contributions to the Public Broadcasting Service, 1972–1976." *Social Problems,* 1978, *25*(5), 504–514.

Espinosa, S. "Girl Scouting Takes a Leap Forward." *The San Francisco Chronicle,* Feb. 24, 1992, p. 1.

"Facts and Figures on the Independent Sector." *Independent Sector Update,* Aug. 1991, p. 5.

Fagan, K. "Compassion Fatigue, Poor Economy Hit Charities." *Oakland Tribune,* Dec. 2, 1990, p. C1.

Fayol, H. *General and Industrial Management (Administration Industrielle et General,* trans. C. Storrs). New York: Pitman, 1949. (Originally published 1916.)

Foundation Center. *The Foundation Grants Index.* (19th ed.) New York: Foundation Center, 1990.

Foundation Center. *Directory of New and Emerging Foundations.* New York: Foundation Center, 1991a.

Foundation Center. *The Foundation Grants Index.* (20th ed.) New York: Foundation Center, 1991b.

Foundation Center. *National Data Book of Foundations: A Comprehensive Guide to Grantmaking Foundations.* New York: Foundation Center, 1991c.

Foundation Center. *Foundation Giving: Yearbook of Facts and Figures on Private, Corporate, and Community Foundations.* (1992 ed.) New York: Foundation Center, 1992a.

Foundation Center. *The Foundation Grants Index.* (21st ed.) New York: Foundation Center, 1992b.

Fox, W. M. *Effective Group Problem Solving: How to Broaden Participation, Improve Decision Making, and Increase Commitment to Action.* San Francisco: Jossey-Bass, 1987.

Fremont-Smith, M. R. "Trends in Accountability and Regulation of Nonprofits." In V. A. Hodgkinson, R. W. Lyman, and Associates, *The Future of the Nonprofit Sector: Challenges, Changes, and Policy Considerations.* San Francisco: Jossey-Bass, 1989.

Fund Raising School. *Study Guide.* San Rafael, Calif.: Fund Raising School, 1977.

Galant, D. "The Entrepreneurs and the Almsgivers." *Venture,* 1987, *9*(10), 72–76.

Galaskiewicz, J. *Social Organization of an Urban Economy: A Study of Business Philanthropy.* Orlando, Fla.: Academic Press, 1985.

Galaskiewicz, J., and Wasserman, S. "Mimetic Processes Within an Interorganizational Field: An Empirical Test." *Administrative Science Quarterly,* 1989, *47*(3), 454–479.

Galbraith, J. *Organization Design.* Reading, Mass.: Addison-Wesley, 1977.

Gannon, M. J. *Management: An Integrated Framework.* Boston: Little, Brown, 1982.

Gardner, J. W. *On Leadership.* New York: Free Press, 1990.

Garner, L. H., Jr. *Leadership in Human Services: How to Articulate and Implement a Vision to Achieve Results.* San Francisco: Jossey-Bass, 1989.

Gerard, D. "What Makes a Volunteer?" *New Society,* 1985, *74*(1193), 236–238.

Goddard, R. W. "Inside the Psychological Employee." *Management World,* 1988, *17*(3), 224–226.

Goodstein, L. D., and Burke, W. W. "Creating Successful Organizational Change." *Organizational Dynamics,* 1991, *19*(4), 5–17.

Gorczyra, M. "Strategic Planning for Voluntary Nonprofits." *Grassroots Fundraising Journal,* 1987, *6*(1), 3–7.

Grande, C. "How to Use Values and Motivation Research to Improve the Efficiency of Direct Mail Fund-Raising." Paper presented at International Conference of National Society of Fund Raising Executives, San Francisco, Mar. 1992.

Greene, S. G. "Just 1 Japanese Company in 5 Calls Itself an Active 'Corporate Citizen' in the U.S." *Chronicle of Philanthropy,* Feb. 12, 1991, p. 14.

Greenfield, J. M. *Fund Raising: Evaluating and Managing the Fund Development Process.* New York: Wiley, 1991.

Gurin, M. G. *Advancing Beyond the Techniques in Fund Raising.* Rockville, Md.: Fund Raising Institute, 1991.

Hall, M. "Newspaper Inserts Produce Loyal Donors for Chicago Charity." *Chronicle of Philanthropy,* Jan. 26, 1993a, p. 31.

Hall, M. "Selling Charity on Television." *Chronicle of Philanthropy,* Jan. 26, 1993b, pp. 27–29.

Hall, M. R. "The Decentralization of Development: Impact on Power, Priorities, Faculty Perceptions." *Teachers College Record,* 1992, *93*(3), 569–582.

Hardy, J. M. *Managing for IMPACT in Nonprofit Organizations: Corporate Planning Techniques and Applications.* Erwin, Tenn.: Essex Press, 1984.

Hart, M. L. "Chalk One Up for DAV." *Fund Raising Management,* 1990, *21*(3), 61–62.

Harvey, J. W., and McCrohan, K. F. "Changing Conditions for Fund Raising." In J. Van Til and Associates, *Critical Issues in American Philanthropy: Strengthening Theory and Practice.* San Francisco: Jossey-Bass, 1990.

Hazenfeld, Y. *Human Service Organizations.* Englewood Cliffs, N.J.: Prentice-Hall, 1983.

Hersey, P., and Blanchard, K. *Management of Organizational Behavior: Utilizing Human Resources.* Englewood Cliffs, N.J.: Prentice-Hall, 1982.

Herzberg, F. *Work and the Nature of Man.* New York: World Publishing, 1966.

Hilgert, C., and Mahler, S. J. "Nonprofit Charitable Organizations, 1986 and 1987." *Statistics of Income Bulletin,* Internal Revenue Service, 1991, *11*(2), 63–76.

Hodgkinson, V. A. *Academic Centers and Research Institutes Focusing on the Study of Philanthropy, Voluntarism, and Not-for-Profit Activity: A Progress Report.* Washington, D.C.: INDEPENDENT SECTOR, 1988.

Hodgkinson, V. A., Lyman, R. W., and Associates. *The Future of the Nonprofit Sector: Challenges, Changes, and Policy Considerations.* San Francisco: Jossey-Bass, 1989.

Hodgkinson, V. A., and Weitzman, M. S. *Giving and Volunteering in the United States: Findings from a National Survey.* (1988 ed.) Washington, D.C.: Independent Sector, 1988.

Hodgkinson, V. A., and Weitzman, M. S. *Giving and Volunteering in the United States: Findings from a National Survey.* (1990 ed.) Washington, D.C.: Independent Sector, 1990.

Hodgkinson, V. A., Weitzman, M. S., Noga, S. M., and Gorski, H. A. *Giving and Volunteering in the United States: Findings from a National Survey.* (1992 ed.) Washington, D.C.: Independent Sector, 1992.

Hodgkinson, V. A., Weitzman, M. S., Toppe, C. M., and Noga, S. M. *Nonprofit Almanac 1992–1993: Dimensions of the Independent Sector.* (4th ed.) San Francisco: Jossey-Bass, 1992.

Homans, G. C. *Social Behavior: Its Elementary Forms.* Orlando, Fla.: Harcourt Brace Jovanovich, 1961.

Hopkins, B. R. *The Law of Fund-Raising.* New York: Wiley, 1991.

Huntsinger, J. *Fund Raising Letters: A Comprehensive Study Guide to Raising Money by Direct Response Marketing.* Richmond, Va.: Emerson, 1982.

"Institute, Firms Accused of Fund-Raising Fraud: State Suit Says Very Little Went to Charity." *San Francisco Chronicle,* Apr. 16, 1992, p. A22.

Internal Revenue Service. *Annual Report 1991.* Washington, D.C.: Internal Revenue Service, 1991.

Jenkins, J. C. "Social Movement Philanthropy and American Democracy." In R. Magat (ed.), *Philanthropic Giving: Studies in Varieties and Goals.* New York: Oxford University Press, 1989.

Jones, J. E. "The Organizational Universe." In J. E. Jones and J. W. Pfeiffer (eds.), *The 1981 Annual Handbook for Group Facilitators.* San Diego, Calif.: University Associates, 1981.

Kaplan, A. E. *Giving USA: The Annual Report on Philanthropy for the Year 1991.* New York: AFFRC Trust for Philanthropy, 1992.

Kaplan, A. E. *Giving USA: The Annual Report on Philanthropy for the Year 1992.* New York: AFFRC Trust for Philanthropy, 1993.

Katz, D., and Kahn, R. *The Social Psychology of Organizations.* New York: Wiley, 1966.

Kelly, K. S. *Fund Raising and Public Relations: A Critical Analysis.* Hillsdale, N.J.: Erlbaum, 1991.

Kettner, P. M., and Martin, L. L. "Purchase of Service Contracting: Two Models." *Administration in Social Work,* 1990, *14*(1), 15–30.

King, W. R. "Strategic Planning in Nonprofit Organizations." In G. Zaltman (ed.), *Management Principles for Nonprofit Agencies and Organizations.* New York: AMACOM, 1979.

Kinkead, G. "America's Best Run Charities." *Fortune Magazine,* Nov. 9, 1987, pp. 145–150.

Klepper, A. *The Corporate Contributions Professional.* Research Bulletin. New York: Conference Board, 1981.

Klepper, A. *Corporate Contributions, 1990.* Report no. 989. New York: Conference Board, 1992.

Klepper, A., and Mackler, S. *Screening Requests for Corporate Contributions.* Report no. 887. New York: Conference Board, 1986.

Knudsen, R. B. *New Models for Creative Giving.* (2nd ed.) Wilton, Conn.: Morehouse-Barlow, 1985.

Koch, F., *The New Corporate Philanthropy: How Society and Business Can Profit.* New York: Plenum Press, 1979.

Koteen, J. *Strategic Management in Public and Nonprofit Organizations: Thinking and Acting Strategically on Public Concerns.* New York: Praeger, 1989.

Kotler, P. *Marketing for Nonprofit Organizations.* (2nd ed.) Englewood Cliffs, N.J.: Prentice-Hall, 1982.

Kotler, P., and Andreason, A. R. *Strategic Marketing for Nonprofit Organizations.* (4th ed.) Englewood Cliffs, N.J.: Prentice-Hall, 1991.

Kotter, J. P. *Power and Influence: Beyond Formal Authority.* New York: Free Press, 1985.

Kramer, R. M. "Nonprofit Social Service Agencies and the Welfare State: Some Research Considerations." In H. K. Anhier and W. Seibel (eds.), *The Third Sector: Comparative Studies of Nonprofit Organizations.* New York: Walter de Gruyter, 1990.

Landy, L. Letter requesting proposals for research to be funded by New York University's Initiative on Nonprofit Entrepreneurship. Feb. 5, 1992.

Lane, F. S., Levis, W. C., and New, A. L. "Funding Fund Raising." *Philanthropic Monthly,* 1989, *22*(5), pp. 20–26.

Lant, J. "Board Stiff: How Some Board Members Really Function." *Nonprofit World,* 1988, *6*(4), 21–23.

Lassey, W., and Sashkin, M. (eds.) *Leadership and Social Change.* (3rd ed.) San Diego, Calif.: University Associates, 1983.

Law, C. K., and Hasenfeld, Y. "The Relationship Between the Public and the Voluntary Sectors: The Case of Refugee Resettlement Services." *Administration in Social Work,* 1989, *13*(2), 15–28.

Lawrence, P. R., and Lorsch, J. W. *Organizations and Environment: Managing Differentiation and Integration.* Boston: Graduate School of Business Administration, Harvard University, 1967.

Leavitt, H. J., and Bahrami, H. *Managerial Psychology: Managing Behavior in Organizations.* (5th ed.) Chicago: University of Chicago Press, 1988.

Levine, J. "Charitable Motives." *Incentive Marketing,* 1986, *16*(9), 16–24.

Levinson, H. *The Exceptional Executive: A Psychological Conception.* Cambridge, Mass.: Harvard University Press, 1968.

Levis, W. C. *Reasonable Fund Raising Cost Percentage Guidelines.* Unpublished Monograph. Nonprofit Management Group, Baruch College, City University of New York, 1992.

Lewin, K. *Resolving Social Conflicts.* New York: HarperCollins, 1948.

Lewin, K., Lippitt, R., and White, R. K. "Patterns of Aggressive Behavior in Experimentally Created Social Climates." *Journal of Social Psychology,* 1939, *10*(3), 271–301.

Lewis, H. "Ethics and the Private Non-profit Human Service Organization." *Administration in Social Work,* 1989, *13*(2), 1–14.

Likert, R. *New Patterns of Management.* New York: McGraw-Hill, 1961.

Lindahl, W. E. "Resource Allocation in University Fund Raising." Unpublished doctoral dissertation, Department of Administration and Policy Studies, Northwestern University, 1990.

Lindahl, W. E. "Differentiating Planned and Major Gift Prospects." In *Connections,* Fall 1991, p. 9. Chicago: American Prospect Research Association, 1991.

Lindahl, W. E. *Strategic Planning for Fund Raising: How to Bring in More Money Using Strategic Resource Allocation.* San Francisco: Jossey-Bass, 1992.

Lindahl, W. E., and Winship, C. "Predictive Models for Annual Fundraising and Major Gift Fundraising." *Nonprofit Management & Leadership,* 1992, *3*(1), 43–64.

Lyman, R. W., and Hodgkinson, V. A. "Meeting the Challenges of the Future." In V. A. Hodgkinson, R. W. Lyman, and Associates, *The Future of the Nonprofit Sector: Challenges, Changes, and Policy Considerations.* San Francisco: Jossey-Bass, 1989.

McClelland, D. C. *Human Motivation.* New York: Cambridge University Press, 1987.

McClelland, D. C., and others. *The Achievement Motive.* New York: Irvington, 1976.

McCoy, P. Consultation with J. R. Mixer and H. A. Rosso, San Rafael, Calif., 1977.

McElroy, K. M., and Siegfried, J. J. "The Effects of Size and Mergers on Corporate Philanthropy." In B. Bock, J. H. Goldschmidt, I. M. Millstein, and F. M. Scherer (eds.), *The Impact of the Modern Corporation.* New York: Columbia University Press, 1984.

McGregor, D. *The Human Side of Enterprise.* New York: McGraw-Hill, 1960.

McLaughlin, C. P. *The Management of Nonprofit Organizations.* New York: Wiley, 1986.

Magat, R. (Ed.). *Philanthropic Giving: Studies in Varieties and Goals.* New York: Oxford University Press, 1989.

"Making Money out of Museums." *The Economist,* Jan. 5, 1991, p. 12.

Manz, C. C., Muto, M., and Sims, H. P., Jr. "SuperLeadership Creates a New Perspective for Managers." *Journal for Quality and Participation,* 1990, 2, 12–15.

Mars, D. *Interorganizational Relations: State of the Art.* Los Angeles: University of Southern California, 1972.

Maslow, A. H. *The Farther Reaches of Human Nature.* New York: Viking/Penguin, 1973.

Mason, D. E. *Voluntary Nonprofit Enterprise Management.* New York: Plenum, 1984.

Mauss, M. *The Gift: Forms and Functions of Exchange in Archaic Societies* (trans. I. Cunnison). New York: W.W. Norton, 1967. (Originally published 1924.)

Mayer, R. R. *Policy and Program Planning: A Developmental Perspective.* Englewood Cliffs, N.J.: Prentice-Hall, 1985.

Metcalf, H. C., and Urwick, L. (eds.). *Dynamic Administration: The Collected Papers of Mary Parker Follet.* London: Pitman, 1960. (Originally published 1941.)

Millar, B. "'Donor Choice' Gains Ground in United Ways." *Chronicle of Philanthropy,* Mar. 12, 1991a, p. 22.

Millar, B. "Japanese Companies Seen Increasing Gifts to Grassroots Community Organizations." *Chronicle of Philanthropy,* June 4, 1991b, p. 7.

Milofsky, C., and Romo, F. P. "The Structure of Funding Arenas for Neighborhood Based Organizations." In C. Milofsky (ed.), *Community Organizations: Studies in Resource Mobil-*

ization and Exchange. New York: Oxford University Press, 1988.

Mintzberg, H. *Mintzberg on Management: Inside Our Strange World of Organizations*. New York: Free Press, 1989.

Mixer, J. R. "Corporate Support of Higher Education." Unpublished doctoral dissertation, Department of Higher Education, University of California–Berkeley, 1977.

Mongon, G. J. *NSFRE Profile: 1992 Membership Survey*. Arlington, Va.: National Society of Fund Raising Executives, 1992.

Moore, J. "As Ellis Island Museum Opens, Fund Drive Prepares to Close." *Chronicle of Philanthropy*, Sept. 4, 1990, pp. 4–5.

Moore, S. "Charity Workers' Job Market Jitters." *Chronicle of Philanthropy*, Apr. 21, 1992, pp. 1, 28–31.

Nash, A., and Carroll, S. *The Management of Compensation*. Belmont, Calif.: Wadsworth, 1975.

National Association for the Exchange of Industrial Resources. *Membership Handbook*. Galesburg, Ill.: National Association for the Exchange of Industrial Resources, 1992.

National Society of Fund Raising Executives. *Research Agenda and Policy*. Alexandria, Va.: National Society of Fund Raising Executives, 1992.

National/United Service Agencies. *Public Attitudes Toward Federated Giving*. Fairfax, Va.: National/United Service Agencies, 1992.

Odendahl, T. "Independent Foundations and Wealthy Donors." In R. Magat (ed.), *Philanthropic Giving: Studies in Varieties and Goals*. New York: Oxford University Press, 1989.

Odendahl, T. *Charity Begins at Home: Generosity and Self-Interest Among the Philanthropic Elite*. New York: Basic Books, 1990.

Odiorne, G. S. *Management by Objectives: A System of Managerial Leadership*. New York: Pitman, 1965.

Ostrander, S. A. "Voluntary Social Service Agencies in the United States." *Social Service Review*, 1985, *59*(3), 435–454.

Ostrander, S. A., and Schervish, P. G. "Giving and Getting: Philanthropy as a Social Relation." In J. Van Til and Associates, *Critical Issues in American Philanthropy: Strengthening Theory and Practice*. San Francisco: Jossey-Bass, 1990.

Ott, J. S. *The Organizational Culture Perspective.* Chicago: Dorsey Press, 1989.

Panas, J. *Megagifts: Who Gives Them, Who Gets Them.* Chicago: Pluribus, 1984.

Paustian, C. "Beloit College Hopes History Will Repeat Itself." *Pensions & Investment Age,* 1985, *13*(25), 51.

Payton, R. L. "Philanthropic Values." In R. Magat (ed.), *Philanthropic Giving: Studies in Varieties and Goals.* New York: Oxford University Press, 1989.

Perlmutter, F. D., and Adams, C. T. "The Voluntary Sector and For-Profit Ventures: The Transformation of American Social Welfare?" *Administration in Social Work,* 1990, *14*(1), 1–14.

Peters, T. J. *Thriving on Chaos: Handbook for a Management Revolution.* New York: Knopf, 1987.

Pfeffer, J., and Salancik, G. R. *The External Control of Organizations: A Resource Dependency Perspective.* New York: HarperCollins, 1978.

Pifer, A. "Philanthropy, Voluntarism, and Changing Times." *Daedalus,* 1987, *116*(1), 119–131.

Popcorn, F. *The Popcorn Report: Faith Popcorn on the Future of Your Company, Your World, Your Life.* New York: Doubleday, 1991.

Richman, T. "Not For Profit." *Inc.,* 1990, *12*(11), 108–117.

Rogers, E., and Shoemaker, F. *Communication of Innovations: A Cross Cultural Approach.* (2nd ed.) New York: Free Press, 1972.

Rosso, H. A., and Associates. *Achieving Excellence in Fund Raising: A Comprehensive Guide to Principles, Strategies, and Methods.* San Francisco: Jossey-Bass, 1991.

Sarason, S. B. *The Creation of Settings and the Future Societies.* San Francisco: Jossey-Bass, 1972.

Scala, R. "Fundraiser's Forum Teams with Ideas." *Fund Raising Management,* 1990a, *21*(3), 28–33.

Scala, R. "Tax Reform Costs Charities Billions." *Fund Raising Management,* 1990b, *21*(3), 11–12.

Schneiter, P. H. *The Art of Asking: How to Solicit Philanthropic Gifts.* Amber, Penn.: Fund Raising Institute, 1985.

Schwartz, B. "The Social Psychology of the Gift." *American Journal of Sociology,* 1967, *73*(1), 1–12.

Scott, W. R. *Organizations: Rational, Natural, and Open Systems.* (2nd ed.) Englewood Cliffs, N.J.: Prentice-Hall, 1987.

"Services Take Aim at Uncollected Pledge Money." *NonProfit Times,* 1991, *5*(6), 10.

Sheridan Associates and Zimmerman Associates. *Study of Cause-Related Marketing.* Washington, D.C.: Independent Sector, 1988.

Sievers, B. "Beyond the Surrogate of Motivation." *Organizational Studies,* 1986, *7*(4), 335–351.

Simon, J. G. "Agendas for Nonprofit Sector Research: A Personal Account." In V. A. Hodgkinson, R. W. Lyman, and Associates, *The Future of the Nonprofit Sector: Challenges, Changes, and Policy Considerations.* San Francisco: Jossey-Bass, 1989.

Skloot, E. *The Nonprofit Entrepreneur.* New York: The Foundation Center, 1988.

Smith, D. H. "Altruism, Volunteers, and Volunteerism." *Journal of Voluntary Action Research,* 1981, *10*(1), 21–36.

Smith, R. "Fund-Raising Force: United Way Quadruples Charities List." *Oakland Tribune,* June 4, 1992, pp. C1, C3.

Spread, P. "Blau's Exchange Theory, Support and the Macrostructure." *British Journal of Sociology,* 1984, *35*(6), 157–173.

Sproull, R. L. "Cost-Effective Way to Spur Private Giving." *Harvard Business Review,* 1982, *60*(2), 62–66.

Staw, B. M. *Intrinsic and Extrinsic Motivation.* Morristown, N.J.: General Learning Press, 1976.

Steckel, R. *Filthy Rich and Other Nonprofit Fantasies: Changing the Way Nonprofits Do Business in the 90's.* Berkeley, Calif.: Ten Speed Press, 1989.

Stehle, V. "Building Endowments for Small Nonprofits." *Chronicle of Philanthropy,* Oct. 16, 1990, pp. 12–13.

Steinberg, R. "Voluntary Donations and Public Expenditures in a Federalist System." *American Economic Review,* 1987, *77*(1), 24–36.

Steiner, G. A. *Strategic Planning: What Every Manager Must Know.* New York: Free Press, 1979.

Steiner, G. A., and Miner, J. B. *Management Policy and Strategy: Text, Readings, and Cases.* New York: Macmillan, 1977.

Tannenbaum, R., and Schmidt, W. H. "How to Choose a Leadership Pattern." *Harvard Business Review*, 1973, *51*(3), 162–180.

Tropman, J. E. *Effective Meetings: Improving Group Decision Making.* Beverly Hills, Calif.: Sage Publications, 1980.

Unseem, M., and Kutner, S. I. *Corporate Contributions to the Nonprofit Sector: The Organization of Giving, and the Influence of the Chief Executive Officer and Other Firms on Company Contributions in Massachusetts.* Program on Non-profit Organizations, Working Paper No. 94. New Haven, Conn.: Yale University, 1984.

Unterman, I., and Davis, R. H. *Strategic Management of Not-for Profit Organizations: From Survival to Success.* New York, Praeger, 1984.

Warwick, M. *Revolution in the Mailbox: How Direct Mail Fundraising Is Changing the Face of American Society—and How Your Organization Can Benefit.* Berkeley, Calif.: Strathmoor Press, 1990.

Weber, M. *The Theory of Social and Economic Organization* (trans. T. Parsons). New York: Free Press, 1947.

Weber, N. (ed.). *Giving USA: The Annual Report on Philanthropy for the Year 1990.* New York: AFFRC Trust for Philanthropy, 1991.

Weiner, M. E. *A Lexicon of Management Theories and Techniques for Human Service Administration.* Hebron, Conn.: Practitioners' Press, 1979.

Weisbord, M. R. "Toward Third-Wave Managing and Consulting." *Organizational Dynamics*, 1987, *15*(3), 5–25.

Weisbrod, B. A. *The Nonprofit Economy.* Cambridge, Mass.: Harvard University Press, 1988.

White, A. H. "Patterns of Giving." In R. Magat (ed.), *Philanthropic Giving: Studies in Varieties and Goals.* New York: Oxford University Press, 1989.

Wilkinson, H. E., Orth, C. D., and Benfari, R. C. "Motivation Theories: An Integrated Operational Model." *Advanced Management Journal*, 1986, *51*(4), 24–31.

Williams, G. "Drop in Charitable Contributions Shown in New Tax Study." *Chronicle of Philanthropy*, Jan. 29, 1991, p. 33.

Wiltsek, N. *Corporate Charitable Behavior of the Small Business Community in San Francisco, Executive Summary.* San Francisco: Nancy Wiltsek (self-published), 1990.

Wolpert, J. "The Geography of Generosity: Metropolitan Disparities in Donations and Support for Amenities." *Annals of the Association of American Geographers,* 1988, *78,* 665–679.

Wood, J. R., and Hougland, J. G., Jr. "The Role of Religion in Philanthropy." In J. Van Til and Associates, *Critical Issues in American Philanthropy: Strengthening Theory and Practice.* San Francisco: Jossey-Bass, 1990.

Wuthnow, R., Hodgkinson, V. A., and Associates. *Faith and Philanthropy in America: Exploring the Role of Religion in America's Voluntary Sector.* San Francisco: Jossey-Bass, 1990.

York, R. O. *Human Service Planning: Concepts, Tools and Methods.* Chapel Hill: University of North Carolina Press, 1982.

Young, D. R. *If Not for Profit, for What? A Behavioral Theory of the Nonprofit Sector Based on Entrepreneurship.* Lexington, Mass.: Lexington Books, 1983.

Young, D. R. "Entrepreneurship and the Behavior of Nonprofit Organizations: Elements of a Theory." In S. Rose-Ackerman (ed.), *The Economics of Nonprofit Institutions: Studies in Structure and Policy.* New York: Oxford University Press, 1986.

Zaleznik, A. "Managers and Leaders: Are They Different?" In H. J. Leavitt, L. R. Pondy, and D. M. Boje (eds.), *Readings in Managerial Psychology.* (4th ed.) Chicago: University of Chicago Press, 1989.

Zander, A. *The Purposes of Groups and Organizations.* San Francisco: Jossey-Bass, 1985.

INDEX